THE ITALIAN RENAISSANCE
A ZEST FOR LIFE

LEGENDA

LEGENDA is the Modern Humanities Research Association's book imprint for new research in the Humanities. Founded in 1995 by Malcolm Bowie and others within the University of Oxford, Legenda has always been a collaborative publishing enterprise, directly governed by scholars. The Modern Humanities Research Association (MHRA) joined this collaboration in 1998, became half-owner in 2004, in partnership with Maney Publishing and then Routledge, and has since 2016 been sole owner. Titles range from medieval texts to contemporary cinema and form a widely comparative view of the modern humanities, including works on Arabic, Catalan, English, French, German, Greek, Italian, Portuguese, Russian, Spanish, and Yiddish literature. Editorial boards and committees of more than 60 leading academic specialists work in collaboration with bodies such as the Society for French Studies, the British Comparative Literature Association and the Association of Hispanists of Great Britain & Ireland.

The MHRA encourages and promotes advanced study and research in the field of the modern humanities, especially modern European languages and literature, including English, and also cinema. It aims to break down the barriers between scholars working in different disciplines and to maintain the unity of humanistic scholarship. The Association fulfils this purpose through the publication of journals, bibliographies, monographs, critical editions, and the MHRA Style Guide, and by making grants in support of research. Membership is open to all who work in the Humanities, whether independent or in a University post, and the participation of younger colleagues entering the field is especially welcomed.

ALSO PUBLISHED BY THE ASSOCIATION

Critical Texts
Tudor and Stuart Translations • *New Translations* • *European Translations*
MHRA Library of Medieval Welsh Literature

MHRA Bibliographies
Publications of the Modern Humanities Research Association

The Annual Bibliography of English Language & Literature
Austrian Studies
Modern Language Review
Portuguese Studies
The Slavonic and East European Review
Working Papers in the Humanities
The Yearbook of English Studies

www.mhra.org.uk
www.legendabooks.com

THE FONDATION BARBIER-MUELLER

The Fondation Barbier-Mueller pour l'étude de la poésie italienne de la Renaissance was created in 1997 through the initiative and generosity of Jean Paul Barbier-Mueller, whose collections of primitive art are known worldwide. Housed in the University of Geneva, it offers scholars free and easy access to an exceptionnal collection of more than six hundred books of Italian poetry printed between 1480 and 1620, most of them very rare. The Foundation's aim is to promote and stimulate research on dozens of poets, often little known, who, in the wake of Petrarch, explored new paths in creative writing and had a wide influence on European sensibility and literature in the Early modern era.

The Foundation edits a journal, *Italique*, and a series of scholarly editions and essays, *Textes et Travaux de la Fondation Barbier-Mueller*, both with Editions Droz in Geneva. There is a scientific catalogue of the collection compiled by Jean Balsamo, *De Dante à Chiabrera. Poètes italiens dans la bibliothèque de la Fondation Barbier-Mueller*, Genève, Droz, 2007, 2 vols. The website www.fondation-italienne-barbier-mueller.org provides an inventory of the books as well as digitised documents.

The Italian Renaissance

A Zest for Life

Edited by Michel Jeanneret and Nicolas Ducimetière

Translated by Viviane Lowe

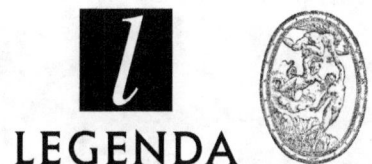

Modern Humanities Research Association
in association with the
Fondation Barbier-Mueller pour l'étude de la poésie italienne de la Renaissance
2016

Published by Legenda
an imprint of the Modern Humanities Research Association
Salisbury House, Station Road, Cambridge CB1 2LA

ISBN 978-1-78188-445-4 (HB)
ISBN 978-1-78188-446-1 (PB)

First published 2017

All rights reserved. No part of this publication may be be reproduced or disseminated or transmitted in any form or by any means, electronic, mechanical, photocopying, recording or otherwise, or stored in any retrieval system, or otherwise used in any manner whatsoever without written permission of the copyright owner, except in accordance with the provisions of the Copyright, Designs and Patents Act 1988, or under the terms of a licence permitting restricted copying issued in the UK by the Copyright Licensing Agency Ltd, Saffron House, 6–10 Kirby Street, London EC1N 8TS, England, or in the USA by the Copyright Clearance Center, 222 Rosewood Drive, Danvers MA 01923. Application for the written permission of the copyright owner to reproduce any part of this publication must be made by email to legenda@mhra.org.uk.

Disclaimer: Statements of fact and opinion contained in this book are those of the author and not of the editors or the Modern Humanities Research Association. The publisher makes no representation, express or implied, in respect of the accuracy of the material in this book and cannot accept any legal responsibility or liability for any errors or omissions that may be made.

Trademark notice: Product or corporate names may be trademarks or registered trademarks, and are used only for identification and explanation without intent to infringe.

© Fondation Barbier-Mueller pour l'étude de la poésie italienne de la Renaissance 2017

Copy-Editor: Richard Correll

Iconography: Caroline Gibert

CONTENTS

	List of Illustrations	x
	Introduction: Crossing the Mountains MICHEL JEANNERET	1
1	La Lippina ETIENNE BARILIER	7
2	Geneva and New York: Two Places of Memory for Pietro Bembo and Ginevra de' Benci LINA BOLZONI	15
3	The Brancacci Chapel: Florence and Poetry YVES BONNEFOY	25
4	Saint Jerome Reading MICHEL BUTOR	35
5	The Dwarf NADEIJE LANEYRIE-DAGEN	45
6	What Was Re-born during the Renaissance? DOMINIQUE FERNANDEZ	55
7	The Meteorite of Orgueil ADRIEN GOETZ	63
8	Niccolò to Himself CARLO OSSOLA	71
9	Petrarch in Naples PASCAL QUIGNARD	79
10	Petrarch on Stage FRANCISCO RICO	85
11	Ludovico's Secret: A Fantasy CESARE SEGRE	93
12	A Feast on Île Barbe: The Italians at the Court of France LIONELLO SOZZI	99
13	Montaigne in Rome: A Fantasy in Four Voices EDNA STERN	109
14	Dark Shadows from the Youth of Giordano Bruno CARLO VECCE	115
15	Filigrana Italiana MARINA WARNER	127
	Index	139

Note: Apart from the essays by Edna Stern and Marina Warner, whose originals were in English, all other essays were translated by Viviane Lowe, either from the French or from the Italian.

LIST OF ILLUSTRATIONS

Fig. 1. Filippo Lippi, *La Lippina*, c. 1437–65, tempera on wood, 92 × 63.5 cm, Uffizi Gallery, Florence. © 2015 Photo Scala, Florence. Courtesy of the Ministero Beni e Att. Culturali.

Fig. 2. Filippo Lippi, *Feast of Herod*, c. 1450–60, fresco, Duomo, Prato. © 2015 Photo Scala, Florence.

Fig. 3. Leonardo da Vinci, *Portrait of Ginevra de' Benci*, c. 1474–78, oil on wood, 38.1 × 37 cm, National Gallery, Washington. Ailsa Mellon Bruce Fund/Courtesy National Gallery of Art, Washington.

Fig. 4. Leonardo da Vinci, *Portrait of Ginevra de' Benci* (reverse), c. 1474–78, oil on wood, 38.1 × 37 cm, National Gallery, Washington. Ailsa Mellon Bruce Fund/Courtesy National Gallery of Art, Washington.

Fig. 5. Hans Memling, *Man with a Roman Coin (Portrait of Bernardo Bembo?)*, c. 1473–74, oil on wood, 30.7 × 23.2 × 0.6 cm, Koninklijk Museum voor Schone Kunsten, Antwerp. © 2015. Photo Scala, Florence.

Fig. 6. Masolino da Panicale, *Temptation of Adam and Eve*, 1426–28, fresco, Brancacci Chapel, church of Santa Maria del Carmine, Florence. © 2015. Photo Scala, Florence/Fondo Edifici di Culto — Min. dell'Interno.

Fig. 7. Masolino da Panicale, *St Peter Healing the Cripple, St Peter Raising Tabitha*, 1423–25, fresco, Brancacci Chapel, church of Santa Maria del Carmine, Florence. © 2015. Photo Scala, Florence/Fondo Edifici di Culto — Min. dell'Interno.

Fig. 8. Masaccio, *The Expulsion from the Garden of Eden*, 1424–28, fresco, Brancacci Chapel, church of Santa Maria del Carmine, Florence. © 2015 Photo Scala, Florence/Fondo Edifici di Culto — Min. dell'Interno.

Fig. 9. Antonello da Messina, *St Jerome in his Study*, c. 1474–75, oil on lime panel, 45.7 × 36.2 cm, National Gallery, London. © 2015 The National Gallery, London/Scala, Florence.

Fig. 10. Antonello da Messina, *St Jerome in his Study*, c. 1474–75, oil on lime panel, 45.7 × 36.2 cm, National Gallery, London (detail). © 2015 The National Gallery, London/Scala, Florence.

Fig. 11. Antonello da Messina, *St Jerome in his Study*, c. 1474–75, oil on lime panel, 45.7 × 36.2 cm, National Gallery, London (detail). © 2015 The National Gallery, London/Scala, Florence.

Fig. 12. Andrea Mantegna, *Camera degli Sposi*, c. 1474, fresco, Palazzo Ducale, Mantua (detail). © 2015 Photo Scala, Florence; courtesy of the Ministero Beni e Att. Culturali.

Fig. 13. Andrea Mantegna, *Camera degli Sposi*, c. 1474, fresco, Palazzo Ducale, Mantua. © 2015 Photo Scala, Florence; courtesy of the Ministero Beni e Att. Culturali.

Fig. 14. Benvenuto Cellini, *Perseus*, 1554, bronze, height 320 cm (excluding base), Loggia dei Lanzi, Florence. © 2015 Photo Scala, Florence; courtesy of the Ministero Beni e Att. Culturali.

Fig. 15. Michelangelo, *Holy Family* or *Tondo Doni*, 1503–04, tempera and oil on wood, diameter 120 cm, Uffizi Gallery, Florence. © 2015 Photo Scala, Florence; courtesy of the Ministero Beni e Att. Culturali.

Fig. 16. Michelangelo, *The Rape of Ganymede*, c. 1533, black chalk on antique laid paper, 38

× 27 cm, Fogg Art Museum, Harvard University Art Museums. Harvard Art Museums/ Fogg Museum, Gifts for Special Uses Fund, 1955.75. Photo: Imaging Department © President and Fellows of Harvard College.

FIG. 17. Jean-Auguste-Dominique Ingres, *Raphael and la Fornarina*, 1814, oil on canvas, 66 × 54 cm, Fogg Art Museum, Harvard University Art Museums. Harvard Art Museums/ Fogg Museum, Bequest of Grenville L. Winthrop, 1943.252. Photo: Imaging Department © President and Fellows of Harvard College.

FIG. 18. Francesco Diofebi, *The Opening of Raphael's Grave in 1833*, 1836, oil on canvas, 54.9 × 70 cm, Thorvaldsens Museum, Copenhagen.

FIG. 19. Hans Hoffmann, *Hedgehog*, before 1584, watercolour and gouache on parchment, 20.7 × 30.7 cm, Metropolitan Museum of Art, New York. Met Purchase, Annette de la Renta Gift, 2005/www.metmuseum.org.

FIG. 20. Engraved portrait of Petrarch with Florence in the background, in Francesco Petrarca, *Canzoniere i Triomphi*, Venice, Albertino Vercellese, 1503, title page. Known as the "three commentaries" edition. Fondation Barbier-Mueller pour l'étude de la poésie italienne de la Renaissance, University of Geneva.

FIG. 21. Petrarch's notes in Cassiodorus, *Berengarius Pictavensis*, Latin manuscrit 2923, folio 178v, Bibliothèque nationale de France, Paris.

FIG. 22. Petrarch's notes (necrology of Laura), in a manuscript of the collected works of Virgil, known as *Virgilio ambrosiano* or 'Petrarch's Virgil', A 79 inf., Biblioteca Ambrosiana, Milan.

FIG. 23. Titian, *Portrait of a Man (Gerolamo (?) Barbarigo or Ariosto)*, c. 1512, oil on canvas, 81.2 × 66.3 cm, National Gallery, London. © 2015 The National Gallery, London/Scala, Florence.

FIG. 24. Nicolas Le Febvre (attributed to), *Lyon Cité opulente, située es confins de Bourgongne, Daulphné et Savoye*, 1555, paper glued to wood panel, 340 × 260 cm, Bibliothèque nationale de France, Paris.

FIG. 25. Anonymous, *Presumed Portrait of Michel de Montaigne*, late sixteenth century, oil on canvas, 13.2 × 14.5 cm, Musée Condé, Chantilly. Photo © RMN-Grand Palais (domaine de Chantilly) / René-Gabriel Ojéda.

FIG. 26. Anonymous, *Portrait of Pierluigi da Palestrina*, late sixteenth century, oil on canvas, 86.50 × 112 cm, Oratorio di San Filippo Neri, Rome. © 2015 Photo Scala, Florence.

FIG. 27. Brueghel the Elder, *Port of Naples*, 1560, oil on wood, 70 × 41 cm, Doria Pamphilj Gallery, Rome. Amministrazione Doria Pamphilj srl con socio unico.

FIG. 28. Walls of Eton Chapel, 1479–87, fresco. From left to right: Amoras sells his wife to the devil; St Elizabeth of Hungary. Reproduced by permission of the Provost and Fellows of Eton College.

FIG. 29. Walls of Eton Chapel, 1479–87, fresco. From left to right: St Ursula; the Empress sees the Virgin in a vision; St Dorothea. Reproduced by permission of the Provost and Fellows of Eton College.

FIG. 30. Walls of Eton Chapel, 1479–87, fresco. From left to right: unidentified female saint; the miracle of the wounded image; St Margaret. Reproduced by permission of the Provost and Fellows of Eton College.

FIG. 31. Walls of Eton Chapel, 1479–87, fresco. The legend of the falsely accused Empress. Reproduced by permission of the Provost and Fellows of Eton College.

INTRODUCTION

Crossing the Mountains

Michel Jeanneret

The story we are about to discover is an old story, a story that has been told countless times in the past five centuries: the story of a pilgrimage across the mountains, to Italy, in search of treasure. For the French, the flow began with the Italian wars of the late fifteenth century, and never stopped. The armies of Charles VIII and his successors, up to Henri II, set out to conquer new territories, but returned empty-handed. However, this apparent political and military fiasco heralded the start of a cultural revolution. The acceleration of exchanges across the Alps allowed the Renaissance, then in full flowering in the lands of southern Europe, to reach the countries of the north. The Italian miracle was infectious: it presaged sweeping changes in society, ideas and the arts. It was, in fact, the dawn of the Modern Age.

Down from the mountains rushed rustic noblemen and clerics learned in the scholastic tradition, to discover cities that were like museums, educated elites, a refined way of life and a modernity of ideas and of style that was as exotic as it was enchanting. Jaded and saturated with images as we are today, we can no longer fully experience the intensity and freshness of their emotions. But we can at least try to picture the radiance and magic of this first contact with Italy as it appeared to the eyes of those pioneers.

From one principality to the next, on the road from Milan to Naples, visitors could not help but notice the role of architects and artists in the disposition of the urban landscape; sculptures, paintings, decorative arts and technical innovations contributed to the beauty of the cities and spread their luxury to private interiors. Refined manners, sophisticated conversation and elegant dress further accentuated this environment. For Italy also witnessed the emergence, within aristocratic circles, of an ideal of court life and the figure of the perfect courtier. Their behaviour and customs were shaped by a model of sociability, which soon became the common code of etiquette of early modern Europe. The civilisation of social life resulted in part from the fact that intellectuals were invited to contribute to the collective well-being. Whereas clerics in northern Europe were generally attached to a specific monastery or college, and, until the sixteenth century, wielded only limited influence on the life of the century, in Italy scholars mingled with the nobility and took part in the affairs of the city. They were consulted and listened to, and could inflect the course of events and use their knowledge to advance progress.

Even before the Age of Enlightenment, the collaboration between scholars and the powerful was directed at building an ideal society, guided by knowledge and reason.

To burnish their own image, as well as that of the state, the princes became patrons; they promoted the study of the classics, founded libraries, collected art, supported teaching and encouraged intellectual debate. Almost everywhere, the visitors saw a style, a vision, an impetus that they would never forget.

Others braved the rigours of the road in order to add to their store of knowledge: these were the scholars in search of books and contacts within academia. Entire cohorts of students — for true scholars are perpetual students — went to Italy to complete their education at the venerable universities of Bologna, Padua or Pavia, and to acquire an intellectual aura. These magistrates and medical doctors, theologians and philologists, named Rabelais, Du Bellay or Montaigne, had in common a boundless curiosity, a thirst for the new, which the academies and libraries did not disappoint. They explored and exploited the resources of contemporary Italy; but traces of the ancient world were visible everywhere, and they also came to discover the vestiges of a civilisation that was seen as a source of renewal. There was no continuity in the transmission from Greece to Rome, and from Roman culture to its heirs fifteen centuries later. Treasures were everywhere for the taking: an undiscovered manuscript, a statue, a medal, each of them a missing link in a history which, if it was to serve as an example, needed to be better understood.

Erasmus was almost forty when he travelled to Italy, from Turin to Rome, searching for knowledge that had not yet passed over the barrier of the Alps. His intention was to study Greek, and he met with the best Hellenists of his time. He had come to save from oblivion Greek and Latin authors, and religious works asleep in libraries; his purpose was more than fulfilled when, during his stay in Venice, he was invited by Aldo Manuzio, the great promoter of classical literature, to assist him in preparing for publication the texts of several little-known or corrupted masterpieces. For anyone who was convinced that the way to create a better world, after the dark night of the Middle Ages, was to appropriate and update ancient models, this opened up vast new perspectives and great hopes.

The travellers had left behind societies and ways of thinking that were overwhelmingly dominated by the Church and the articles of faith. The Italians, in contrast, were as interested in the city of men as in the city of God, if not more so. As the Middle Ages receded into the distance, these scholars no longer expected theology or ecclesiastic tradition to hold the answers to all problems, and marked out instead a separate space in which they attempted to offer profane solutions to the questions posed by man and nature. The movement of emancipation was long and drawn out — think of Galileo — but the example of Antiquity offered a first point of entry, which left ample leeway for human enterprise and intellectual curiosity. Significantly, among the Italian masters who sowed the first seeds of the European Renaissance, Dante, whose work is suffused with metaphysics, theology and Christian symbolism, had far less impact than two other authors, who were more keenly attuned to immanent realities: namely, Petrarch, a spiritual, contemplative writer, who, though he worshipped Antiquity, tirelessly explored the human subject, and his values and personal life; and Boccaccio, whose *oeuvre* was almost entirely profane.

When it was time to turn toward home, the visitors did not travel empty-handed. Artists and scholars no doubt carried their treasures home in their eyes and minds, but the princes and soldiers hauled back vast quantities of objects, both ancient and modern, which they used to decorate their dwellings. A significant trade in books, artworks and things seen thus flowed toward the countries of northern Europe and progressively modified their appearance. Did you say architecture? In France, the castles burgeoning along the banks of the Loire were less and less gothic in form and more and more Italianate. Painting and drawing? The school of Fontainebleau was a pure product of styles and techniques first developed in the workshops of Italy. Whether in garden design, ornamental fashions — the vogue for grotesques, for instance — the promotion of good manners, the idea of civility or the refinement of court life, the Italian masters' imprint was recognisable everywhere. According to the ancient legend of *translatio studii* — the transfer of culture — the sciences and arts were transferred from the Orient to Greece, then from Greece to Rome, and finally from the Romans to their successors, the modern Italians. The northern states in turn hoped to capture some of this legacy. The Italian-style palaces, with their frescoes, festivities and mannerist style, represent a sort of symbolic appropriation, as if displaying these attributes could beget a better future and, through artistic sovereignty, ensure political supremacy.

Not content with importing artworks, the Northerners also persuaded scholars, architects, artists and craftsmen to cross the mountains in order to transplant the Italian miracle under different skies. François I masterfully — and at great expense — orchestrated this exodus of brains and hands. Leonardo da Vinci accepted his invitation, followed by many other painters, sculptors, cabinet-makers and carvers of ornaments. The king also surrounded himself with philosophers, scholars and poets, to whom he offered pensions and protection, thereby transposing to France a form of patronage — the political use of culture — modelled on that of the Italian courts. He had learned in Italy that the arts and literature were the most effective means of conveying the magnificence of the sovereign, celebrating the prosperity of his reign and, more importantly, exalting him as the epitome of a fully realised life. For both in reality and in the image his sycophants painted of him, the prince had to be a complete man, equipped to play every role. As a soldier, he must demonstrate the strength and courage of a hero and the masculine power of the condottiere; as a statesman, show the intelligence, prudence and wisdom of a politician; and in the face of hardship, exemplify the moral virtues — justice, integrity and self-control. Not only did this ideal master possess the qualities of a leader, he also cultivated his mind, counselled with philosophers (like Lorenzo de' Medici with Marsilio Ficino), read or wrote poetry (again, like Lorenzo il Magnifico), and withdrew occasionally from active life to elevate his mind above everyday concerns through contemplation and meditation. '*Homo sum: humani nihil a me alienum puto*'. This humanistic motto, borrowed from the Latin author Terence, clearly expresses the ideal of completeness embodied at the time by the Italian prince, whose virtues shone sun-like over society.

More than any other area, poetry was infected by the contagion, engulfed by a Petrarcan tidal wave. Petrarch's bitter-sweet complaints, his modulations on the love of the distant lady, were widely imitated and continued to echo in European lyric poetry for the next three centuries. The triumph of the sonnet, invented in Italy and perfected by Petrarch, further accentuated the phenomenon. If this fashion met a need and touched a large audience, it was no doubt because it offered new ways to explore the inner life and plumb the human heart. Like the lover of the *Canzoniere* detailing his sorrows, poets probed the workings of the human psyche, examined the barometer of emotions and scanned the yardstick of feelings. To describe the nuances of inner life, they developed a lexicon, a language even, capable of expressing the movements of the soul in all its states. For several generations of writers, Petrarch showed how a man in love might — with great difficulty and turmoil — discover his own truth. By exploring the enigmas of the self to better fathom the mysteries of man, the Italian Renaissance had taken a decisive first step toward what would become one of the main projects of European modernity.

★ ★ ★ ★ ★

That transalpine itinerary — to Italy and back with full hands — parallels the journey undertaken by Jean Paul Barbier-Mueller. Surrounded by an exceptional collection of sixteenth-century French poetry, he has spent many years studying Ronsard and his satellites, rivals and disciples, as confirmed by the erudite, multi-volume *Ma Bibliothèque poétique* (eight in-folio volumes, 1973–2015) and the remarkable *Dictionnaire des poètes français de la seconde moitié du XVIe siècle (1549–1615)* (six volumes, 2015–17). This research inevitably led him to the Italian sources, namely Petrarch and his imitators of the *Quattrocento* and *Cinquecento*, whose mannered, codified lyricism gathered a large following and permeates the love poetry of the French Renaissance. Confronted with these palimpsests, intent on untangling each of these many voices, Jean Paul Barbier-Mueller also crossed the Alps, in a manner of speaking; for an enthusiastic collector like him, this meant tracking down and assembling all the first editions and rare books of Italian poetry he could lay his hands on, from the early age of printing to the baroque period. From the 1980s, he hunted through dozens of antiquarian bookshops and brought back hundreds of priceless works that he wished to share with others.

That is how the collection became a foundation. Jean Paul Barbier-Mueller and I initially established it in 1998, with the help of Jean Balsamo, Massimo Danzi and Nicolas Ducimetière at a later stage. Located at the University of Geneva, the Foundation aims to facilitate the work of researchers, for while copies of Petrarch's *Canzoniere* are easy to come by, it is much harder to find one's way among the multitude of poets who followed in his footsteps, and were often dispersed or forgotten. Yet in the sixteenth century their lines echoed in readers' memories and shaped scholarly culture. Arranged on shelves in steel bookcases, this collection of rare books, numbering six hundred volumes and still growing, is less eye-catching than some other witnesses of the flowering of the Italian Renaissance: the châteaux of the Loire Valley, the works of Leonardo and Titian in our museums, or the first operas. But comparisons are odious. In the cultural history of early-modern Europe, these small volumes played a central role in literature and in shaping sensibilities.

Once celebrated, they have become the preserve of specialists. To replace this all too secret garden in its original context of ideas, forms and uses, we invited creators and scholars — all of them writers — to choose a work, an author or an episode from the Italian Renaissance and engage in an exercise of informed invention, calling on their imagination to illuminate history or subjecting history to their imagination. They were given carte blanche on the condition that they share with us their conversation with the shadows of the past.

CHAPTER 1

La Lippina

Etienne Barilier

I am rather proud of the cause of my death: they say I expired after dancing to excess on the night of my second wedding. I am less happy with the fact that I am as good as dead to posterity. Who today, scholars excepted, has ever heard of *Pulchro et amore*, by one Agostino Nifo, born in Calabria, probably in the year 1469, and died in 1538, assuredly, in the glorious circumstances mentioned above, though it might have been after the dance, and the hands and the lips of the young bride?

Who reads me? Almost no one. And yet my work was decisive. A cataclysm, a blasphemy, trumpeted in the adoring silence of Christian Platonist thought, to the face of a priest in thrall to virtuous ecstasy, Marsilio Ficino — God is not beauty! Goodness maybe, but nothing more. Perceptible beauty is not a lost trace of the intelligible, dear Marsilio! To deny the body, to abstract oneself from it, is not to join supreme beauty but to abandon it forever:

> Nihil praeter hominem pulchrum dicendum est; nihil erit pulchrum quod ad cupidinem non referatur.
> [Nothing may be called beautiful if not man; there is no beauty without desire.]

These words did I, Agostino Nifo, dare write. This and more: I described, sung and detailed every aspect of human beauty; ever the fearless philosopher, I evoked its most elusive and ephemeral mystery:

> Nihil citius senescat gratia.
> [Nothing ages faster than grace.]

No one understood this with greater force, depth and despair than Michelangelo Buonarroti, in an anguished madrigal written around the same time as my *De Pulchro et amore*:

> ... ché grazia per poc'or doppia 'l martire.
> [... how grace, in her few hours, doubles the agony.]

But I am not as gloomy as him. I salute from afar the crucified genius. For my part, beauty gives me life before it kills me. And I laugh as I fall while dancing with her held fast in my aged hands. Knowing death simply makes me love life better. Is beauty but human? Is she but mortal? Why, then, should I not love her all the more? Why should I not worship her as my eternal goddess? Plato, Marsilio, don't

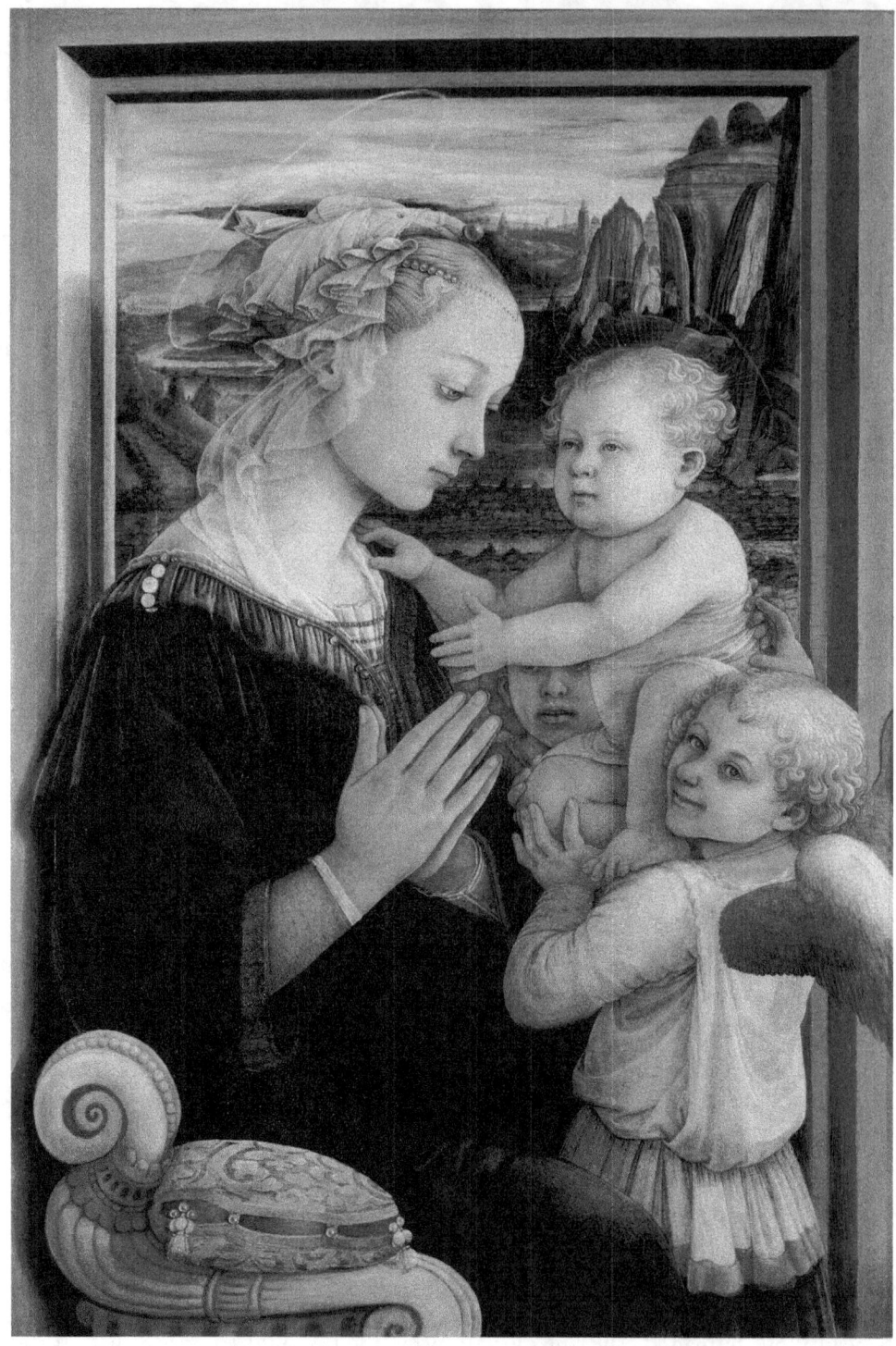

Fig. 1. Filippo Lippi, *La Lippina*, c. 1437–65, tempera on wood, 92 × 63.5 cm, Uffizi Gallery, Florence. © 2015 Photo Scala, Florence; courtesy of the Ministero Beni e Att. Culturali.

lose yourself in vain hopes. Returned to the arms of death, beauty will shine with the most perfect radiance.

★ ★ ★ ★ ★

Nevertheless, from beyond the grave, I confess: had I been alone, I would not have found the strength to dare. There was one who came before me, was always ahead of me, far ahead. His work changed the world, and will continue to change it, far more than mine. But before I name and praise him, let me tell you where we stand today, we the philosophers. And not only the philosophers, but the courtiers as well. Far too timid and fearful every one of us to admit the true nature of beauty. Consider this: even Baldassare Castiglione, who should have no academic scruples, struggles mightily to break away from Platonic propriety. In the *Cortegiano*, he admits that love is carnal. But he concedes the point only to persuade himself, and us, of its opposite: a kiss is permissible only if the lover is an *amante razionale* and not an *amante sensuale*, for only then can it become a passageway for the soul!

It therefore comes as no surprise that his *Cortegiano* puts into the mouth of Pietro Bembo a conventional eulogy of love, more like a prayer to the God of all that is good, which has no place here. What really matters, he preaches, is inner beauty; ugliness is evil, and so on. *Nugas agis*, Baldassare! Neither my dear friend Mario Equicola, in his *De amore*, which I find too much of a cunning compilation of the Ancients, nor even Tullia d'Aragone, in her otherwise bold, free and funny *Dialogo dell'Infinità d'Amore*, manage to break free from Marsilio's touchstone: *anima erit homo*, the soul will become man! As if the soul could exist without the body! There is one thing that eludes them, one thing they should have seen but did not.

★ ★ ★ ★ ★

What should they have seen, you ask. Why, only the pages that changed the world, and forever gave human beauty her rightful place, the first place, the only place: are these not the *Dialoghi d'amore* of the great Leo the Hebrew? Did any philosopher before him venture to show a man and a woman, Philo and Sophia, conversing as equals? Did any before him so boldly portray a man speaking the truth of love because he is in love? A man, Philo, who tries to convince Sophia because he wants her to love him back? A man who speaks instead of sighing, reasons rather than cry? A man whose intelligence beats to the pulse of his tormented heart? A man who, racked with desire, nourished with hope, in the words of Pontus de Tyard's beautiful French translation, loves a woman of flesh, and has no intention of forgetting it? Consider this wonderful scene at the end of the first book: Philo, with noble restraint, lets Sophia sleep after he has showered her with words while receiving no shower of kisses in return. He stands over her, loving her sleep, respecting her unconsciousness, alone in *gracious and anxious contemplation*.

Leo the Hebrew was undoubtedly a great man: perspicacious, powerful and deeply humane. Though he was not my true master (patience, I'm getting there), I admit he inspired me: like him, I proclaim that man and woman are absolute equals. Like him, I believe that reciprocal love between them is composed of *admirable attraction and deep admiration in equal parts.* Like him, finally, I dream of a union between man and woman that is not a dissolution or forgetting of self, but rather a transformation of one by the other, one in the other:

> Accensus amatae totus adhaeret; adhaerens denique in amatam transformatur.
>
> [Inflamed by love, he binds himself wholly to his beloved, and by this bond, he is transformed in her.]

I wrote these words, but I owe the idea to Leo, the philosopher of love. He found the irreplaceable words — the *shibboleth* of love, if I may be so bold to call it so — recognisable only to true lovers, words that were destined for eternity, as you will see. This is what he wrote, one day, in exile in Naples or perhaps Venice, a Jew fleeing the realm of the very Catholic Kings of Spain. Here are his words, in their original splendour:

> La propria diffinizione del perfetto amore de l'uomo e de la donna è la conversione de l'amante ne l'amato, con desiderio che si converti l'amato ne l'amante.

And here their poor echo:

> [This, then, is the true and proper definition of perfect love between a man and a woman: it is a conversation between a lover and his beloved that aims to convert the beloved into a lover.]

This unrivalled masterpiece of amorous and philosophical thought, first published in 1535, in Rome, very quickly passed into Spanish, the language of Leo's native land, for which he never ceased to yearn. To complete this transformation, his words, like ring-neck doves, spread their wings and flew across the oceans all the way to Peru. Indeed, these precious pages were translated by the son of an Inca princess in the twilight of the sixteenth century. Garcilaso de la Vega l'Inca, the author of *Comentarios Reales*, chose to render into Spanish (enriched with Quechua), the monumental dialogue of Leo the Hebrew, recognising in him a fellow exile whose tormented, suffering and generous nature he shared. Here is the same unrivalled sentence in the words of the Inca princess's son:

> La propia definición del perfecto amor del hombre y de la mujer es conversión del amante en el amado con deseo de que el amado se convierta en el amante.

Does this sound familiar? Yes indeed, for it is one of the most beautiful poems ever written, known to all who walk this earth, not to mention all who, like me, lie below it:

> ¡ oh noche que juntaste
> amado con amada,
> amada en el amado transformada !
>
> [Oh, night that joined Beloved with lover, Lover transformed in the Beloved!]

You will certainly have recognised *La Noche oscura,* by John of the Cross, a poem as grave and barely less gloomy than Michelangelo's — trembling, peaceful, anguished. Juan de la Cruz and Michelangelo Buonarroti, kindred martyrs of love, though only Juan manages to smile through his torment. *Conversión del amante en el amado... amada en el amado transformada!* It is unlikely, however, that John of the Cross, who went to his eternal silence in 1591, read the translation penned by the Inca princess's son. But that he knew Leo the Hebrew and found in him an intense mystical fervour, that he offered this up to his God in words even more beautiful and imploring, is beyond the shadow of a doubt.

★ ★ ★ ★ ★

What does this signify? What am I, Agostino Nifo, trying to demonstrate? I, who claim to have freed beauty from the heavenly realm of Ideas so she may be purely and simply human again? I, who claim to reject Marsilio's teachings and Platonic hope? Do I not contradict myself by praising to the heavens such Judeo-Christian-Platonic high mysticism? If Leo the Hebrew was my true master, am I not drawing some strange conclusions from his teachings?

I don't think so. And, as I said, my true master is elsewhere. I will tell you of this master soon. He allowed me to love Leo the Hebrew's inspired and generous prose, John of the Cross's gracious and anguished verse, with all my force and, I dare say, with all my soul, by giving them a completely human meaning. Who is my true master? In fact, she is a mistress. Her name is *la Lippina*. Don't waste your time searching for her among the courtesans and great ladies of my age. *La Lippina* is not the name of a girl, but the name of a painting. Here is her story.

When I was young, I taught in the city of Padua, home of the brave Pomponazzi, whom I followed: he denied the immortality of the individual soul. Consequently, one of his books was publicly burned in Venice. Hoping to escape a similar fiery fate, I made a few cowardly concessions: I penned a laboured refutation of Pomponazzi, *De immortalitate animae libellus adversus P. Pomponacium*, demonstrating his alleged errors. In the meantime, I had fled Padua for the Papal City.

More to the point, on my way to Rome I passed through Florence. It was there I saw a painting whose creator, I was told, was one Filippo Lippi, a defrocked monk. It was made around 1465, a few years before I was born. I must confess: this extraordinary sight made me ashamed of my weakness. I berated myself: you dare not assert that the soul is mortal, yet this simple fellow, through the sole power of love, had the audacity to paint such a radiant blasphemy? How is this possible? When I heard the whole story, my question only grew more urgent, my wonder greater and my admiration deeper.

Fra Filippo Lippi, a lover of life and of women, a monk by necessity rather than choice, was chaplain of the convent of Santa Margherita in Prato. One day, he encountered a face of all-powerful gentleness, a rose amid the thorns of the crucifixion. The name of this young nun is known: she was Lucrezia Buti, the daughter of a respectable family. Twenty, perhaps thirty years his junior. Too beautiful, I knew in a heartbeat, not to awaken in him a desire to capture her for himself and transform himself in her, by transforming her in him. But also to transform her in herself through the precise and most jealous attention of painting. To capture her, but only in the way that a dancer catches his partner, who makes herself as light as a leaf for her carrier — Fra Filippo remembered this when he painted his beloved as a dancing Salome.

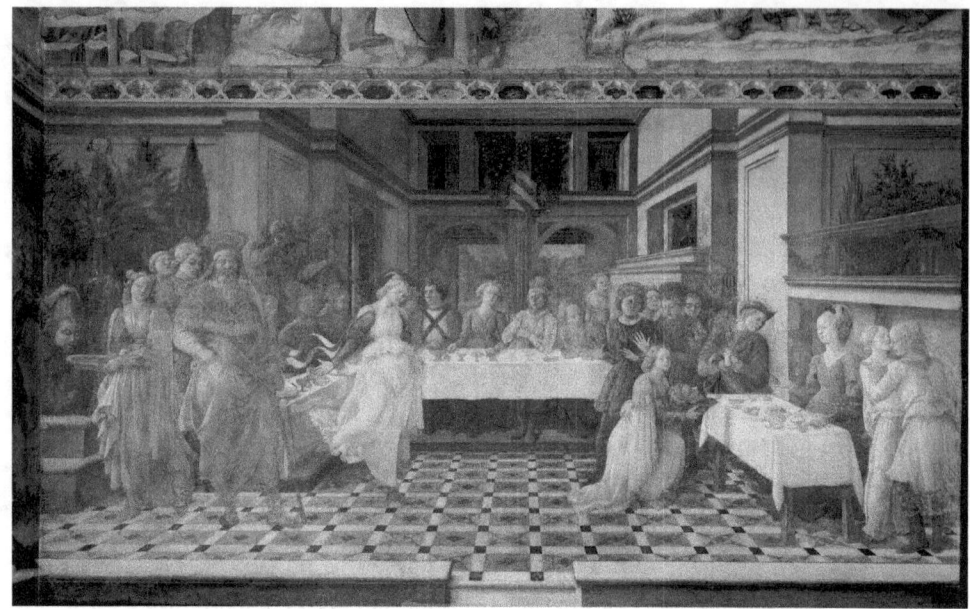

Fig. 2. Filippo Lippi, *Feast of Herod*, c. 1450–60, fresco, Duomo, Prato.
© 2015 Photo Scala, Florence.

What a scandal this was in Florence! The punishment for seducing a nun could be terrible. However, Pope Pius II Piccolomini, himself the author of a charming little book entitled *Story of Two Lovers* and thus predisposed to clemency, lent a friendly ear to the intercession of Cosimo de' Medici and released both the monk and the nun from their vows. Once free, they didn't marry but had a son nonetheless, Filippino, who also became a painter. What else was a child of love and art to do?

Ah, but the painting I saw in Florence! Even today, though centuries in the grave should have dimmed my wonder, I can hardly believe my memory. *Madonna col Bambino e angeli, detta Lippina*. Now, here is the inevitable, albeit not essential, starting point: this woman is beautiful, as beautiful as truth — though not being a Platonist, I shouldn't really say this! Let us give thanks to Fra Filippo, for not keeping her beauty to himself alone, but offering it to us instead, so that we might transform ourselves in her! Sometimes in my writings I invoke the memory of Petrarch's Laura. What a stroke of genius it was for Lucrezia, whose lover undoubtedly painted a faithful likeness of her, to resemble Laura:

> Fuor i biondi capelli allor velati,
> et l'amoroso sguardo in sé raccolto.
>
> [Your blond hair took the veil immediately,
> Your loving gaze withdrew into itself.][1]

But she was the genius of her own beauty first of all, for it is unimaginable that Fra Filippo, with all his love and talent, could have painted a portrait of such definitive

---

[1] In the translation of Mark Musa, *Petrarch Canzoniere* (Bloomington: Indiana University Press, 1996), p. 13.

purity, like the purity of a perfect silence, had Lucrezia not embodied it perfectly herself: in her face, on her forehead and behind her forehead! However, the most extravagant, audacious and blasphemous aspect of this work, the most decisive too, lies elsewhere.

Where, then? What was it about this painting that gave me the courage to believe and to proclaim: *nihil praeter hominem pulchrum dicendum est; nihil erit pulchrum quod ad cupidinem non referatur*?

★ ★ ★ ★ ★

Open your eyes! For the first time in the history of Christianity, the holy Virgin is given the traits of the most desirable and most desired of women, a beauty whose extreme delicacy is also carnal in the extreme, carnal enough to awaken a dead man like me. Before her, the Virgin could be beautiful, but never desirable. Real women undoubtedly served as models — how could they not — yet they remained nameless, effaced in every sense of the word. A transient, physical vessel for hyperdulia. Before Fra Filippo, in areas other than painting, divine honours had been rendered to a few real women, it is true: Laura and Beatrice, for instance. Then again, *L'amor che move il sole e l'altre stelle* — love of this kind is not carnal in the least. As creations of language rather than painting, the *Canzoniere* and the *Commedia* could more easily escape into Platonic abstraction. Language, alas, is the first form of abstraction.

Fra Filippo, on the other hand, painted a woman of flesh, using a *sfumato* that was never equalled until Leonardo, a *sfumato* of the most diabolical precision — or rather, human, simply human precision. The simple precision of carnal truth. He painted a woman whose name is known, who we know is young and will grow old, is alive and will die some day — lucky Fra Filippo, who was certain to die before her. What Virgin is effaced in this way by her model? None before her.

Then what? Does it matter? The bright rift had been opened, the transgression committed. What is surprising is how long it took for people to notice. In fact, for many years, philosophers and theologians simply didn't want to know. Can't you see that everything has been turned upside down, as if Heaven were now the ground under our feet? Does this mean that Heaven is mortal? Don't you see that the *pulchrum* will never again exist *praeter hominem* — *et feminam*? And that with a single brushstroke of genius, desire, love, the Renaissance became what it will remain forever: a religion of beauty — human, perishable beauty?

I can hear my detractors, Marsilio chief among them, asking: why should Heaven lie, mortal, at our feet? Why shouldn't the earth rise, immortal, to Heaven? Could it be that the Virgin gave Lucrezia her beauty? Did Fra Filippo perhaps understand that desire itself is a desire for God? Did he understand, long before Leo the Hebrew and John of the Cross, that the body of man, longing to join with the body of woman, is but the human soul longing to join the perfection of God? Is *la Lippina* in fact a lesson in Platonism and Christianity?

Why not? Just look at Lucrezia Buti, I tell you, look at her again. Now, you must admit that if the Virgin created woman in her image, this woman certainly returned her the favour. And returned it well, so terrifyingly well that we should have the courage to accept the consequences. You are free to believe what you wish, dear Marsilio. Assuredly, Platonism and Christianity are treasures that do great honour to the human dream. But there may be a higher dream, a dream more desperate and therefore more demanding, a dream that impels us to seek the absolute, knowing that it took the form of your face, Lucrezia, and that we will die without ever reaching it, that we will die as you did, for all eternity. Nevertheless, we give you thanks, for you were, and remain, full of grace.

CHAPTER 2

Geneva and New York: Two Places of Memory for Pietro Bembo and Ginevra de' Benci

Lina Bolzoni

There are places and times, books, paintings, and people one encounters which leave their mark on one's life and one's history as a researcher. Places can serve both to anchor a recollection, as the ancient art of memory rightly understood, and to tell a story: they carve out a space both in our minds and in the text. It has always struck me as remarkable that Leonardo Sciascia chose to call his book on the amnesiac of Collegno *The Theatre of Memory*, a title which, by his own admission, was inspired by Frances Yates's work.[1] While acknowledging that, as a twentieth-century man, his memory was necessarily modelled on Proust and Pirandello, Sciascia used a quotation from the *Rhetorica ad Herennium* (III, 16): 'Constat igitur artificiosa memoria ex locis et imaginibus' (The art of memory is therefore based on places and images) as a sort of refrain or formula to structure and guide his narrative.

As I looked back on the years of research which led to the publication of my book *Il cuore di cristallo Ragionamenti d'amore, poesia e ritratto nel Rinascimento* (Turin: Einaudi, 2010), I became aware — *si licet parva componere magnis* — that two places regularly sprang to mind, two cities which played an important role for me: Geneva and New York.

I shall start in Geneva, on the morning when, for the first time, I entered the small room containing the Barbier-Mueller Foundation's splendid collection of Italian Renaissance poetry. To return to my first image, I felt like I had entered the heart of a veritable *thesaurus memoriae*, filled with books, many of them priceless, which I would otherwise have been obliged to hunt for, often unsuccessfully, in many different libraries around the world. Among these was a first edition of Pietro Bembo's *Gli Asolani* from 1505, whose elegant illuminated initial immediately drew my attention to the dedicatory letter to Lucrezia Borgia introducing the work. As Jean Balsamo explains in his wonderful catalogue, this miniature was added in the nineteenth century — not a forgery so much as a collector's 'retrospective' fancy.[2]

---

1   L. Sciascia, *Il teatro della memoria* (Turin: Einaudi, 1981); Frances A. Yates, *L'arte della memoria* (Turin: Einaudi, 1972) / *The Art of Memory* (Chicago, IL: University of Chicago Press, 1966).

2   *De Dante à Chiabrera: Poètes italiens de la Renaissance dans la bibliothèque de la Fondation Barbier-Mueller*, catalogue edited by Jean Balsamo (Geneva: Droz, 2007), p. 105.

What I had before me was a perfect illustration of the role played by the reader's eye and taste, and the degree to which they sometimes shape the image of the text according to the reader's desires, reinforcing the magical capacity that the act of reading possesses to enable us to converse with the ancient authors and transport ourselves to their world ('I deliver myself entirely to them', Machiavelli wrote in his famous letter to Vettori).[3]

This observation led me to a realisation, or rather, a new methodological approach. It is a well-known fact that only some copies of *Gli Asolani* printed in 1505 include the dedication to Lucrezia Borgia. The reasons for this disparity have been thoroughly researched, and several explanations offered. Leaving this essential question aside for the moment, however, I thought it might be interesting to examine this ancient text from a different perspective. Imagine you are a sixteenth-century reader buying this book: you can choose from two different versions, with or without the dedication letter. Pietro Bembo's love affair with Lucrezia Borgia notwithstanding, the presence or absence of this letter changes the point of view on itself that the book creates, and proposes to the reader. Let us see how this plays out in the first printed copies of *Gli Asolani*, which do not include the letter. Following an introduction, in which he explains the circumstances and significance of the book, Bembo immediately launches into a detailed depiction of Asolo and the wedding festivities celebrated there by the Queen of Cyprus:

> The fair and pleasant castle of Asolo, built in the foothills of our mountains overlooking the marches of Treviso, belongs, as everyone should know, to my lady the Queen of Cyprus (with her family, which goes by the name of Cornelia and is much honored in our city of Venice, my own is joined by blood as well as friendship and familiarity). At Asolo, where she went for her diversion last September, it befell that she married off one of her maids of honor, a beautiful, well-bred, gentle girl whom the Queen, having brought her up from childhood, cherished with a most tender love. Accordingly she had preparations made there for a large and brilliant wedding; and after all the more eminent men of the surrounding country had been invited with their ladies, and those of Venice likewise, to the full satisfaction of them all she prolonged the celebrations day after day with music, singing, dancing and most solemn feasts.[4]

The celebration of a brilliant wedding is, in a sense, a faithful image of court festivities, the epitome of all that is refined, honourable and pleasant about life at court. Naturally, everything there is beautiful, genteel and grand. There could be no more suitable place or occasion for a discourse on love. This opening image remains largely unchanged in later versions of *Gli Asolani*. But Bembo's original manuscript contains some profoundly significant differences, namely in the part about the queen, which is more fully developed. Asolo, he writes:

> belongs (as you most certainly know) to my lady the Queen of Cyprus, who, since the death of her late husband King James, remained in a state of childless widowhood until long past youth, she then entrusted the governance of her kingdom to the Signoria, to the satisfaction of her entire people, and returned

---

3 N. Machiavelli, *Lettere*, ed. by F. Gaeta, in *Opere*, Vol. III (Turin: UTET, 1984), p. 426.
4 P. Bembo, *Gli Asolani*, trans. by R. B. Gottfried (Bloomington: Indiana University Press, 1954), p. 8.

to her native Venice to see her parents and spend her remaining years in her homeland, close to her family. She was warmly welcomed by them and received from the Signoria many valuable gifts, including this castle, which I consider pleasant and agreeable above all others due to its situation, the surrounding countryside, and its healthy air.[5]

Here again, the tone is idyllic and the story highly idealised. However, we also learn that the queen, who is celebrating the wedding of her maid of honour, has suffered a double loss: that of her husband and that of her kingdom. The setting is still as splendid and refined, yet the image of the court immediately appears more fragile and illusory: the court of Catherine is merely a gift to her from the Republic of Venice on its own territory. In the published text, as we have seen, the history of the Queen of Cyprus has been removed. The events that precede the present moment in the narrative are part of the common memory and therefore can be omitted from the narrative to avoid creating an atmosphere of insecurity around the court and the rituals celebrated there. It is fascinating, nonetheless, to observe that certain themes banished from the story — death, loss, separation and substitution — re-emerge in a different form in the dedication to Lucrezia Borgia. Returning to the opening section of *Gli Asolani*, in the version mentioned at the beginning of this essay, let us now consider how the dedication introduces the text that follows.

Bembo starts by apologising for his lateness in delivering 'these discourses which I promised, last year in Ferrara, that I would send you'. The reason for this delay is his grief over the death of his younger and much beloved only brother, Carlo,

> who, out of his great love for me making every wish of mine his own, had no greater care than to relieve me of all my cares, so that I might give my whole time and thought to the literary studies which he knew were dear to me above everything.

She — Lucrezia — had also suffered terrible loss recently, and therefore could understand his pain:

> But how much these things have continually deepened my wound, Your Highness may easily estimate from those two blows which a malicious fortune has dealt to you in so short a space of time.[6]

The text of *Gli Asolani*, which this letter accompanies, both represents and ideally substitutes for the author, who is away from Ferrara. Moreover, it has the effect of reproducing reality, in that it depicts a court wedding in all points similar to the one Lucrezia had just organised:

> [I] send these discourses, such as they are, to you, and all the more readily at this time, as I have recently learned that Your Highness has married off your worthy Nicola. For I consider them no unseemly gift at such a season, when, although my employments now prevent me from taking part in your celebrations, these may speak and argue in my place with Your Highness, with your dear and worthy Lady Angela Borgia, and with the bride, perhaps not without the assistance of Master Ercole Strozzi and Master Antonio Tebaldeo,

---

5 Translator's note: no published translation of this manuscript is available.
6 *Gli Asolani*, pp. 1–2. The sorrows that Bembo alludes to are the loss of a stillborn daughter, in 1503, and the death of Lucrezia's father.

the familiars and followers of Your Highness, much loved of me and honored by the world.[7]

Gli Asolani thus makes up for an absence: it speaks and debates in place of its absent author. In the context of the actual wedding at the court of Ferrara, the participants in the dispute on love are also three men (Bembo through his text, Ercole Strozzi and Antonio Tebaldeo) and three women (Lucrezia, Angela Borgia and the bride). Bembo emphasises that the two situations are both very different and very similar, and in many ways reflect each other:

> And it may well be that the very things which *other* young men have discussed with *other* ladies during the festivities for *another* marriage, you in *your* festivities will read with *your* maids of honor and courtiers as they have been written down by me, who am likewise *yours*.[8] (Italics added)

The nature of the author's ties to Lucrezia imbues this reflection with a more powerful and secret meaning, emphasised by the repeated opposition of 'other' and 'your'. Meanwhile, the theme of absence and distance is strongly coloured by its direct association with death and the inexorable loss it implies. *Gli Asolani*, but also literature as a whole, are closely connected to this dimension: Bembo's younger brother managed Bembo's affairs for him, leaving him free to write ('so that I might give my whole time and thought to the literary studies which he knew were dear to me above everything'). *Gli Asolani* carries to the court of Ferrara the memory of this brother, to whom the book owes its very existence.

Copies of the first editions of *Gli Asolani* that include the dedication to Lucrezia Borgia therefore generate a more complex and tragic perspective on the text. The description of the wedding festivities at the court of the Queen of Cyprus is recreated within the space of writing, and we return to the scene of another wedding only after crossing the dark threshold of death.

It is now time to move on to the second place of memory: New York. In the autumn of 2005, the Frick Collection presented an exhibition of the portraits of Hans Memling.[9] I had to wait for quite a long time to get in; the rooms in which the paintings hung were small and the crowd waiting was large, so that only a few visitors were admitted at a time. I remember walking down a rather narrow staircase and stopping suddenly in front of a portrait of a youngish man with an intense, severe expression, holding an ancient coin in his left hand. 'Portrait of Bernardo Bembo (?)', said the label on the wall. What was Pietro Bembo's father doing here, and why the question mark?

I was nonplussed. I had been looking forward to visiting a small, exquisite exhibition of portraits by one of the Flemish masters of the genre, and here I was, inexplicably drawn to a figure intimately connected with the topic I had been researching for several years: Pietro Bembo and *Gli Asolani*, his dialogues on love, an archetypal theme of Italian Renaissance literature. This encounter with that wonderful portrait encouraged me to cross the boundaries of the geography and

---

7 Ibid. p. 2.
8 Ibid. p. 2.
9 *Les Portraits de Memling*, ed. by T. H. Borchert (Gand and Amsterdam: Ludion, 2005). The exhibition at the Frick Collection in New York took place from 6 October to 31 December 2005.

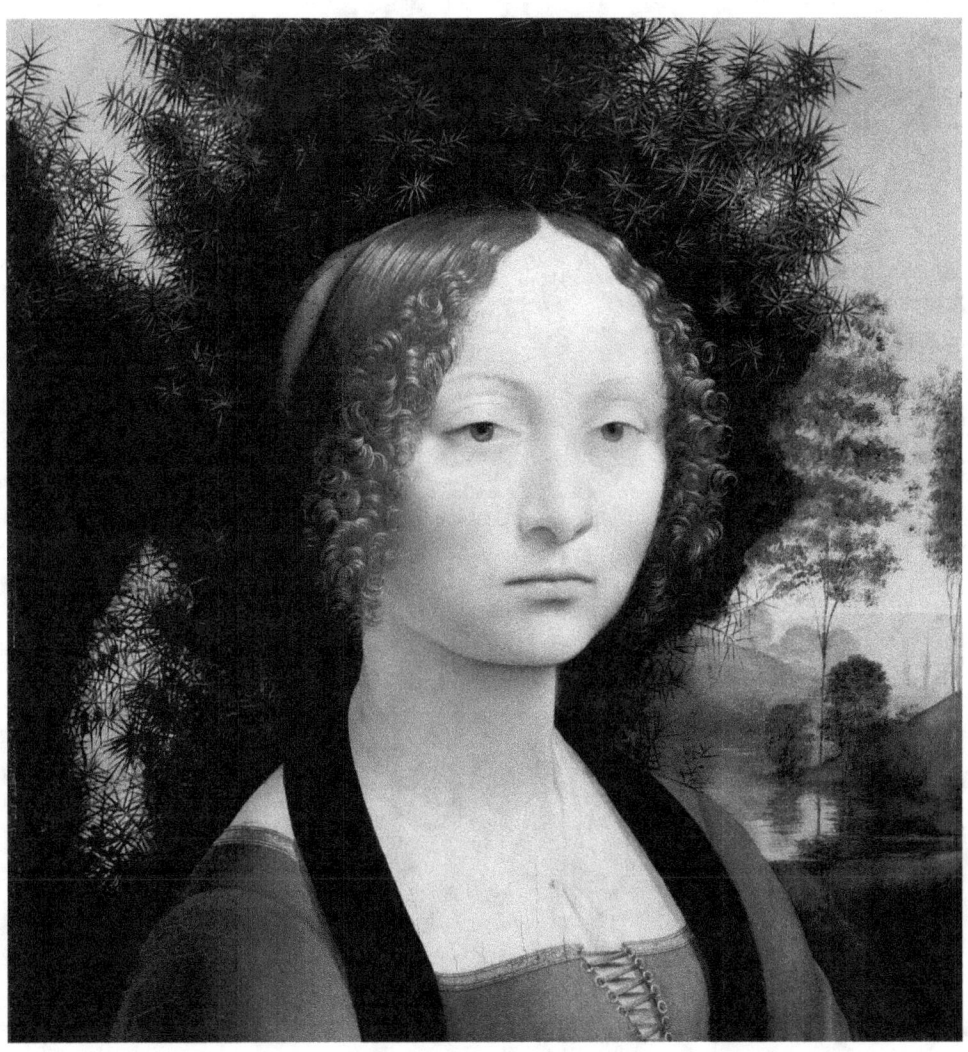

FIG. 3. Leonardo da Vinci, *Portrait of Ginevra de' Benci*, c. 1474–78, oil on wood, 38.1 × 37 cm, National Gallery, Washington. Ailsa Mellon Bruce Fund/Courtesy National Gallery of Art, Washington.

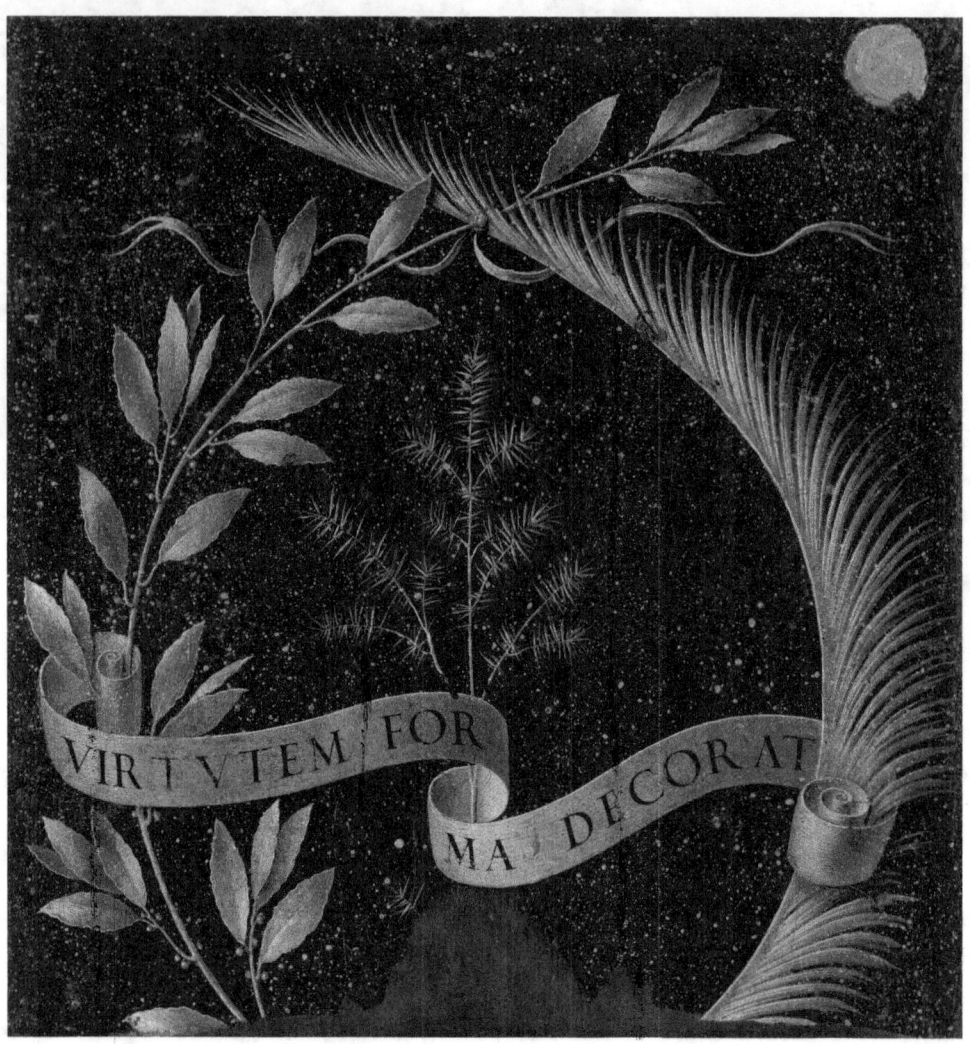

FIG. 4. Leonardo da Vinci, *Portrait of Ginevra de' Benci* (reverse), c. 1474–78, oil on wood, 38.1 × 37 cm, National Gallery, Washington. Ailsa Mellon Bruce Fund/Courtesy National Gallery of Art, Washington.

history of Italian literature. I wondered what influence the great artistic flowering of the countries of northern Europe might have had on Bernardo Bembo when he was ambassador to Burgundy, at the court of Charles the Bold, and what complex and fascinating connections might exist between words and images, literature and art. On the one hand, my aim was to reveal what one might call the dual nature of *Gli Asolani*, which appears not only in its structure but also in the way that its main themes emerge when one penetrates the deep layers of the text. My hypothesis is that *Gli Asolani* present a sort of 'double portrait' of love, poetry, and court life, a bit like a type of fifteenth- or sixteenth-century portrait that features a second, allegorical or emblematic imaged painted on the reverse, or occasionally on a lid.

The very structure of these portraits forces the viewer to engage in a process of 'reading', which not only takes time but also involves the body in a series of actions necessary to interpret them. A famous example is the portrait of Ginevra de' Benci, by a young Leonardo da Vinci, now in the National Gallery in Washington, DC. On the back of this portrait, a crown of laurels and palm fronds surrounds a sprig of juniper and a scroll inscribed with the motto '*virtutem forma decorat*'. The portrait was originally dated 1474, the year of Ginevra's marriage. However, several studies have since highlighted the central role Bernardo Bembo played in commissioning it. He was ambassador to Florence in 1475–76 and again in 1478–80, at which time literary sources unequivocally attest that he began a platonic relationship with Ginevra.[10] In particular, the image on the reverse has been crucial to establishing the date the portrait was painted, and has opened a new chapter in the history of art and literature between the fifteenth and sixteenth centuries, with many fascinating implications. Moreover, infrared reflectography has confirmed Bernardo's role in the painting: his motto '*virtus et honor*' appears under the motto we see today, '*virtutem forma decorat*'.

In this case, too, I took an approach similar to the one I used to analyse the effect on *Gli Asolani* of the dedicatory letter's presence or absence. Leaving to one side the complex and still unresolved question of who ordered the two parts of this painting, and when, I asked myself how this double portrait functioned: how was it intended to be received by viewers in either case, that is, with the motto of Bernardo Bembo on the reverse, or with the motto referring to Ginevra, as it appears today? What is fascinating is that an entire community of friends formed around the platonic love of Bernardo and Ginevra, and, in a way, around this portrait, too. This group of poets and philosophers from the court of Lorenzo de' Medici sang and commented their relationship in terms drawn from the Neoplatonic code the couple adhered to; they constituted a sort of 'community of interpretation' devoted to identifying the bonds of *similitudo*, or hidden associations, which served as the foundation of their love of that circle of friends. It is also remarkable that, after returning to Venice for good, Bernardo Bembo did not forget Ginevra, as attested by an annotation in his hand in the margin of a manuscript of Ficino's commentary on Plato's *Banquet*

---

10 For the preceding biography see also D. A. Brown, 'Ginevra de' Benci', in *Italian Paintings of the Fifteenth Century*, ed. by M. Boskovits and D. A. Brown, Collections of the National Gallery of Art (US) (Washington, DC: National Gallery of Art; Oxford: distributed by Oxford University Press, 2003), pp. 357–68.

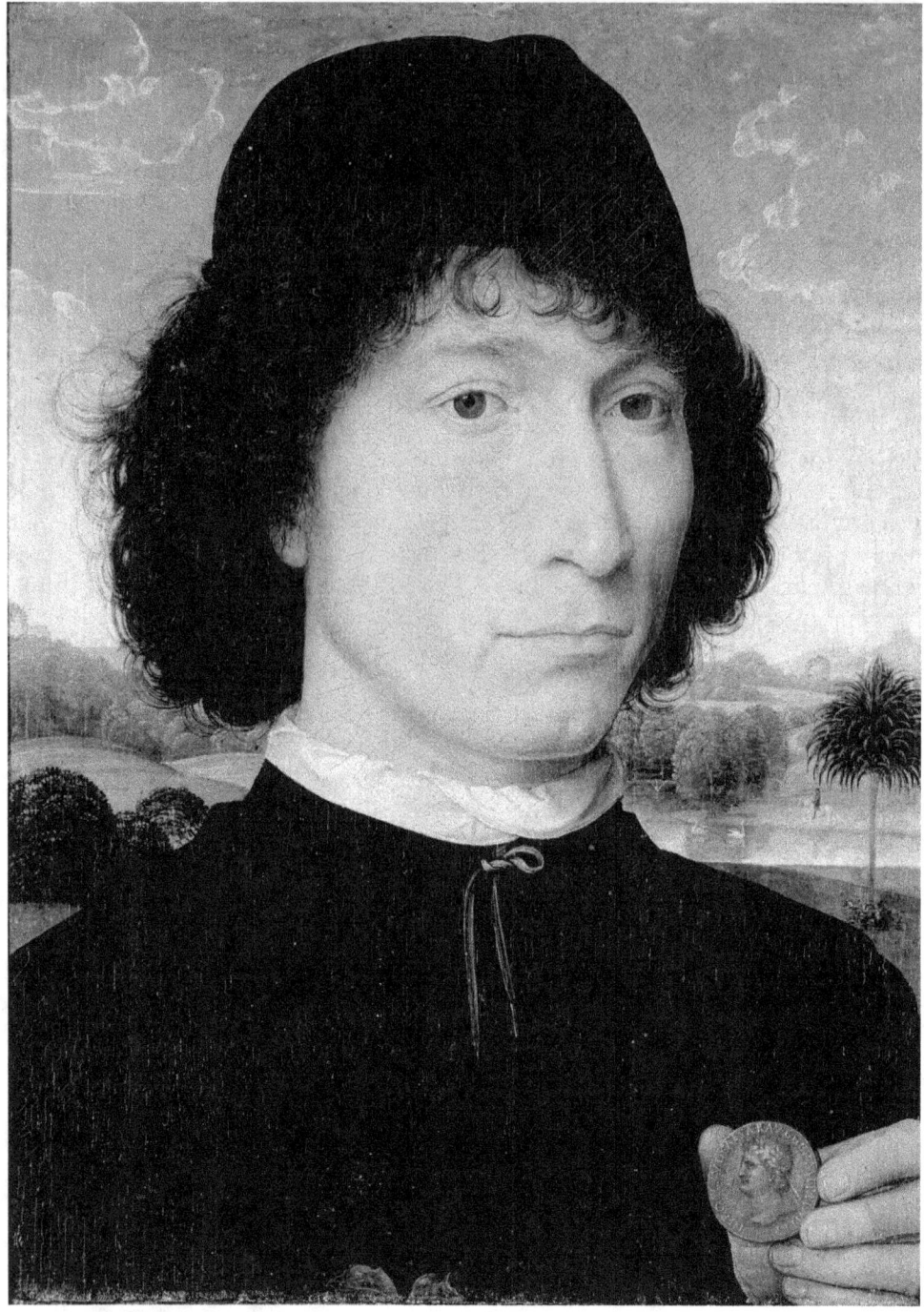

Fig. 5. Hans Memling, *Man with a Roman Coin (Portrait of Bernardo Bembo?)*, c. 1473–74, oil on wood, 30.7 × 23.2 × 0.6 cm, Koninklijk Museum voor Schone Kunsten, Antwerp. © 2015. Photo Scala, Florence.

(Bodleian Library, Oxford, Can.Class.Lat.156, c.21^r), in which he praises Ginevra as 'the most beautiful and virtuous of women'.

Around the same time — the final years of the fifteenth century — Bernardo's son Pietro started working on *Gli Asolani*. This book presents a dispute among friends, who also happen to be poets and philosophers, on the nature of love. They alternately condemn and celebrate love before finally opting for a life of strict asceticism, a choice influenced by Neoplatonism. These elements — the discussion of love, the learned circle of friends, the appeal of Neoplatonism — remind me of Ginevra, the double portrait by Leonardo, and the many texts on love produced in the circle around Bernardo and Ginevra. I thought that one could perhaps re-place this experience behind the text of *Gli Asolani*, so to say, and in this way reconnect several places of memory: Geneva and New York, of course, but also Florence, Venice and the far North.

CHAPTER 3

The Brancacci Chapel: Florence and Poetry

Yves Bonnefoy

I

Florence, late 1950. One of my most treasured memories: via di Santo Spirito, Borgo San Frediano, those long, narrow streets of a whole winter in Oltr'Arno. Night was falling. A sparse yellow light trickled from the shops onto the pavement, glistening in rain puddles and on the occasional patch of snow. I took no notice of the passers-by; it was too cold; they were in a hurry; I was alone. I was in the habit of stopping at the door of a grocer's for a piece of the flat, oily bread they told me was called *scacciata*, though this was not what they called it in Sicily. Florence lay mostly on the other side of the river.

This was the neighbourhood where I lived, in a *pensione* on via dei Serragli with a garden overlooked by vague, time-blackened statues, and on the white wall of my room, a large coloured lithograph of Raphael's *Transfiguration*. Almost every evening, I walked through these streets or others just like them to the Chiesa del Carmine to see the frescoes of Masaccio and Masolino in the Brancacci chapel. At this late hour, the great church was empty. There was only the sacristan hobbling around in the growing dark with his small lamp. Later, cradling the feeble light in his hands, he would come tell me they were closing. But by then I had already had a long time to myself in that enclosure of paintings, which I could illuminate for a few lira. Why did I go there so often, at an hour, moreover, when the paintings were barely visible? I hardly glanced at them, for I knew them by heart. I sat with them, keeping them company of a fashion, taking notes for stories I thought I might someday write.

Why did I return, again and again, to the Brancacci chapel at nightfall? For the simple reason that almost every day I had an appointment of almost equal importance at a different chapel, the Sagrestia Nuova di San Lorenzo, where Michelangelo had worked. The appointed time was noon, after I left the *mensa universitaria* or a small *trattoria* I frequented nearby, on via San Gallo. How different from Masaccio's work was the approach embodied in Michelangelo's almost subterranean statues! I had to walk either around or through the perpetually lively and noisy market bordering the church. And, I don't know why, in my memory, the sky at this hour was almost always clear, with a pale sunlight filtering through the cloths that flapped over the vendors and their wares. A few steps away loomed the austere walls of the church and its sublime façade of naked brick. That sunlight was perhaps not of this world.

My two great memories are joined. My Florence was perhaps not of this world. I would leave my room early in the morning, cross the river, and, until the hour of the Brancacci Chapel, remain among the museums and streets of the city of Giotto and Brunelleschi, returning again and again to a few spots I particularly loved. During these months, I could not imagine living anywhere but Florence, surrounded by the daily and nightly mystery of Italy, and this was probably a way for me to take possession of the city within a dream. I was beset by so many dreams at the time, though I struggled to control them. I was trying to serve out this apprenticeship under Masaccio and Michelangelo — the latter no doubt very much aware of the former, for they shared a concern with transforming life — and was beginning to understand, through them, the nature of poetry and, at the same time, of Tuscan art. Let me try to explain how I arrived at this understanding.

II

Many years have passed since that long-ago winter, that distant spring, and I feel better equipped today — or at least, I have the illusion that this is the case — to explore the reasons that led me so often from the Brancacci chapel to the tomb of Giuliano de' Medici. First of all, what explains the powerful and lasting attraction of Santa Maria del Carmine? Clearly not the genius of Masaccio so much as the presence, in the same space, often side by side on the same wall, of his vision and Masolino's.

Indeed, the two painters shared the chapel in a rather surprising way. Hoping to understand them better, I sought answers from historians whose thinking and methodology I respected, but found nothing sufficiently enlightening in their work — though to be honest, at the time I had not yet discovered the *Fatti di Masolino e di Masaccio*. These historians and critics rightly point out the disparity between the two artists. Masolino da Panicale, they suggest, represents a narrative that flourished in the period known as the late gothic, in which religious imagery focused on supernatural events and miracles. This required artists to circumvent rather than confront the obvious facts of objects and bodies: they concentrated, therefore, on the outline of figures without addressing their mass, and this outline became the thread stitching together a narrative that seemed designed, in its complacent unreality, to embellish, but never contradict, the theologians' discourse. And indeed, this is quite visible in Masolino's frescoes. His representation of Adam and Eve at the moment of temptation, for instance, the elegant proportions of their bodies and the negation of three-dimensional space, offer no intimation of the burden of the flesh or of their existing in a time that will soon come crashing down on them.

Facing these figures that appear to withdraw from life as it must be lived, Masaccio's work displays a clear desire to break through the screen of representation, to go straight to the facts as they truly are under the veil of legend, to stand squarely in the unavoidable space of the simple human condition. He substitutes a concern

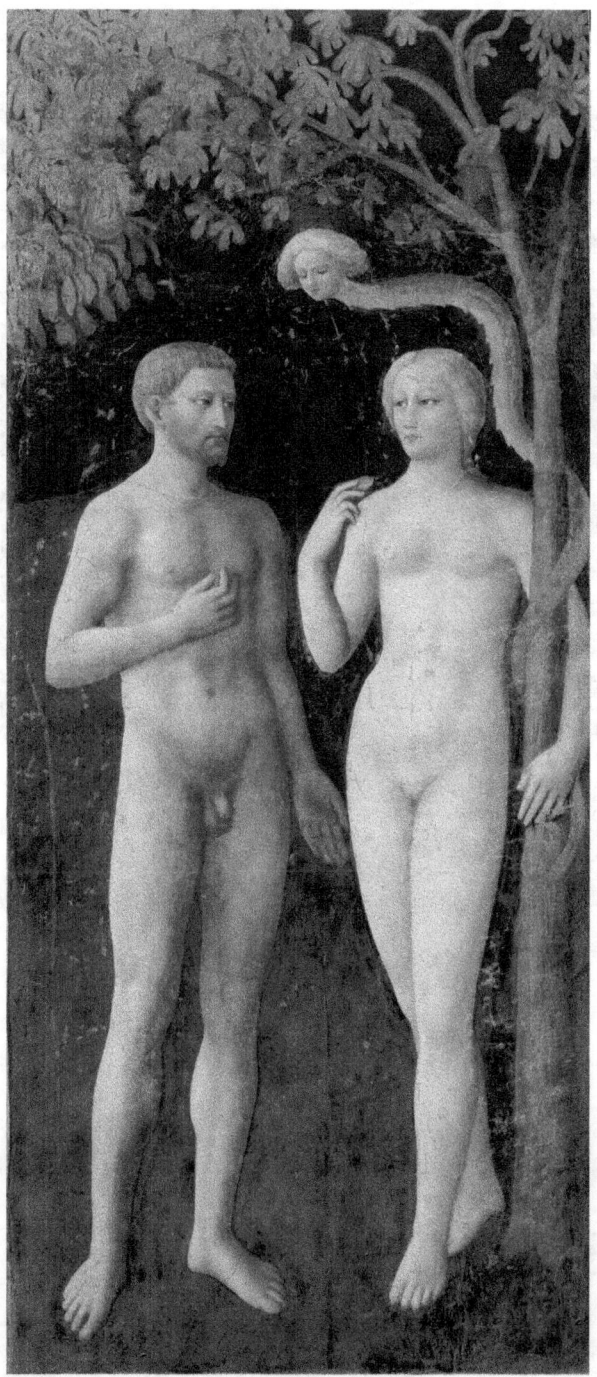

Fig. 6. Masolino da Panicale, *Temptation of Adam and Eve*, 1426–28, fresco, Brancacci Chapel, church of Santa Maria del Carmine, Florence. © 2015. Photo Scala, Florence/ Fondo Edifici di Culto — Min. dell'Interno.

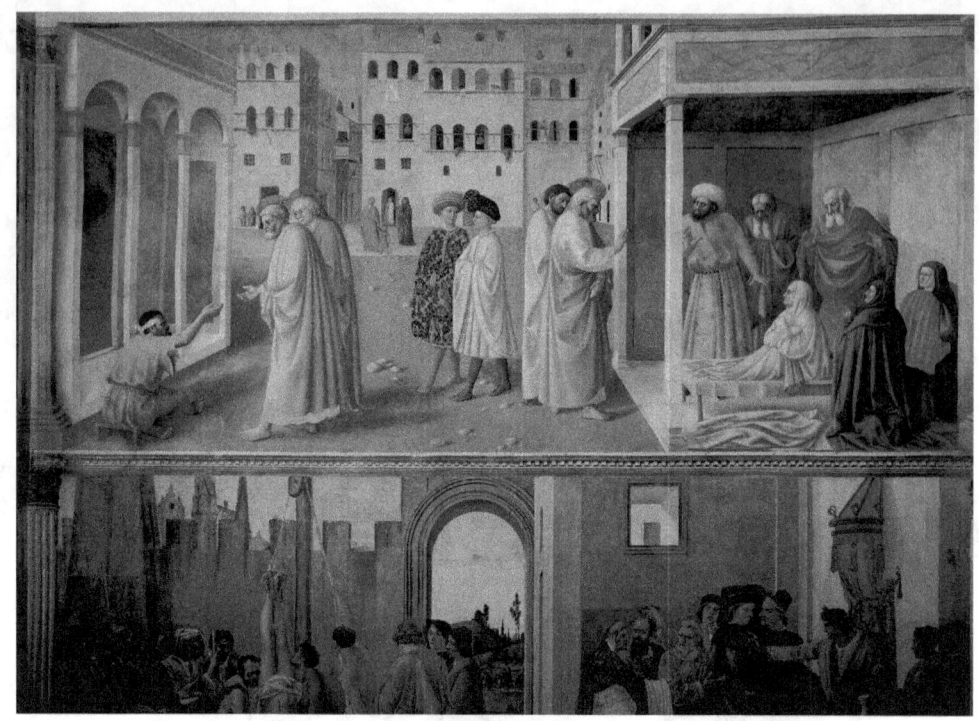

Fig. 7. Masolino da Panicale, *St Peter Healing the Cripple, St Peter Raising Tabitha*, 1423–25, fresco, Brancacci Chapel, church of Santa Maria del Carmine, Florence. © 2015. Photo Scala, Florence/Fondo Edifici di Culto — Min. dell'Interno.

with perspective, which explores both the horizon and the world close at hand, for the pleasure of a beautiful line, which evades it. Like Donatello in Santa Croce and Orsanmichele, he focuses on the fullness of bodies that are less than beautiful. There lies the indisputable differences between two painters who worked side by side. In addition to this characterisation of their respective poetic approaches, historians also bring up issues of historical chronology. Indeed, the transition from Masolino, the master, to Masaccio, the pupil, represents a sudden and decisive shift from the Middle Ages to the budding Renaissance. Leaving behind the endless rituals of the monasteries and their dull, repetitive sermons, we enter a world of bankers and merchants pursuing their business in guilds and town halls, a world that thirsts for knowledge, the world, in short, of the first humanists. In this small chapel where two painters, who were also friends, worked side by side, we see the wheels of time turning.

This is all well and good, but I know now that the understanding I was seeking in the twilit chapel, like the moment when sleep overcomes us and we glimpse the first shimmering outcrops of the unconscious, was of a different, more timeless kind. Today, I would say that what I perceived, beginning with Masolino, what held such power and fascination for me, was not so much the charm and seductiveness of those dream-soaked tales as the fact of the dream itself, the dream as dream, the dream as a fatality of language. When established ways of thinking rob words of their close relationship to objects, replacing them with very incomplete figures, the mind is inevitably tempted to lay claim to this incompleteness, and opportunistically build entire universes of desiring imagination within its crevices. The need to dream, stimulated in this way by the ossification of reason, may follow channels traced by time or environment, yet remain constant in its eagerness to transfigure everything it encounters, to become the fever and trembling that animate the representations created by painters; in particular, the need to dream is always eager to channel the forces that arise from deep within the speaking subject and drive us to radically transform the very nature of life — which is of necessity finite, as we are — rather than transform a specific way of life.

What I glimpsed in Masolino's frescoes was a desire for a reality that was not contained in the tales he was telling. I saw it, for instance, in the tall houses, with their rows of dark windows, which haunt the background of *The Healing of the Cripple*. From the first instant, more than anything else in the chapel, the provocative beauty of this backdrop to the main scene captivated me. As in certain paintings by Giorgio de Chirico, which had fascinated me in the same way ten years earlier, I experienced these façades, between two of which, at the end of a street, appear more façades, as a doorway from a place here on earth to a metaphysical realm. Here, in the foreground, among the richly dressed young men with their fashionable *mazzochio* hats, live the hopes and inventions of ordinary dreams, a superficial imagining, so to speak. But there, in the background, on the horizon not of the city but of the visible, a deeper dream comes into sight, a dream that seeks its satisfaction beyond the world as it is, on another level of reality, in an existence delivered from the chains of matter. I could be mistaken, but in *The Healing of the Cripple* I detected, freely and explicitly expressed, the elemental dream of a mind inescapably shackled to language: a dream of freedom from conceptual thought, which is the cause of our crippled existence. And all of a sudden, I saw it everywhere in Masolino's other frescoes, in his *Adam and Eve*, for example, their bodies less a thing of flesh and blood than a musical exercise.

But what is Masaccio's role in all this? I would say, first of all, that the elemental dream becomes explicitly visible in Masolino's frescoes not only because the great artist filters it through legends or tales from the Bible, but also because it appears as if heightened or thrown into relief by Masaccio's work, which is itself illuminated by the gaze he directs at his friend and fellow artist. Is the Masaccio of the Brancacci Chapel, as historians would argue, simply the master of a form that focuses narrowly on the volume and weight of male and female bodies in order to signify and celebrate their materiality in all its historical contingency? No, for he perceives in these figures, which he restores to their here-and-nowness, a presence, so to speak, the possibility of their non-being in the face of the stubborn fact of their being; and before such a mystery the need to dream dissipates. By lowering the horizon line and arranging his figures within the three-dimensional space of human activity, in the light and dark of an ordinary day, Massacio hollows out the old dreamy image, and thereby emphasises and accentuates the linear nature of Masolino's art, the way it embroiders a dream instead of consenting to reality. Masaccio shows us Masolino. His *Adam and Eve* expelled from the Garden of Eden, their hunched and unlovely bodies in visible pain, placed exactly opposite Masolino's *Adam and Eve*, seems designed to function with it as a diptych that demonstrates the intuitions and the truth of a new kind of painting. A painting that appears almost aware of what it aims to surpass.

Two forms of art are juxtaposed in these two scenes. They overlap on a level that seems to me far removed from the action-versus-dream debates that flourish in an ordinary, historically defined society. In their interplay, the gnostic need to escape from life is opposed to a desire for full presence to oneself and to others within life. However — and this may have been what I found disconcerting about the Brancacci Chapel — there is nothing polemical in the gaze that the younger artist directs at the work of his master, for two reasons, which I believe I now understand.

III

Firstly, in this fresco — but equally in the others — Masaccio seems fully aware that the fullness of presence he strives for is out of reach, as evidenced by the way space appears to curve around the bodies, weighing on them rather than helping them express their power, containing them as if in a sort of crypt. This space that deprives the figures of their full radiance, the chiaroscuro that dampens the light, an indefinable air of sadness and depression in the faces: by these means, Masaccio signals his inability, at least as a painter, to create real presence; he can only record his desire, his intention to do so, and though these may act as a premonition or an evocation of presence, they must nevertheless concede that they too are but a dream, and can signify their existence only by consenting to the imaginary. Another of his paintings comes very close to recognising this. The first impression of the *Tribute*

Money is one of full presence, notably in the figure of Christ at the centre of the composition and the way he gestures with apparent freedom towards the massed disciples. But there is something non-spatial, even unreal, in the way the men are juxtaposed, a Masolino-like line that no longer circumscribes the figures but dreams them horizontally, so to speak. As for Christ's face, its beauty here is entirely conventional, leading some historians to hypothesise that it was painted by Masolino.

Masaccio understands that as long as his painting remains a world of simple images, the fatality of representation will undermine his desire to signify presence in it. Consequently, Masaccio's relationship to Masolino's art is less polemical than dialectical. The younger artist clearly sees that, as much as his intuition and intention differ from his master's, the methods he uses to express them are subjected almost everywhere in his work to a form of substitution caused by a seemingly irresistible fatality of mind, whereby a figure, a simple idea, is substituted for the direct encounter, in a shared moment, between a self fully aware of its finiteness and an other caught in the act of existing. Masaccio realises that he is not as different from Masolino as he would like to be. In the work of both artists — who may well have been searching together, side by side, in a similarly instinctive manner — I think I also glimpsed areas of overlap, in fact areas of sharing, such as their use of perspective.

I think I glimpsed? Perhaps the dream was mine and mine alone, from the beginning. Yet I know this to be true: what I glimpsed — yes, that is the right word — in the growing dark of the Brancacci Chapel, was just such a relationship of confrontation and reconciliation in an otherwise ordinary work of art; this is what fascinated me and seemed so rich with significance, so meaningful for me personally. This is what I believe: the experience that these painters shared, side by side, is exactly what emerges from the purpose of poetry. A purpose I was just beginning to understand, or so I thought.

IV

In other words, what did that city in winter, the sparsely lit streets on the poor side of the river, teach me, if not a lesson that Ravenna would later confirm through the paradox of its mosaics and tombs: that all there is, all there can ever be, is the person in the here and now, in the grip of this great mystery? That poetry, moreover, is what remembers this and, within the conceptual discourse, a discourse of generalities without substance, attempts to recreate a relationship of living words between an individual and his or her own finitude, and the finitude of those he or she loves? Understanding this, I nevertheless indulged in reveries that spun their specious images in my head, and though I recognised them as such, I was powerless to stop their endless spooling. I could see what poetry was, but realised to my dismay that its practice was not easy, and that the intuition that sustains poetry is fated to sink and flounder in the poem. This was the realisation that slowly took shape in the dark mirror of evening in the Brancacci Chapel.

This much is clear: like presence on Masaccio's horizon, total poetry is inaccessible. Under the sign of poetry, all we are entitled to is the lucidity that turned the younger painter into a compassionate witness of his elder, and, for those of us who adopt it as our beacon, the obstinacy to search constantly for something that is always denied us. What a school the Brancacci Chapel was for me, in those long-ago days; what a difficult lesson I learned there, and how little I put it into practice! Every morning I crossed the Arno — the weather was always fine in the morning — and saw the campanile of Santa Maria Novella rising confidently into the clear blue sky, its proportions clearly aspiring to take its rightful place in the superior and absolute reality of nature that the gnostic Plato, scorning this world, called Numbers, the realm of the intelligible. That striking monument, which a year earlier had suddenly determined the future course of my life, embodied the first great leap towards the platonic dream that replaced the phantasmagoria of the gothic night in Florence. But an idea from the here and now soon took form against it. Nanni di Banco, Jacopo della Quercia and especially Donatello were searching for something beyond the social and historical contingency of the person, Florentine humanism's favourite subject of exploration and improvement, in order to invoke the intimate relationship to the self in its absolute finitude. And not far from the campanile of Santa Maria Novella stood the wall I have already mentioned, the wall that was constantly on my mind, the naked brick façade of San Lorenzo. Though often described as unfinished, a cause for some worry in Florence, it is as definitive as any moment when truth comes within reach, for it expresses the very substance of matter, of non-being, that which lies below all dreams. Only by becoming conscious of the possibility of this vacuum can one escape it for a new place to live, and lay the foundations for a human being that might evade its grasp at last.

Florence is the dream but also the lucidity that condemns the dream. Did Brunelleschi imagine a building of perfect form and proportions, and did the choice of dusky *pietra serena* immediately occur to him as a necessary element of this dialogue of light and dark surfaces, a choice that Michelangelo would later recall? What emerges from this great debate is the intensity of the conversation among architects, painters and sculptors in Tuscany, the way they brought to the discussion a vision of the artist struggling between dream and presence, the two terms of the debate. The artist marvels and racks himself, reducing himself in this way to painful subjectivity, yet occasionally manages to translate his excessive dreaming into an overabundance of life in his relationship to himself, and into an experience of presence — albeit perhaps negatively, in the image of Masaccio's cringing Adam — a way forward, in other words. The great subjectivity — which was ravaged by the metaphysical dream and suffered its grappling iron, which searched and almost found — was born in Florence, and would go by the name of Botticelli (the artist of the Munich *Pietà*) and, later, Rosso Fiorentino or Pontormo. Cleary, this was the subjectivity that asked me to descend into the Platonic crypt, after I had passed through the dramatic façade of San Lorenzo. In this other chapel, which was like a meditation on the Brancacci Chapel on the other side of the river, Michelangelo carried the search for presence and unity to a pinnacle of intensity in the pure formal beauty of the tomb he created, all the while realising that what he had fashioned was but its dream — he admits as much in *Night*'s sublime expression of generous sorrow. Now that my life lies mainly behind me, I try to remember how

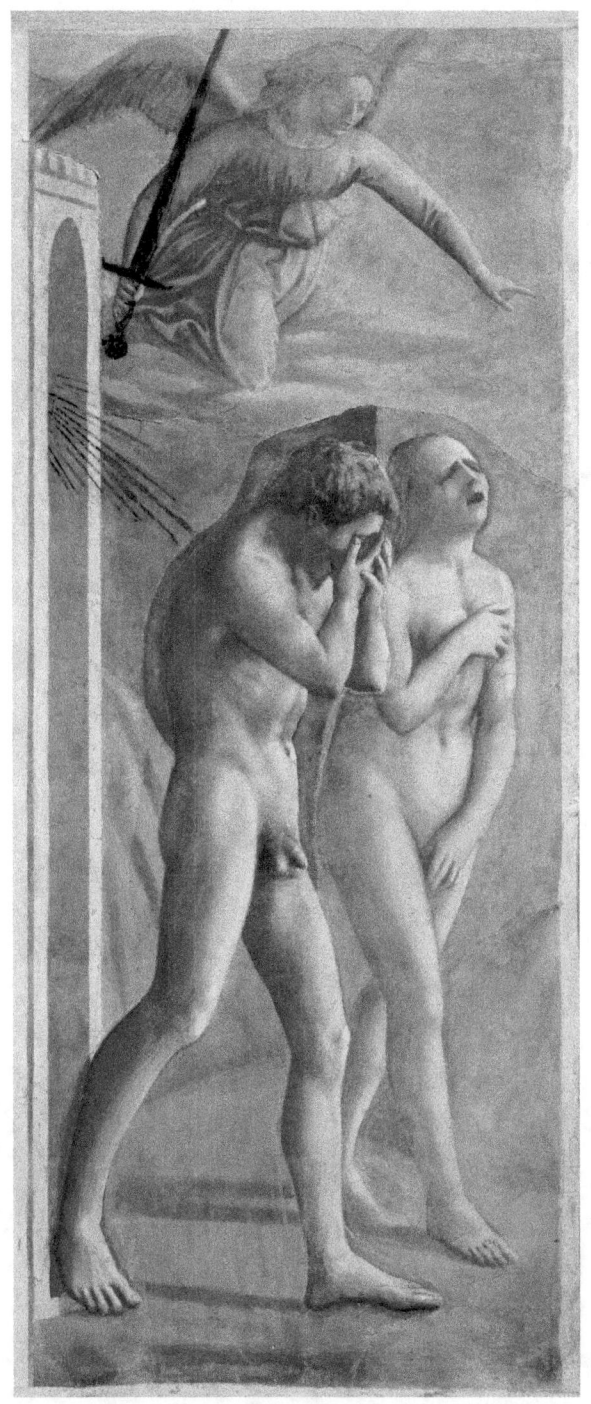

Fig. 8. Masaccio, *The Expulsion from the Garden of Eden*, 1424–28, fresco, Brancacci Chapel, church of Santa Maria del Carmine, Florence. © 2015 Photo Scala, Florence/Fondo Edifici di Culto — Min. dell'Interno.

I responded to this revelation, as the bells struck noon. In this chapel too, I was alone: in 1950, the war was barely over, and tourists were still a rarity. I scribbled in notebooks that later I tore up, for they were just a way of distracting myself, of losing my way, yet nonetheless I received and stored away what you might call advice.

Florence in 1950 was Masaccio and the discovery of poetry in its wish. But it was also Michelangelo's sculptures, that is, poetry in its fact. At work between the two were all the dialectics of language wrestling with the illusions of language. In other words, I had 'provisions for the journey'. Florence was the city where I would have wanted to live, was my thought on the night I left, unwillingly, by the last train, pulling slowly out of the station past the lighted campanile. If nothing else, Florence was my teacher, a true one, of the kind that gives meaning to a life.

CHAPTER 4

Saint Jerome Reading

Michel Butor

For Michel Jeanneret
In memoriam Antonello da Messina

I. The doorway

The painting is framed by a gothic wall surrounding an ogee-arch doorway surmounted with a finial. The doorway is in two parts: the inner part is more ornate, with a design of capitals in profile. The stones appear generally symmetrical, but are in fact asymmetrical in their detail. A peacock and a partridge are sunning themselves in front of the raised doorstep, next to which is a metal bowl for their food and water.

The peacock is often a symbol of pride, the partridge a symbol of sensuality. They are banned from the interior of the convent but tolerated at its threshold and fed out of mercy.

II. The architecture

It is undoubtedly a convent, but there is no one to be seen aside from the saint. He seems perfectly alone. The doorway opens onto a vast gothic hall, at least two spans deep and three wide. The double columns are crowned with capitals in the shape of monsters' heads, as if the vault of the church rested on the corpses of the old, vanquished deities. At the end of each span, a double dormer window offers a view of the sky and passing birds. Doves or crows?

The central column of the window in the middle is offset slightly from the vertical central axis defined by the apex of the ogee arch and the tiles covering the floor. There are three types of tiles — plain blue-grey, a black oblong on a white ground, black with a few white marks — arranged in a complex pattern reminiscent of Islamic architecture.

The asymmetrical shift is even more evident in the two outer spans. Everything here seems designed to emphasise perspective, through the use of false symmetries that one notices only after a while. The painting behaves like a labyrinth. Like a kinetic artwork, it is animated by a sort of vibration. We find ourselves in a moment of disequilibrium. Though everything appears calm, everything can change.

To the right, a vaulted doorway gives onto a second gallery with slender columns and no upper storey, its vaulted ceiling illuminated by light reflected off a tiled floor or perhaps a fountain.

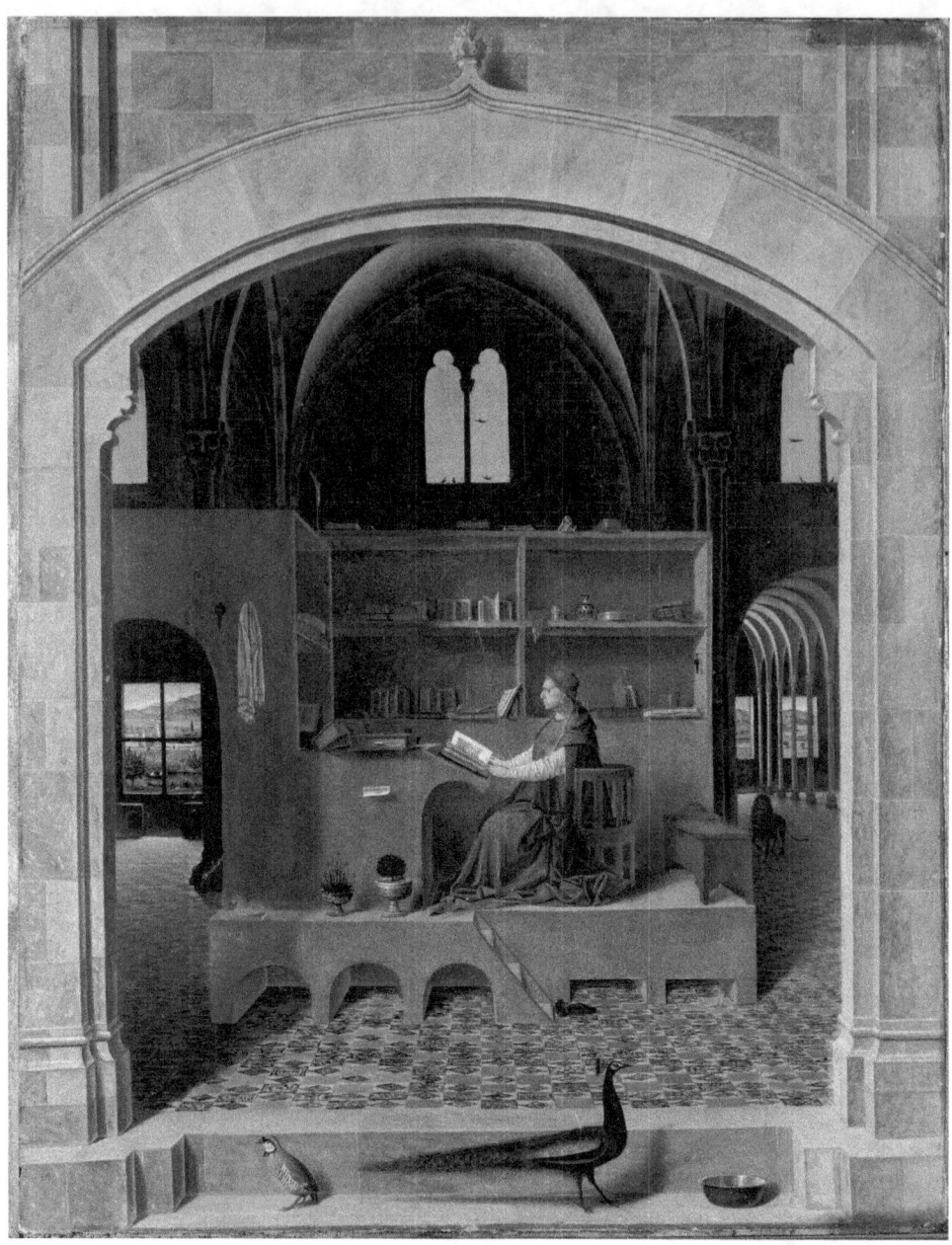

Fig. 9. Antonello da Messina, *St Jerome in his Study*, c. 1474–75, oil on lime panel, 45.7 × 36.2 cm, National Gallery, London.
© 2015 The National Gallery, London/Scala, Florence.

At first glance, the archway on the left appears symmetrical with the one on the right, but it soon becomes clear that it is much closer, and that the rectangular window is on the same level, as is the double window above, whereas the window on the left is much farther away, at the end of the second gallery.

An almost equally strong reverberation illuminates the central span, suggesting an open window on the lower level at least as large as the one on the left, whose light is reflected by a continuous expanse of tiled floor. The light shining in from the place where the viewer stands is complemented by another, partially hidden source emanating from the other side of the door-frame: the radiance of the landscape.

III. The open study

It is a platform resembling the stage of a theatre (or a university amphitheatre), supported on the left by three small round arches and on the right by two rectangular ones, and reached by a staircase of three steps. The side panel of the desk where the saint sits reading a book is slightly set back from the edge. Above it, a bookshelf with two deep compartments extends to form the vaulted doorway on the left. A second, shallower bookshelf faces the viewer; its four compartments are strewn with books and objects of learning, and its lower edge coincides with the horizon of the landscape beyond. These shelves rise higher than the first bookshelf and extend behind it.

The saint is seated in a semi-circular chair. The hands holding the book occupy the geometrical centre of the entire composition.

The painting is generally known by the title 'St Jerome in his Study'. But this implies an enclosed space, whereas everything here is open to the convent, which in turn opens onto the garden-world in the distance and the place where the viewer stands, on the other side of the doorframe, which has no closing system.

IV. The clothes

His cardinal's hat rests on a small bench behind him.

He wears a long crimson robe and matching skullcap. The sleeves of a fine pleated shirt emerge from the shoulder slits of the robe, and over it he wears a fur vest. His shoes have been left at the bottom of the steps.

The Golden Legend explains why his costume has been given such particular attention:

> After Jerome had reprimanded some clerks and monks for their lascivious conduct, they became highly indignant, and laid traps for him. According to John Beleth, they used the clothing of a woman to mock him in a most shameful way. When he rose as usual to go to matins, he found a woman's clothing laid by his bed, which had been placed there by those who envied him, and believing they were his, he put them on and so attired went to the church. However, his enemies had done this so that others would believe that he had a woman in his chamber.

The saint retired to the desert, but was plagued there by temptations equal to Saint Anthony's: 'Though my only companions were scorpions and wild beasts, I often imagined myself surrounded by maidens, and my cold body and dead flesh burned with the fire of lechery.'

According to the hagiography, Jerome remained a virgin until his death, yet Jacobus de Voragine himself reports that in a letter to Pammachius he wrote: 'I carry virginity to Heaven, though I do not possess it.'

Notice the towel hanging on a hook, like the one that a Flemish painter might have added next to a ewer. It is set slightly above his reach. One imagines a fountain hidden behind the left-hand bookshelf.

V. The books

Though Jerome was far from indifferent to women, his great passion was books. In a letter to Eustachia, he writes:

> At the time, I spent my days reading Cicero and my nights reading Plato, because I found the rude style of the books of the prophets unpleasant. Halfway through Lent, however, I fell prey to such a sudden and violent fever that my body grew cold and the warm life drained from my breast. Arrangements for my funeral were already being made, when I found myself suddenly summoned before the court of the Supreme Judge. Asked what I was, I readily replied, 'I am a Christian.' 'You lie,' said the Judge. 'You are a follower of Cicero and not of Christ, for where your treasure is, there is your heart.' At that moment I was struck dumb, and the Judge ordered me to be whipped very harshly. I cried out: 'Have mercy upon me, Lord, have mercy upon me!' Meanwhile, the bystanders began pleading with the judge to take pity on me. I made this oath: 'Lord, if ever again I possess worldly books, or if ever again I read such books, I have denied you.' After this oath, I was dismissed and suddenly returned to life... Since then, I have read the books of God with the same zeal that I previously devoted to the books of pagans.

But in what language?

With the exception of the signature cartouche, none of the texts in Jerome's library can be identified. But considering that he spent 'forty-five years and six months' translating the Bible, which gave us the Vulgate, these texts are no doubt ancient versions of the scriptures in Latin, Greek or Hebrew, three languages that he mastered perfectly, reviving his acquaintance with them through regular immersions for a good cause. Consequently, when people began studying the classics again, at first they read Cicero and Plato in order to elucidate the Vulgate and the Septuagint.

The shelves are not very full. Except for the thick volumes on the desk, the books are displayed like precious objects; propped open vertically, they present their text like steles or mementos or windows onto other worlds.

Jacobus de Voragine transcribes this account by Severus Sulpicius, a contemporary of Jerome: 'Saint Jerome [...] was learned not only in Latin and Greek but also in Hebrew, so that none can compare to him in any science there is [...]. He was always occupied with reading, always among books, resting neither by day nor by night. He was always either reading or writing.'

In this image he is reading, perhaps re-reading his own translation, trying to improve it, writing while reading, writing not his own text, but rather the entire diverse tradition, which he improves even as he transmits it, making it his own even as he humbles himself before it.

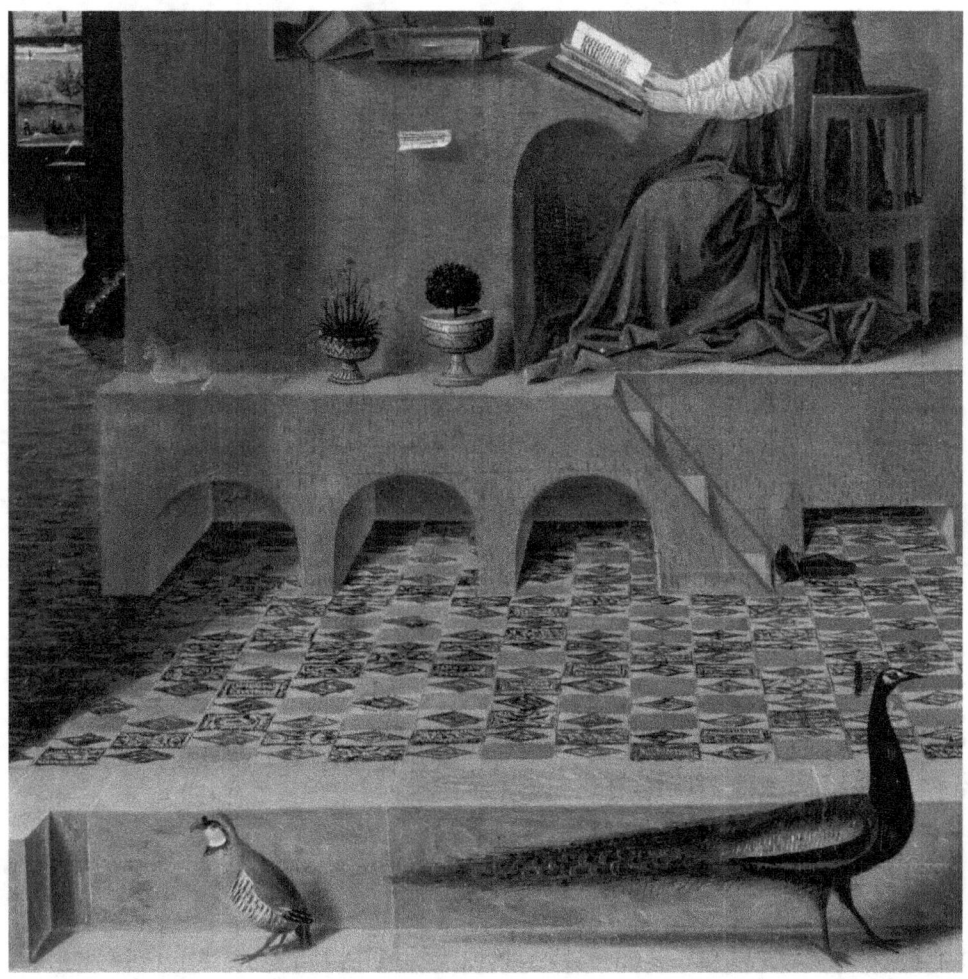

Fig. 10. Antonello da Messina, *St Jerome in his Study*, c. 1474–75, oil on lime panel, 45.7 × 36.2 cm, National Gallery, London (detail). © 2015 The National Gallery, London/Scala, Florence.

VI. Plants and animals

On the edge of the platform, in front of the desk, are two chalices containing a bunch of flowers — carnations perhaps, though I'm not sure — and a small, round-clipped bush, possibly myrtle, which no doubt allude to the virtues required for the saint to complete his colossal task.

The peacock and the partridge are excluded from his study but tolerated at its threshold, cared for and admired, even. The presence of a cat on the platform itself is more surprising, as it could be seen as a negative example of sloth, gluttony and sensuality — it is, after all, a favourite of witches.

But the cat is also cherished by 'ardent lovers and austere scholars'. It hunts among the books without disturbing them and keeps the scholar company while he works.

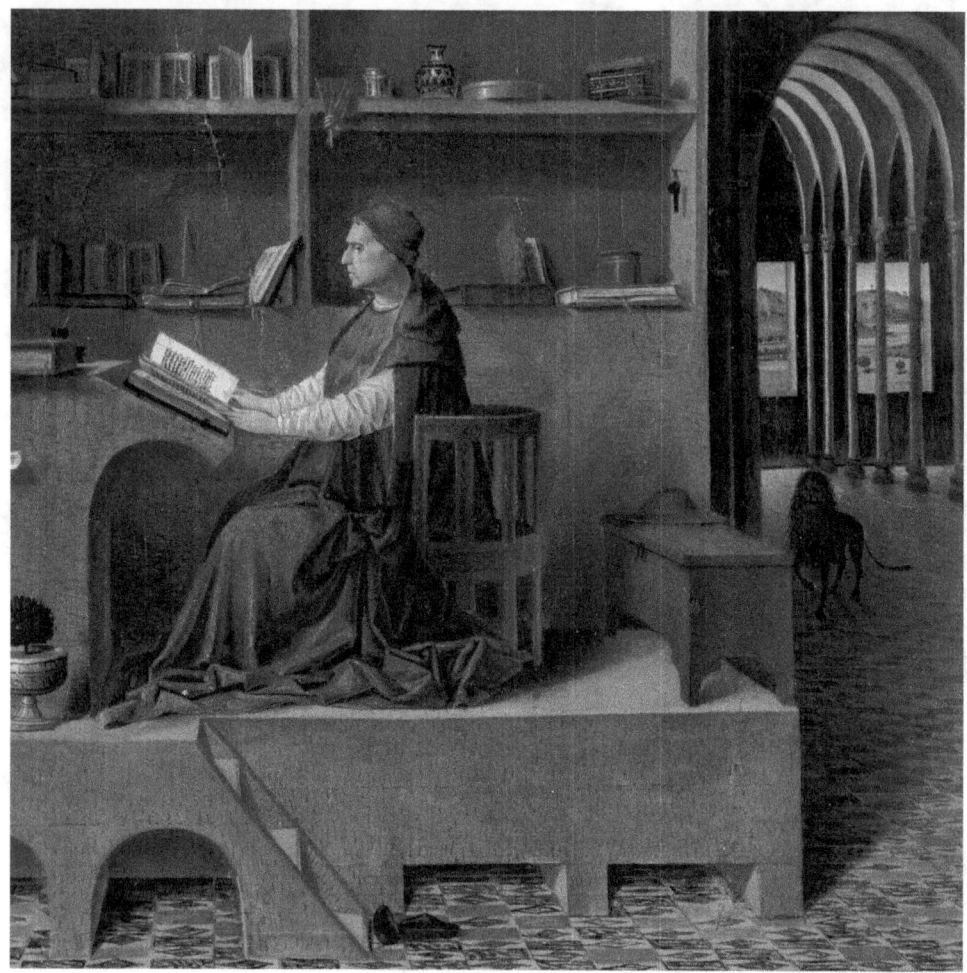

Fig. 11. Antonello da Messina, *St Jerome in his Study*, c. 1474–75, oil on lime panel, 45.7 × 36.2 cm, National Gallery, London (detail).
© 2015 The National Gallery, London/Scala, Florence.

Here, however, its main function is to represent in miniature a far more imposing animal, which is central in the legend and can be glimpsed in the gallery on the right, unobtrusively slipping away, as if metamorphosing into a cat.

One imagines him as a desert companion, like those that appear in the lives of other hermits. But no. Though he represents the wilderness of the land of scorpions, here he appears inside the monastery:

> One day, towards evening, as St Jerome sat with his brothers listening to a holy lesson, a lion came limping suddenly into the monastery. When the brothers saw him, they all fled, but Jerome came towards him as he would with a guest. The lion showed him his hurt foot, and Jerome called his brothers and commanded them to wash the lion's feet and search carefully for the wound. They found that he had torn the soles of his feet on thorns. They employed

every means to cure the lion, and when he was healed, he remained with the community as a tame beast.

After the lion is unjustly accused of a crime, he manifests his innocence by demonstrating his many qualities, yet recognises his error nonetheless, so that when the truth is revealed, he offers not only a lesson in strength, the cardinal virtue he shares with Saint Mark, but also a lesson in humility:

> Then the lion began to run joyously throughout the monastery, as he was wont to before, and kneeled down before every brother. As he fawned them with his tail, he seemed to be asking forgiveness for an offense that he had not committed.

VII. The landscape

After four years of temptations and penitence, Saint Jerome finally found in translation a solution to his intellectual dilemma. He decided to settle near Bethlehem to devote himself to his great task within the confines of his monastery. The view from the two windows should therefore depict the landscapes of Judea. But how was the painter to imagine it, and make the viewer imagine it as well? At the time, the Crusades were long past. The Ottomans were approaching. Byzantium was trembling. He could have painted palm trees, as Van Eyck did. But this is neither Sicily nor Venice. All commentators agree that it looks very much like Tuscany.

In the left window, like a brilliant miniature from a book, against a backdrop of receding hills, rises a city of churches, ramparts, tall square towers like those of San Giminiano, with fruit trees on the banks of a canal in the foreground, two men rowing a boat, a white dog running by the water, a man on horseback, cypresses. Everything in this landscape is an invitation to a meditative stroll.

Just as the reverberated light illuminates the vaulted ceiling of the gallery with the wandering lion, so too does the landscape illuminate the tiled floor, which becomes like a river, flowing through the shadow cast by the doorframe.

Bethlehem and its translation workshop is a window onto the Promised Land, which eventually led us to discover new ways of reading, hearing and perceiving our daily lives. Antonello's peep box is designed to bring about a rebirth, in the same way that Jerome brought about a rebirth of the Bible by translating it into the vernacular. The time has come to do this again, by drawing on all available sources, everywhere and in all languages.

Rebirth

For Michel Jeanneret

We could feel the world growing old
The year one thousand came and went
And nothing happened after all
We must have miscalculated
Yet the fact remained that the end
Of our stay was soon approaching
Though we had no way of knowing
How soon in years or centuries

Certain improvements were made
Cathedrals taller than before
Whose sculpted stones turned into flames
So many wars and yet we were
Still so far from the promised peace
Were these already the prodromes
Of the Antichrist's deceptions
Announcing the Day of Judgment

What kept him at bay was that
The world was expanding so fast
Asia had grown so much larger
Africa extended southward
Much farther than anyone had
Ever imagined possible
There was even talk of new
Continents being discovered

For the Church to be able to
Call itself universal
It was important to ensure
All nations received the Gospel
So many missions were dispatched
To acknowledge and save them all
Vertiginous perspectives
Opened up towards a point

That was forever vanishing
More alarming than this perhaps
Was the disorder in the sky
Caused by our straining to perceive
The sweet harmony of the spheres
To improve the accuracy
Of astrological forecasts
We kept adding more and more

Complicated epicycles
The seasons had shifted forward
The feast days no longer aligned
With the spectacle of Nature
It would soon be necessary
To modify the calendar
To dispel the drifting fog
Of neglect that permeated

Every corner of the school
Which is why we had to break
The locks fastening all the books
That had survived the flood
To save Latin through Greek
To illuminate the Gospel
In this moment of darkness
Through the window of its tongues

And the Septuagint through Hebrew
And all things that came from the time
Of these revelations stricken
As they were with a deep unease
Could mend our reddened eyes
Which no longer served us to see
Not only the books but also
The ancient statues and paintings

Emerging from the foundations
What a fountain of youth it was
The nakedness of ancient gods
Like that of new-born babies
Or Indians from the New World
Offered a new kind of baptism
Translations proliferated
Gleefully exorcising
The biblical curse of Babel

CHAPTER 5

The Dwarf

Nadeije Laneyrie-Dagen

My name is Anna. In Mantua, where I lived for most of my life, they call me Diamantina. Four and a half centuries have passed since Master Andrea Mantegna painted my likeness. Since then, I have looked down upon the world from where I stand high above the ground. On the fresco I'm three feet high. In life I was no taller. For by God's will, I was a born a dwarf.

I was born in Selva Gherdëina in the Dolomites, near the source of the Adige, where they speak a dialect called *Ladino*. This part of the Alps, extending from Merano to Bressanone, is famous for goitres and cretins. There is some truth in this. I am one of the monstrous progeny of the mountain, albeit with a smallish goitre, and not as dumb as initially assumed. In the land of my birth, food is scarce and poor. For meat, there are goats and the ibex that the men poach. Grains are plentiful but often rotted by excessive rain or harvested early and green for fear of the storms that destroy the crops. And then our blood is tainted. The valleys are narrow, the mountains difficult to cross, so the peasants intermarry. At best, they might look for a bride in the next hamlet. But there are only three villages in the valley where I came into the world.

My mother married an uncle, so my father was also my great-uncle. I was the youngest child but one, coming after three brothers, plus two who died. My older brothers were still living, I think, when Mantegna painted me. They all married cousins of some kind. A last girl arrived several years after me; she never married. She was half-witted, born after a labour that took my mother's life. No one wanted her, of course. She took my place in the village priest's house and served him to the best of her abilities. One day, a baby popped out from between her legs, although no one had noticed her grow big. The priest had the infant taken to the orphanage in the town. Yet I doubt it was placed in the foundling wheel where parents who wish to remain anonymous may leave a baby. The time was early spring and snow still covered the roads, yet the men charged with this errand returned three days later, unusually quickly for the round-trip.

This was the same priest who raised me. Or rather, let me live in his house. When it became clear that I was not growing, my father and my mother decided there was no room for me at home. As in the case of my sister's child, there was must have been some discussion of leaving me at the hospice. But the elderly woman who served the priest took pity on me. And the priest allowed her to take me in.

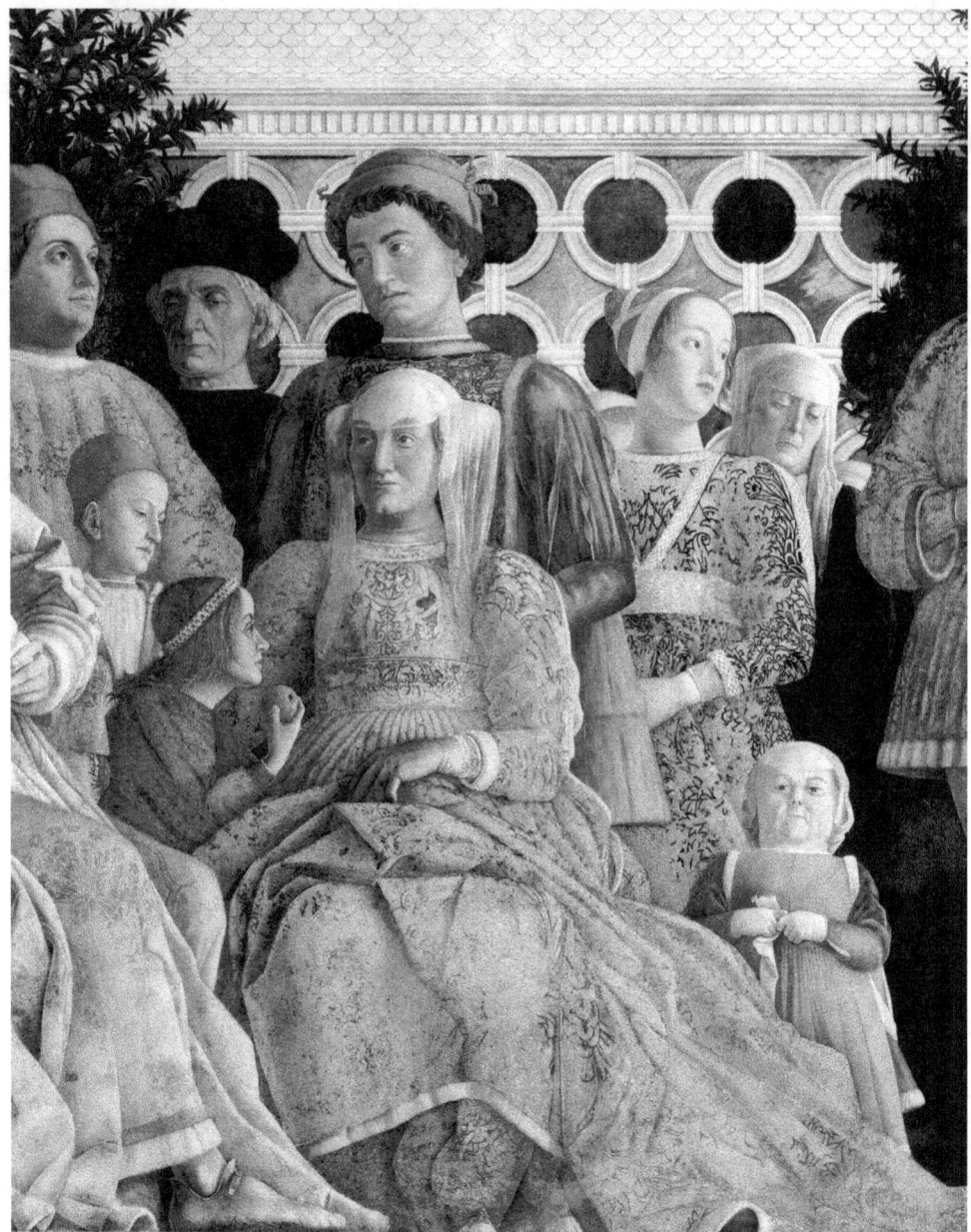

Fig. 12. Andrea Mantegna, *Camera degli Sposi*, c. 1474, fresco, Palazzo Ducale, Mantua (detail). © 2015 Photo Scala, Florence; courtesy of the Ministero Beni e Att. Culturali.

I spent eight years in the house next to the church. During the day, I would follow the priest almost everywhere. He called me his little familiar. He spoke to me in German rather than Ladino, which is how I came to know that language. At night I slept with Anna. She gave me my name, which was also hers — I have no idea what I was called before then. We slept above the stable, in the rising warmth and sharp stink of the straw trampled by a mule and two goats, whose milk I greedily drank during those first years of my life.

I was a healthy child. Surprisingly healthy, given the body I was given. For it stubbornly refused to grow. At the age of eight, I had to stretch my arm as high as it would go to unlatch the stable door. Seated on the ground, I could suck directly from the teats of Maddalena and Marta, the goats, and I amused myself by standing under the mule's belly and trotting between her legs when she rode out with my master on her back. I lasted for only a few strides, of course, for I was not only small but also so misshapen that I walked with a lopsided gait. My spine arched back instead of growing straight. My short legs twisted when I walked. My arms and hands also remained small. Only my head was of a normal size, but, when I was older, it seemed huge in relation to my torso. My face was similarly ill-favoured, with a deeply indented bridge and a bulging forehead that made my eyes seem smaller than they were. To speak plainly, I was ugly.

When I turned ten, the priest declared that it was time for me to leave. What would become of me if I stayed in the village? No one would marry me, I couldn't follow the flocks to the summer pastures, and I was useless even in a house: the pots and pans where too big and heavy for my short arms, knives looked gigantic in my hands, and I could barely reach the top of the table to set the plates upon it. So, at the end of that summer, I left with some men who were heading to the plains to find work as farms labourers.

The city was called Bozen. I travelled there on the back of a donkey, in a basket filled with small leather goods that the women made during the winter to sell for cash. My soul was untroubled: I was going to the orphanage, my fate was sealed, I had not a care in the world. My attention was entirely focused on what I saw around me. Bozen was a large town in the eyes of a humble peasant girl like me. It stood in a broad valley at the confluence of two rivers, the Talfer and the Eisach. For the first time in my life, I saw the mountains open up and the horizon spread out before my eyes. When I was removed from the basket, it was a revelation: I saw that the ground under my feet could continue this flat for a great distance, that the world was huge, and the sky above my head endless, not strangled by rocky peaks as it had appeared to me until then. I had no idea then that later, in Mantua, on the Paduan plain, I would gaze at the straight line of the horizon and sorely miss my mountains, those accidents of geography with their tattered crown of clouds.

We walked straight to the hospice. The Franciscan nuns refused to take me in: I was too old to be placed among the little ones, not tall enough to join the ranks of the young girls they were preparing to enter the novitiate and care for the orphans. On the square where we were promptly turned out, the men argued angrily about what to do with me. One wanted to leave me in the street or on a church bench. The two others, my relatives obviously, refused to abandon me to my fate. From my thigh-high station, I listened, powerless, to this quarrel of giants. I hurried to keep up with them as they walked among groups of men and women whom I could see only from the belt down, while their eyes passed, unseeing, far above my head. My clogs, made especially to my size for this trip, clattered on the paving stones: I found this terribly amusing, for until then I had known only the thud of my bare feet on the dirt and mud of the village, never the sound of shoes on smooth stones. The houses on either side were like rocky cliffs and their windows like the mouths of caverns.

When we reached the marketplace, the men set out a mat and arranged the goods we had brought on it. Having reached no decision about me, they turned me loose. Did they secretly hope I would disappear, I wonder? I had never seen so many goods for sale, or so many different kinds of people. I wandered among the groups, feeling no shyness (in my mountain home I had never been mocked), even as children, young girls, men and women began to look at me curiously. I was no longer invisible: on the contrary, all eyes were focused on me. People laughed and pointed. There were cries, jeers, cruel words; I heard 'monster', 'pygmy' (I had no idea what this was), even 'creature of the Devil'. I was bewildered: it was my first experience of cruelty. I tried to find my way back to my countrymen, but found myself lost in the great market. Finally, the three men came in search of me, alerted to my whereabouts by the clamour. Instead of removing me from the throng, however, Michael (for that was his name) picked me up and stood me on a greengrocer's stall. Next to me on the table were yellow melons, a fruit I had never seen, still less tasted. Michael, who seemed to know the merchant, seized one. He cut a slice and stuffed it into my mouth before setting the melon down again. He then took two more melons which he piled on top of the first to form a tower taller than me.

The crowd roared with laughter. They were no longer mocking me but marvelling at my small size. They asked to hear my voice: could I speak, they wanted to know, or was I dumb? I spoke. Thereafter, my intelligence no longer interested them. My hair, my only beautiful feature, attracted their attention next: unknown hands stroked my head and shoulders. At one point I had to remove my clogs so the women could pass them around, laughing at their diminutive proportions. Then Michael picked me up again. The crowd stood back as he swung me round. My legs went flying, my head was spinning, but I loved it, and my laughter won me the sympathy of my audience. When my feet touched the table again, of my own accord I pulled up my sleeves to show off my arms and hands. I wiggled my fingers: the crowd gasped at their minuteness. Thrusting out my chest, I even improvised a few dance steps among the melons, and was reward with applause. To my amazement, some onlookers even threw coins. I had never touched money of any kind. Although, in fact, these coins went straight into Michael's pocket.

Considering my minders' lack of interest in my well-being, if there had been only the chance of this market, would I have spent the rest of my life as a human curiosity, wandering from city to city, village to village, amusing the crowd? I wonder. Later, at Mantua Castle, I would meet creatures who could have been my companions in misfortune: dwarves like me, giant men, a bearded lady who was displayed nursing her equally furry baby, and all kinds of performers, normal people who were acrobats or jugglers, violin players or wild animal trainers.

But this was not to be my destiny. Noticing the intense curiosity I provoked (the whole market had gathered around to gawk) and the unexpected gracefulness of my movements, Johann, the cleverest of the three who had brought me to Bozen, had an idea. He knew — but how did he, cooped up as he was in the mountains all winter? — that the noblemen of this country liked to surround themselves with creatures like me, midgets and giants, hunchbacks and freaks. Their strangeness added interest to the wildly popular *tableaux vivants*, known as 'mysteries', organised every year to celebrate the nativity and death of Our Lord. Many ordinary citizens of Bozen participated in these spectacles, but 'monsters' such as myself (I would hear the word repeated again that day) played a special role by representing devils and demons, sorcerers and executioners.

Johann, therefore, asked where he might find a nobleman. The city was governed by the merchants and the bishop, was the answer; the ruler of the land, the Count of Tyrol, lived somewhere far from there. He was directed to the bishop's palace and the houses of the rich merchants. Neither the bishop nor the merchants received us, but an officer at the town hall suggested we try our luck at Maretsch Castle, just outside the town. The family there was no longer rich, but it was noble, and well regarded by the Count, he said. The men led me to a fortress, ancient and menacing to my eyes. For the fourth time that day we knocked, and for the fourth time Johann explained that he wanted to give me away. The man he spoke to was a type of steward. His master was not at home, he explained, and he could take no decisions in his absence. Johann offered to leave me anyway, and promised to return if the Lord of Maretsch didn't want to keep me. He never returned.

I remained for a short time in Bozen but took part in no religious celebrations. Clearly, this was not the fate God had chosen for me. After about three weeks at the castle (they gave me a bed, decent clothes, the first bath of my life and plenty to eat), the master, being informed of my arrival, sent a letter requesting for me to be sent to a city further north, called Innsbruck. Again, I was carried somewhere new, not that I had any say in the matter. The voyage was comfortable, in a cart with a real seat and a roof over my head this time, and lasted three days. Innsbruck at the time was smaller than Bozen, yet it was here that the Count of Tyrol lived, in a very frugal manner. The nobleman who had acquired me also owned a modest house in the same city. However, it was not for either of these nobles that I had been summoned, but for a princess.

The princess, or rather, the lady (as she was still a child, this was her title), was named Barbara. She was the daughter of the Margrave of Brandenburg and the niece of Emperor Sigismund. At the age of eleven, she had been removed from her palace and her family, in a city in the north called Kulmbach, to be married in Italy. Her personal escort had stopped at Innsbruck, from where she would be escorted to her new home by the envoys of the Duke of Mantua's son, whom she had married by proxy. The future duchess spoke only German, her new escort only Italian. However, the girl had taken a dislike to the two attendants authorised to accompany beyond this point, a governess and a nobleman, who had arrived in

Innsbruck before her. She constantly asked for the dwarf who had kept her company and entertained her since she was small, but the poor woman had left Kulmbach in poor health and died along the way. I was expected to gain the girl's affection and dry her tears by taking the dead woman's place.

I was nothing: a country bumpkin, lost at court, unfamiliar with its rituals. Besides, I was myself barely out of childhood, probably not much older than the girl I was expected to serve, though I did not know my exact age. Madonna Barbara... her body was as large as mine was small. Later she would grow taller than her husband, much to his displeasure. Her face was long, her nose ungracefully large. Her hair fell lank and straight on either side of her face. The russet hue of her hair, which was braided into coils over her ears, and the high colour of her face were a peculiarly unattractive combination. On the day of my presentation to the princess, they dressed me as prettily as possible in a red dress with a large white collar and a green ribbon for a belt around my graceful waist (I was slim back then, not stout as I have grown since), leaving my hair loose and cascading down to my hips as befitted my virginal state.

Thus attired, I seemed to make a good impression. *Madonna* herself burst into laughter when she saw me. She poked the low bridge of my nose with her index, right between the eyes. There was no ill intention in this. When she spoke to me, I understood her with difficulty. She, in turn, struggled to understand my reply, for the German I learned from the priest of Selva Gherdëina, mixed with my native dialect, was not quite the same as the language she spoke.

Barbara was sitting up in bed when I was introduced. At the time, I found this surprising, but I would soon become accustomed to being received in this half-reclining position, for the grand castles where noblemen live are often bitterly cold. The room was crowded with people; after ordering the men to leave, she asked me to undress, and observed my body with great curiosity, her eyes serious. Seeing that I was shivering, she lifted the covers and invited me into her bed. She caressed my skin, cupped my breasts in her hands — mine were round and firm, whereas she was still flat-chested and not yet nubile — and ran her fingers lightly over the downy hair of my lower belly. Though I felt some pleasure, I remained perfectly still, unsure what to say, not daring to move. She went no further. She never again asked to see me undressed, nor welcomed me to her bed. We had become acquainted: I was accepted. In the days after this, I remained with Barbara. When she continued her voyage, I travelled in her carriage. And during the years that followed — forty in all — I never left her side.

How quickly those years passed... For the first few seasons, Madonna was allowed to grow into adulthood. Her husband Ludovico had not yet assumed power (Duke Francesco was still living) and was himself very young. He was learning to be a soldier, riding to battle in faraway lands. The duchess received instruction in Italian, and I learned the language along with her, as I was present for all her lessons. But she only spoke German with me, and corrected my mistakes. Skipping back and forth between languages all day long in this fashion, I became quite a chatterbox. I also discovered the written word: before coming to Mantua I had no idea of what a book was, whereas my German princess was wild about them. I never learned to read, but I loved listening to my mistress or her lector read letters out loud. I learned to sew and took a liking to needlework. In fact, I became far more accomplished than my mistress in the art of embroidery: why then did Mantegna depict me clutching a strip of cloth that looks more like the rag you would give a child?

At the end of several winters, Madonna's breasts had grown. She began to bleed. Ludovico returned. One night, shortly before Francesco's death, the future duke and his wife were put into bed together. A first son was born, and then a second. Eight more children followed, half boys and half girls, thank goodness. I don't know if my mistress enjoyed the hours she spent in the marital bed, but she always complied. Her ample body carried the fruits sown by her husband and she gave birth with little visible pain. Ludovico loved her in his way. He was unfaithful to her, no doubt, but he appreciated the way her fertile womb ensured the continuity of his line. He also enjoyed her conversation. He spoke with her often about hunting, about his dogs and horses, but also about politics, and his frequent military campaigns. In San Giorgio castle, where they established residence (the former duke had lived elsewhere), they occupied separate apartments connected by the room that Mantegna was commissioned by the duke to decorate, and where he painted my likeness. When Ludovico and Barbara retired for the night to their curtained bed, the main item of furniture in this room, I stood watch over the duchess's chamber, while the duke's favourite dog guarded the door to his rooms. Because this dog (or rather, the generations of dogs that filled the position during my time in Mantua) was red, the duke called him Rubino. 'He has my wife's hair', he used to say, and one day, for fun, he called me Diamante. The nickname stuck; it comes from those tiny rocks that are cut into facets so that they sparkle. Ruby and Diamond: we were two wonderful gems beloved of the duke and duchess.

I too have known a man. Ludovico had a dwarf who occasionally looked after the dogs, but mainly tended to the hunting birds; his nickname was Gigante. He gained our master's favour after fighting a huge monkey from the palace menagerie with his bare hands. Ludovico had to intervene to stop the fight, which he had started in jest, and ordered Gigante to spare the beast, whom he had pinned to the ground and was about to strangle. Gigante was older and much taller than me, a powerful man, with hair all over his body and, despite his diminutive size, endowed with an impressive male apparatus. The duke, who had recently succeeded his father, was determined to marry me to him. A new red dress, Barbara's colour, was sewn for me, and Gigante received an outfit of grey and pink, the colours of Mantua. At the same time, a suitable mate was selected for Rubino, and the two celebrations — the human wedding and the canine coupling — were combined. At least we dwarfs enjoyed the privilege of a ceremony in the chapel of the castle.

Did I love Gigante? We made love: I found the experience not entirely unpleasant. But we did so only seldom, as he preferred women of regular size, and they did not disdain him. My belly was infertile, which displeased the duke. I, on the other hand, thanked the Lord that I was unable to give birth to a creature who would certainly have been even tinier than me. After three years of marriage, Gigante was kicked by a horse as he was readying Ludovico for the hunt, and died. I grieved briefly, and then enjoyed being the sole mistress of the room that had been arranged especially for the two of us, with a bed, furniture, and even crockery to our size. In his painting, Master Mantegna placed me next to Duchess Barbara and in front of her daughter, Barbara the Younger. Dressed again in red, grown stout from the fine food at court, I gaze resolutely away from both my mistresses. I have no desire to smile — no one is smiling in this painting — or to look at anything or anyone inside the painting. Indeed, shortly before Mantegna painted my portrait, the Duchess had told me that I would have to leave her. My likeness, she added, would remain as a token of all the years I had spent with her, as a memory she would cherish. I would remain by her side in effigy, while Barbara would send news of me in the letters she was sure to write.

Barbara the Younger was the beloved daughter of Barbara the Elder, the child she named after herself, the eldest of three daughters born after four strapping boys and a little Cecilia who didn't live. The fate of the young Barbara was the mirror image of her mother's: born in Mantua, she was promised to a German prince. In 1470, when Master Mantegna undertook to finish this part of the fresco ordered by the duke, she was already officially betrothed. 'She will leave soon — she is almost twenty, after all — and join her future husband.' Barbara the Younger spoke better Italian than German: 'With you she will speak the language of her childhood.' And 'She has known you since infancy; you are attached to her, and she loves you. You must go with her and be the one who speaks to her of us.' So spoke the Duchess. I had to obey. It was my duty: I had no choice, no right to refuse, no possibility of saying no.

These were the thoughts running through my mind as I posed for Mantegna, not surrounded by the family but perched alone on a ladder at the exact height of the false cornice where he had arranged the members of the court. I made no effort to look pleasant, but my unhappy expression concealed my submissiveness. I did not know that Ludovico would die so soon afterwards: for some reason I assumed that the Duchess would pass away before him. Was this the true cause of my dismissal, I wondered? Her last-born daughter, Paola, was strange. This appears clearly in the portrait of the court: her spine is more curved than her father's, who leans closer and closer to the ground in spite of himself as he grows older, and it seems obvious that she does not have all her wits. The artist placed a golden apple in her hand, a beautiful symbol that means she should be cherished, like the treasures of the garden of Hesperides in a story that my mistress loved to have read to her. How could I refuse an order that I imagined was the final wish of my dear Monna Barbara, light of my heart?

I had to leave. Two winters later (Mantegna's work continued on another wall, seemingly with no end in sight), we celebrated the wedding of Barbara the Younger. In the old basilica of Sant'Andrea, which was torn down shortly after the ceremony and later magnificently rebuilt, she received a ring from the hand of a nobleman representing her husband, the faraway Duke of Württemberg. It was a few days before Easter. Nature was alive with flowers, the sun shone brightly, the bells pealed long and merrily. There were great banquets, jousting, dancing... and the two Barbaras cried.

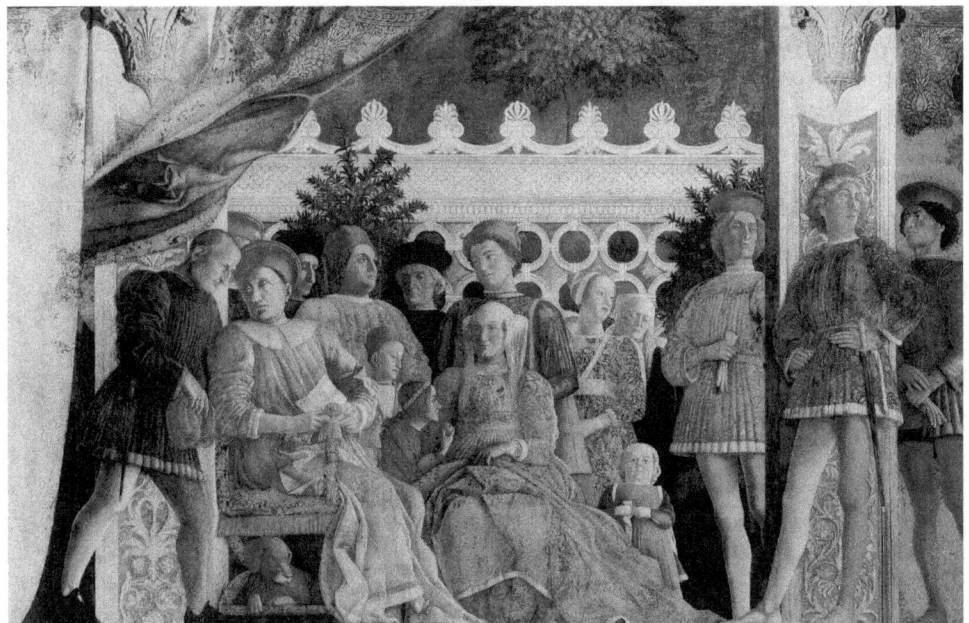

Fig. 13. Andrea Mantegna, *Camera degli Sposi*, c. 1474, fresco, Palazzo Ducale, Mantua. © 2015 Photo Scala, Florence; courtesy of the Ministero Beni e Att. Culturali.

The bride's company left three days later. We travelled for many weeks, stopping at length along the way for further celebrations. By a strange twist of fate, we stayed especially long at Innsbruck. Though I was terrified of suffering the same fate as the dwarf for whom the Margrave's daughter had grieved forty years before, I did not die on the way. I was back in the mountains, albeit not those of my childhood but others, more wooded, not as high, and colder in winter. The castle where I spent the last years of my life was a fortress named Urach, a sound as guttural as the German they spoke there, which I could never become accustomed to. As Barbara's mother had foretold, her daughter, whom I was bold enough to call Barbarina, spoke only Italian to me. The pleasure this gave her was a great consolation to her: she missed Italy as much as I did.

I spent at least five more winters in Urach, perhaps more. I don't remember. My soul was elsewhere, on the other side of the Alps. Shortly before I died, I made a will and requested that my remains be carried home so that I could rest in Mantua, next to Duchess Barbara. Of course, no one heeded to the wishes of a dwarf. Nevertheless, Barbarina had me buried with considerable ceremony under a stone in the church where she prayed. A century later, the church was destroyed. Christians who were angry with the pope pried open the stones and dispersed the bones. Barbara's remains, buried in the same church thirty years after mine, suffered the same fate. But neither her ashes nor mine were carried across the mountain by the northern winds.

All that remains of Barbara, my ugly and beloved Duchess, of Barbarina, the mistress I followed faithfully, of myself, precious diamond of a dwarf, is the image you are looking at now. All that remains of the line born of the Duke and Duchess, the sons and daughters who were Ludovico's pride, whom he dreamed would one day rule Italy, are powdered pigments painted on a wall by a divine hand, chipped and cracked by the centuries, but never destroyed. We all suffered the same fate, regardless of rank or reign: Ludovico and Barbara, the Duke and Duchess, their children and servants, Rubino the dog and Diamante the dwarf. Faded ghosts, living still through the grace of art.

CHAPTER 6

What Was Re-born during the Renaissance?

Dominique Fernandez

Around 1540, Michelangelo, then approximately sixty-five years old, sent the young Tommaso dei Cavalieri a love poem (sonnet no. 98) that ends with this line, 'Resto prigion d'un cavalier armato':

> Se vint' e preso i' debb'esser beato,
> maraviglia non è se nudo e solo
> resto prigion d'un cavalier armato.

Roughly translated, these three lines mean: 'If I must be conquered and taken to be happy, it is no marvel that I, naked and alone, remain the prisoner of an armed cavalier'. A French translator, Adelin Charles Fiorato, rendered them as this lovely tercet:

> Si vaincu et pris je dois être heureux,
> ce n'est merveille que solitaire et nu
> je sois captif d'un chevalier en armes.[1]

But why does he feel the need to explain, in a note, 'Naked, that is, unarmed'? *Nudo e solo* is perfectly clear. Another objection: 'chevalier' is far too noble a term and translates neither the crudity of *cavalier* nor the pun.

Michelangelo's poems were not published until long after his death, by his great-nephew, in 1623, at the height of the Counter-Reformation, a time of intense moral repression. A faithful edition appeared only in 1897, thanks to the efforts of the scholar Karl Frey. Only then was the extent of the great-nephew's meddling revealed: he had led it to be believed that the poems to Tommaso were addressed to the poet's female friend Vittoria Colonna. The 'armed cavalier' and his too-obvious 'weapon' were clearly hard for the great-nephew to swallow, so he shamelessly bowdlerised the last line to read: 'I remain the prisoner of a burning heart'.

Among the poems dedicated to Tommaso, one of the most explicit — the majority are complex and obscure in the extreme, due to a taste for hermetic allusion but also a need for secrecy and an instinctive prudence — ends with the

---

1 Michel-Ange, *Poésies/Rime*, ed. and trans. by Adelin Charles Fiorato (Paris: Les Belles Lettres, 2004). A literal translation of the French into English would read: 'If conquered and caught I must be happy | It is no marvel that solitary and naked | I am captive of a knight in arms'.

following two tercets:

> Happy will that day be, when it comes!
> Let time and the hour stop for a while,
> The day and the sun arrest their ancient course,
>
> So that I may hold — underserving though I am,
> My dear, tender lord, the one I desire,
> Forever in my unworthy and eager arms.

In other words, Michelangelo hopes to hold his lover in his arms but believes he doesn't deserves such happiness — but the poem is clear enough to require no explanation.

Next to the statue of David on Piazza della Signoria in Florence, in the Lanzi Loggia, is another symbol of the re-birth of something that was in principle forbidden: Benvenuto Cellini's *Perseus*, also stark naked. The model for this beautiful youth was the sculptor's student and lover, Fernando da Montepulciano, whom he also used to illustrate the great myths of classical pederasty: the rape of Ganymede, Apollo and Hyacinth, and Narcissus.

Michelangelo and Cellini didn't hide, or barely bothered to hide. Cellini, accused by a jealous colleague of being an 'infamous sodomite', responded with cutting irony: 'You, madman, are going too far. Would to God that I understood so noble an art: they say that Jove used it with Ganymede in paradise, and here on earth it is the practice of the greatest emperors and kings. I am but a poor humble man with no hope of aspiring to a thing so admirable.' This trumps even the discourse of Pausanias and Alcibiades in *Plato's Banquet*.

Leonardo da Vinci, on the other hand, made only few allusions to sexuality in his notebooks: it seems he found the sexual organs deeply repulsive. 'The act of intercourse and the parts used for this purpose are so ugly that, were it not for the beauty of human faces, nature would have abandoned the human race.' Relationships were clearly not to the taste of this solitary man. 'Alone, you belong entirely to yourself, but if you have even one companion, you belong to yourself by half.' It can easily be imagined why the author of this statement might have been very discreet about his private life. Nevertheless, his sexual inclination must have been well known: Lomazzo, one of his earliest biographers, imagined the following dialogue between Phidias and Leonardo: 'Did you and he ever play the "game in the rear" that the Florentines love so much?', the Greek sculptor asks. 'Many times!' Leonardo answers (he was stunningly handsome as a youth, especially around the age of fifteen). 'Are you not ashamed to admit to it?' — 'No! Why should I be ashamed? Among men of merit there is no greater cause for pride.'

The pagan cult of boys had a marked influence on the Florentine and Roman Renaissance. While Venice had a clear preference for women and the opulence of female flesh — consider the profusion of Venuses, Danaes and bathing Susannahs turned out by Giorgione, Titian, Veronese and Tintoretto — Florence and Rome expressed a predilection for androgynous males. Botticelli himself, despite his celebrated Venus, was suspected of this heresy, a suspicion that his slim, ambiguously seductive angels would seem to substantiate. In the background of the painting of the Holy Family known as the *Tondo Doni*, Michelangelo couldn't help but include

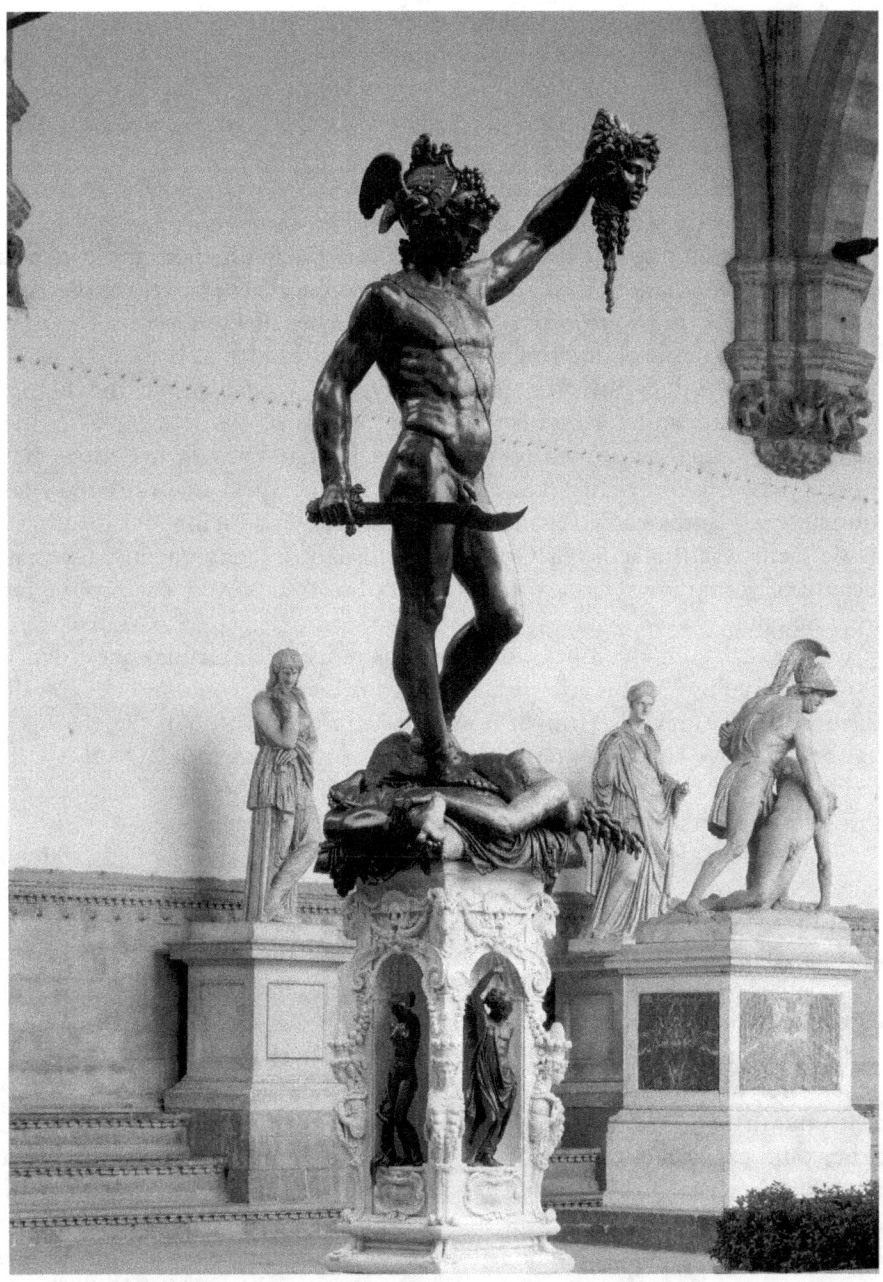

Fig. 14. Benvenuto Cellini, *Perseus*, 1554, bronze, height 320 cm (excluding base), Loggia dei Lanzi, Florence. © 2015 Photo Scala, Florence; courtesy of the Ministero Beni e Att. Culturali.

— or rather, had the audacity to include — five nude male figures. These small but ravishingly beautiful boys playing and fondling each other appear as a double tribute to pagan antiquity and Greek mores inside a work whose explicit aim was to exalt a symbol of Catholic Christianity — the mystery of the Nativity reconfigured as a Virgilian eclogue!

Officially, homosexuality was condemned. Preachers denounced it from the pulpit. One of the most virulent was the Dominican monk Savonarola. Men who debauched minors (as most painters and sculptors did with their apprentices and students) could be sentenced to the stake. A philosophical alibi was therefore needed to justify practices that were officially reproved. One of Florence's great accomplishments was to devise a doctrine that recast the forbidden as licit.

In the latter third of the fifteenth century, the Tuscan priest and humanist Marsilio Ficino, a translator and commentator of Plato, codified the doctrine of Neoplatonism, which attempted to reconcile Christianity with the pagan beliefs of antiquity. Because of man's central position in the world, the doctrine exalted the human body and awarded it the greatest dignity. For Ficino and his disciples, the male form was the acme of God's glory in nature; consequently, celebrating the beauty of young boys was a way for the soul to find its way back to the realm where it belongs.

By way of such subtle casuistry, sodomy was recast as a spiritual quest. Michelangelo made free use of this alibi in declaring his love for Tommaso dei Cavalieri: 'God, in His grace, reveals Himself nowhere better than through the charms of a mortal body; I love this body only because He is reflected in it.' On the basis of such thinly veiled rhetoric, however, prudish commentators deny that there was anything more than a chaste friendship between the two men.

Michelangelo made a wonderful and justly celebrated drawing of the abduction of Ganymede to send to Tommaso. This theme was also justified by a philosophical explanation that fooled no one: the abduction of the beautiful youth was presented as an example of *furor amatorius*, and his erotic kidnapping as the flight of the intellect delivered from the bonds of flesh and intoxicated by contemplation. More impudently, Jupiter's favourite was sometimes assimilated to St John the Apostle carried up to heaven by Christ. Michelangelo's friends, Sebastiano del Piombo, for instance, offered some advice that he was not hypocritical enough to follow: 'It seems to me that the Ganymede would look good at this spot; if you gave him a halo, he could pass for Saint John of the Apocalypse transported to heaven.' Others justified Jupiter's actions by quoting the gospel verse 'Let the little children come to me' — one hopes in jest.

Michelangelo's Ganymede has no halo, nor the gentleness of the apostle: the artist was content to celebrate male beauty and the passion it awakens in the eagle's heart. The naked youth has been snatched up by a great bird of prey; he spreads the boy's legs and encircles his torso in the curve of his neck and powerful beak. Spread legs, talons, beak, thick plumage, rising movement: stripped of any idealising intent, these are the means and stages of erotic conquest or sexual aggression.

Whereas Michelangelo's paintings and sculptures of men — the Sistine Chapel's *Ignudi*, the slaves of the tomb of Julius II, the Greek heroes — are highly eroticised,

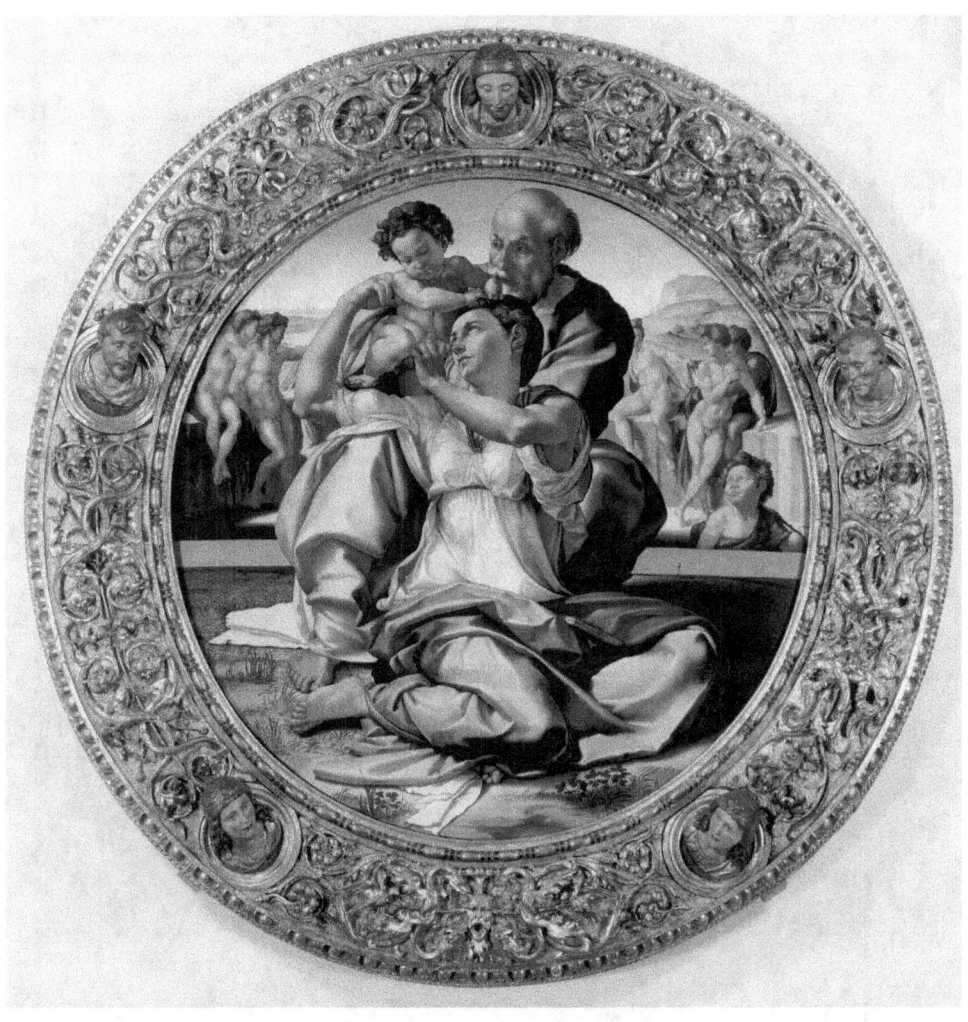

Fig. 15. Michelangelo, *Holy Family* or *Tondo Doni*, 1503–04, tempera and oil on wood, diameter 120 cm, Uffizi Gallery, Florence.
© 2015 Photo Scala, Florence; courtesy of the Ministero Beni e Att. Culturali.

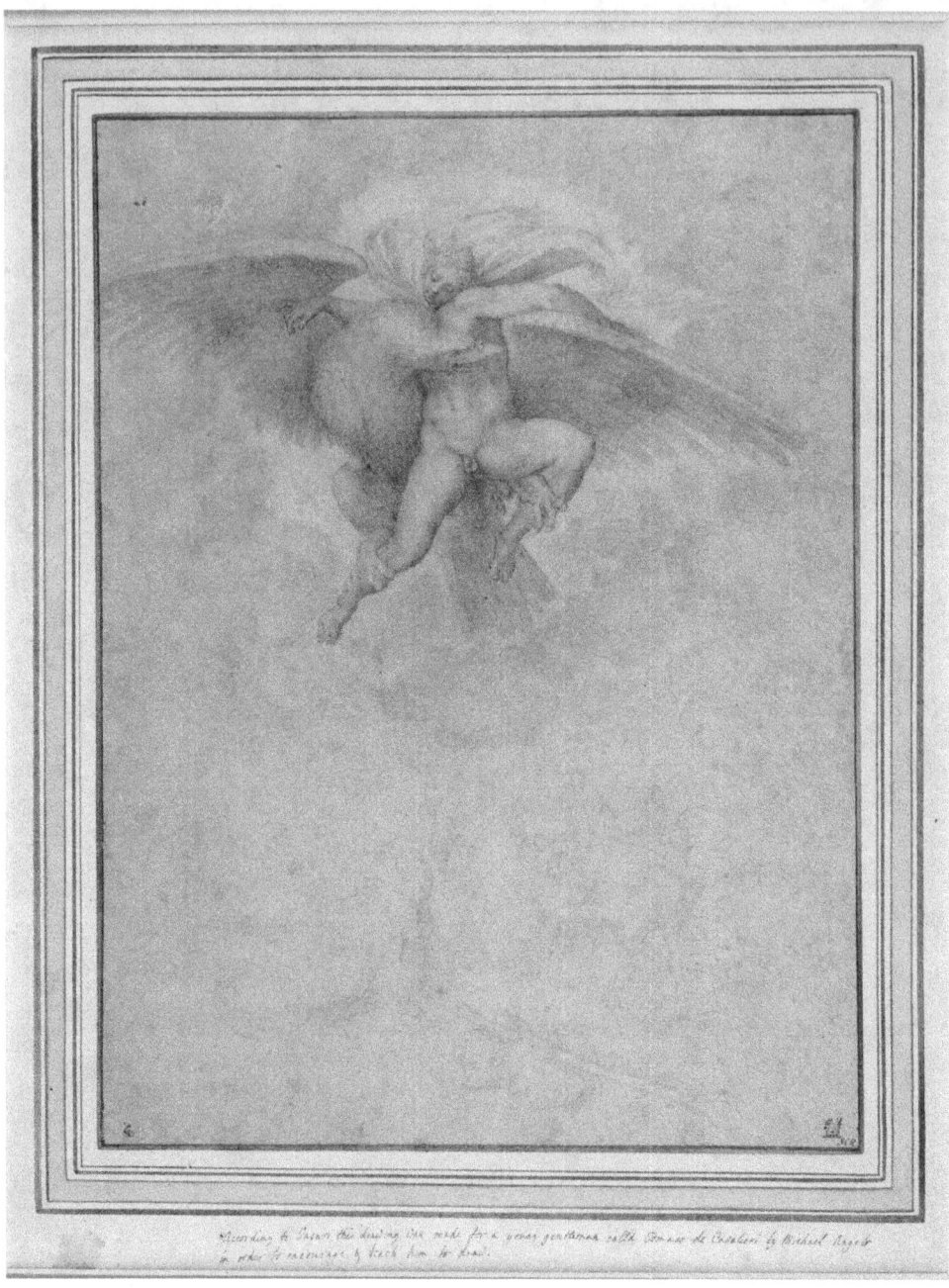

FIG. 16. Michelangelo, *The Rape of Ganymede*, c. 1533, black chalk on antique laid paper, 38 × 27 cm, Fogg Art Museum, Harvard University Art Museums. Harvard Art Museums/Fogg Museum, Gifts for Special Uses Fund, 1955.75. Photo: Imaging Department © President and Fellows of Harvard College.

his women have an air of grave dignity with little sexual attraction. They are draped and gaze off into the void, unlike his males, who are always nude and active. The two female nudes in the Medici Chapel, for instance, *Dawn* and *Night*, are heavy and ungraceful, if not frankly ugly. The maker of *David* could never have created a Venus. He painted wonderfully pure and gentle Madonnas (in Saint Peter's of Rome, Bruges, the Medici Chapel in Florence) precisely because they were no longer women: he could represent their youth and beauty only insofar as they had transcended their femininity and acquired a supernatural dimension.

Michelangelo's sex life is well documented: the list of his known lovers includes Giovanni Pistoia when he was working on the ceiling of the Sistine Chapel, Gherardo Perini whom he met in 1522, Tommaso dei Cavalieri in 1532, Febo di Poggio, who died in 1535 and whose name (*Febo* means Phoebus/the Sun, an epithet of Apollo, *poggio* means hill) gave the poet an opportunity for more puns ('When Febo spreads his light and warmth on the summit of my life...'). Finally, ten years later, there was Cecchino Bracci, who died in the full glow of his youthful beauty.

Regarding Leonardo, a prince of mystery in both his life and his work, the utmost circumspection is necessary. While still a student of Verrocchio, and probably his lover, he was jailed for having carnal relations with Jacopo Saltarelli, aged seventeen, who was known as a prostitute. In fact, it seems likely that he hired the young man as a model for a clay bust of Christ Child, and this sacrilege may have been the true cause of his arrest. The incident took place in 1476, when Leonardo was twenty-four.

We know of another boy who played an important role in his life: his name was Gian Giacomo Caprotti, and he was ten years old when the master took him into his house, in 1490. He remained with Leonardo until his departure for France in 1516. A pretty child with a head of curls, later a beautiful young man, he was also a good-for-nothing and a delinquent. He stole money, filched silver nibs from the workshop, and sold a piece of Turkish leather that Leonardo intended to make into boots so as to buy sweets. In his notebooks, the painter refers to this boy with the face of an angel by the strange name 'Salaï', a nickname probably inspired by *Morgante*, an epic poem in Italian, published in 1483. The author, Luigi Pulci, was a friend of Lorenzo the Magnificent. The name Salaï appears in the poem as an alias of Satan. (Proust coined the term 'salaïstes' to describe the descendants of the 'damned race'.) Leonardo cared for the little devil with astonishing patience, recording what he spent on the boy's clothes and shoes, and taking notes on his lies and larcenies with an obsessive attention to detail that fascinated Freud. For lack of more extensive information, however, we must see what answers we can find in Leonardo's art.

The drawing *Allegory of Pleasure and Pain* depicts two men with two heads and four arms but one torso and one pair of legs, in an intimate union of male bodies. The front half is an old man and the back half a youth with the face of Salaï, holding a reed in one hand and scattering gold coins from the other. Leonardo provided an explanation of his allegory: 'It represents Pleasure together with Pain, and shows them as twins, as if united together, because one is never without the other. They are back to back because they are opposed to each other. If you choose pleasure, be aware that he has behind him one who will bring you suffering and repentance.' This sounds like a clear allusion to Leonardo's tormented homosexuality. Furthermore, the reed is a phallic symbol of the young man's physical appeal, while the gold coins symbolise his expensive tastes. In the drawing, lover and beloved are forever separated by their inability to look directly at each other.

Another of Leonardo's drawings of an old man facing a youth evokes the *erastes* and *eromenos* of ancient Greece. The curly-haired youth in this drawing is also a portrait of Salaï. This time, the two figures look at each other, but with such an expression of hardness in the eyes! Is the old man reproaching the young rascal? Is the youth staring back with insolent coldness? Beyond the biographical reading, does this drawing express, once again, Leonardo's difficulty with sexual relationships and the impossibility for him — or his refusal — of complete union?

More secretive than Michelangelo, notwithstanding the fictional dialogue attributed to him by Lomazzo, Leonardo left no explicitly homosexual paintings. In the words of the great art historian Rudolf Wittkower, 'All Leonardo's conscious efforts were focused on reining in sensuality, Michelangelo's on intensifying it.' Although Leonardo would never have decorated the ceiling of the Sistine Chapel with *Ignudi*, he betrayed himself in the suspiciously ambiguous bodies and faces that appear in his paintings. Take the Louvre's *St John the Baptist*, for instance. Male or female? Difficult to say, with his coy smile, wistful, enticing eyes, luxuriant curls, the feminine roundedness of his shoulder and arm, finger pointing to the heaven — or is it beckoning the viewer to a more earthly tryst? Similarly, his plump, nude *Bacchus*, also in the Louvre, has almost womanly breasts, an androgynous face, unisex hair, and that finger, again, which could be inviting us in to a place that is not the kingdom of God...

Last but not least, the *Mona Lisa*. If this portrait has so frequently been copied, lampooned, deformed and misappropriated in so many ways, it is no accident. Satirists have detected, behind the appearance of a young woman, a mother in labour, a nun, a bearded man, a male transvestite, even Salaï; and indeed, she is all of them at once, and everything but a creature of a single gender. We need look no further to explain the impression of mystery that emanates from this painting.

Rome had the papacy and the tight lid of the Catholic cupolas; Florence, with its massive and forbidding palaces, their thick bossing and square towers, had the air of a fortress. Paradoxically, however, there emerged in both cities — the first dominated by the doctrine of the repression of the flesh, the second by its severe cityscape — a culture diametrically opposed to both the moral orthodoxy and the so-called masculine virtues. Paganism, and its erotic corollary, were thus re-born exactly where they were least expected.

CHAPTER 7

The Meteorite of Orgueil

Adrien Goetz

I had to sort through my entire library in order to find my volumes of Pietro Bembo. They were purchased mainly in Italy, when I was director of the *Académie de France*. At the time, I wanted to surround myself with beautiful books and the authors I often quoted, like so many friends. My books followed me to Paris, though I open them less often now. I had not opened the Bembo volumes until today. Earlier this evening, next to the fireplace, they glowed in front of the flames like embers.

I own a translation of his collected works that I had bound in red moire, the colour of his cardinal's robes, the colour of fiery passion. Bembo is a blazing star. I love his Italian poetry, have always struggled to read him in Latin, and yet I find him enchanting. I used to recite his songs out loud in my studio. I know that Raphael, whom I adore, was his friend: the thought alone delights me.

Bembo wrote the painter's epitaph; I wonder who will write mine. I know it by heart. I would often go to the Pantheon, the most beautiful building in Rome, especially to read it.

This was the first place I visited after returning to Rome, to escape Paris and the critics — jealous, mediocre, arrogant, spiteful critics who wanted to nothing better than to tear me down. *Ille hic est Raphael timuit quo sospite vinci rerum magna parens et moriente mori* — 'Here lies Raphael by whom Nature feared to be conquered while he lived, and when he was dying, feared herself to die'. I translate as best I can, attempting an elegant turn of phrase, though I am incapable of writing poetry and have long since forgotten the little Latin that the Christian brothers of Montauban tried to teach me in school.

I have painted Raphael in love, in his workshop, embracing La Fornarina, the beautiful woman who was probably the cause of his death. Heaven seems almost jealous of the Earth when she robs it of men like Raphael or Mozart before their time. Whereas I have been forgotten even by Hell: born under King Louis XVI, I am eighty-four, and when death comes, I think it will be a great surprise. I am remarkably healthy and take my walk every day, for I like my Quai Voltaire. I walk to the Seine and admire the glistening dome of the Institute as I cross the bridge. It reminds me of the battles I have fought. I continue through the Louvre, which his Majesty the Emperor has so wonderfully embellished and is still enlarging; it is the most beautiful palace in the world, a temple to the Arts, and I am sure my paintings will hang there some day when I am dead, next to those of the Master of Urbino, whose student I would have liked to be. I arrive finally at the Imperial

Library, where at my request the librarian fetches volumes of engravings, which I trace for my own pleasure. I like copying: it exercises my hand. As long as I live, I will not let a day pass without tracing a line.

The passage I wanted to reread this morning is the dialogue in which Bembo recalls a journey to the slopes of Etna when he was twenty years old. I wanted to see how he describes the volcano. I remember something about fireworks in the sky. I remember the images, but have forgotten the words.

My hometown gazette, which I received yesterday, tells of a very similar event, something extraordinary that occurred this week on the shores of the Tarn. If only I had Pietro Bembo's talent to describe it. If only I had Raphael's colours from his fresco *The Fire in the Borgo* to render the lights and cries of that night of terror in my native land, my peaceful countryside with its tranquil villages. If only I were an astrologer to read the omen written in this upheaval of the stars in the sky of my birth.

A volcano: that is what the divine Raphael was for the men of his time, for painters like me, who live in his shadow. As I collected Bembo's books, Raphael's death was always on my mind. I have just set hands on my copy of a very old translation of Bembo's *Asolani*, published in Lyon during the Renaissance. It was a gift to me from Paul Flandrin, a painter from Lyon, in memory of our discussions in Rome, on the Pincio, at sundown. For me, it is also a book of friendship.

I opened it again this morning: it speaks of love, and nothing but love. One character says that love is bitter — I cannot disagree — while another strives to explain that we can find true love only in the contemplation of beauty. All my life, I have believed this. I have observed Raphael's paintings and frescoes as if he had painted them especially for me, to make me feel what this world can give us from time to time, if we are lucky: a glimpse of perfect beauty. As painters with eyes wide open, we have a sacred duty to allow others to catch a glimpse of it too. And if the Philistines criticise us, if they fail to understand, too bad. Let them chatter; I watch, I move on. The beauty I wanted to paint was the beauty of that woman's body, which some said was too long — as if I cared two figs for medicine and anatomy. My aim was to render pure beauty visible, beauty as I know it, as I carry it inside me. 'When I set out to paint beauty I have a type in mind', Raphael wrote to his friend Castiglione.

I have painted the Virgin with her lovely rounded face and her large eyes lowered to the white disk of the Host. I am currently putting the last touches on a canvas in the same format, a round painting of female nudes that is like a collection of my memories, the vestiges of a life devoted to the love of forms. Sacred love and profane love are connected, as they were in my life and in the pages of Cardinal Bembo; the beauty of bodies, the beauty of faces, are the intermingled images of the heavenly beauties I hope to discover very soon — if I manage to avoid the flames of Hell.

Cardinal Bembo owned a strange relic, which healed nothing — particularly not love. I saw it in the Milan library once, when I was young. Preserved under glass was a lock of blond hair, a severed curl found between the pages of a letter. This strange object was a reliquary of Lucrezia Borgia's hair.

Is it a comet? A volcano emerging amid the hills of my youth? I reread Cardinal Bembo's *Etna*, but found no answers there.

Astonishing news, but more astonishingly, it reached me through the pages of the *Journal de Tarn-et-Garonne*, which I subscribe to in order to receive some news of my beloved valleys. It was lying on a silver platter in my drawing room, under the large photograph of me — over three feet high — by Mr Disdéri, which I have hung right in the middle of the wall, so as to frighten the visitors who wait for me to emerge from my study. The paper rarely brings us interesting news, but though my darling Delphine makes fun of me for it, I enjoy reading the names of villages and of people I once knew, many of whom are the great-grandchildren of my old playmates.

I asked my colleague at the Institute, Monsieur Le Verrier, discoverer of Neptune and my favourite member of the Academy of Sciences, to tell me all he knows about comets and aerolites. I'm expecting him to arrive at any time now. I plan to ask him whether, peering through the telescopes of the Paris Observatory, astronomers have noticed a great ball of fire as large as the full moon, with Lucrezia's blonde mane for a halo.

The incredible event occurred on Saturday 14 May 1864, the eve of Pentecost, in the village of Orgueil, between Montauban and Buzet. I know the town and many of its inhabitants well. So as not to be consigned to the circles of Dante's *Inferno*, the peasants of Orgueil call themselves 'Orgueuillois', rather than 'Orgueilleux', which means proud or arrogant. (In fact, they seem rather proud of the name.) They were unprepared for the tongues of fire that rained down on their rustic retreat.

It was like an earthquake, the newspaper writes. A blast like the thunder of a cannon, like fireworks, like a volley of bullets. The Orgueillois reported lights in the sky like the trail of a phosphorus match, which turned into fiery pinwheels upon reaching the ground. A rock larger than a cannon ball fell from the sky and blasted a crater in a field. It started a fire.

Amid the disorder of my books, I found another book that was a gift from Flandrin, who likes to haunt the old bookshops of Lyon: a volume of poems published in Besançon in 1594. I wonder if it is rare. The poet is long forgotten. His name is Jean-Baptiste Chassignet. He wrote at least this one book, *Contempt of Life and Consolation against Death* — the title caught my attention.

> Our bodies oppressed by the weight of the grave,
> When the thundering roar of the trumpet will sound,
> Raining down fire on the earth all ablaze,
> The sky pure and amazed, its torches extinguished [...]

I thought then of Raphael's tomb, ringed with torches, under the open dome of the Pantheon in Rome, and returned to my study. This is where I keep what I consider the most sacred of reliquaries. A glass box in a golden frame. My pride and joy.

On 9 September 1833, Pope Gregory XVI, who has since proclaimed his infallibility, requested the exhumation of the tomb known as Raphael's. Above the sarcophagus in the church that our Roman friends call Santa Maria della Rotunda, stands Lorenzetto's statue of the *Madonna of the Rocks*, which I don't much care for, incidentally. The vicinity of the tomb was cordoned off with a fence. The only light in the lanternless cupola fell from the sky. I have visited the place so often that I can picture it perfectly.

My friend Horace Vernet, my predecessor at the head of the *Académie de France*, was among the witnesses to the event; he made a very good print of it, which he gave me with a kind dedication. The sculptor Thorvaldsen, a friend of Vernet's, was apparently also present as the representative of the *Académie de Saint-Luc*; he sculpted the bust of Cardinal Consalvi for the Pantheon. Incidentally, the cardinal's marble face bears some resemblance to that of his young nephew, Hannibal de Bréauté-Consalvi, universally known as Babal, who paid me a visit the other day. In Francesco Diofebi's rather ghastly but accurate painting of this unique event in the history of the arts, Thorvaldsen, standing among the spectators, can be easily recognised thanks to his white hair. The painting captures the moment on 14 September, a few days after excavations began, when the pope himself arrived, escorted by two Swiss guards, just as the sacred body was about to appear. A chair was brought for him to sit on while he watched the exhumation. Also present were Mr Overbeck, Mr Camuccini, the sculptor Fabris, and Cardinal Zurla, who was similarly provided with a chair. When the bones of the divine Raphael first emerged from the unsealed tombstone, the pope rose to his feet and removed his cap.

Until then, the members of the *Académie de Saint-Luc* had believed that the skull they kept in a crystal box belonged to my darling Sanzio. On this day, however, they were forced to admit that it was a fake; or rather, that it was merely the skull of Canon Desiderio d'Adiutorio, founder of the Congregation of Virtuosi who sit in the rotunda of the Pantheon. Fabris made a mould of the real skull, with its prominent forehead and perfect teeth.

I received a few fragments of Raphael's bones from the Holy Father — an immense honour. I recite the verses of Pietro Bembo over them, like a prayer. Thorvaldsen, for his part, received a cardboard box containing a bit of the lime with which the tomb had been whitewashed.

I keep this reliquary at home. After my death, I intend to bequeath it, along with my paintings and my precious books, to my beloved city of Montauban. I hope that people will pray for me and draw in front of these remains of Raphael, in the city where I was born, as a most humble servant of his altar.

The people of Orgueil picked up their rock. They too may decide to keep it in a modern sanctuary, one of those glass cabinets that are the reliquaries of science: it was a gift from God, after all, was it not? Artworks, on the other hand, are reliquaries without relics. In my native province, hundreds of relics and reliquaries were destroyed during the wars against the Huguenots, before Montauban rebuilt its white cathedral, where my painting now hangs — my *Vow of Louis XIII*, the ex-voto that made my reputation. This may be why I wanted to keep these sacred fragments always near me, as protection against death and evil temptations; I have never been parted from them for more than a day.

When I entered the Pantheon for the first time after returning to Rome as the new director of the Villa Médicis, it was raining. The crowd was laughing at the noise. No mass was being said, and the bronze doors were wide open. Water

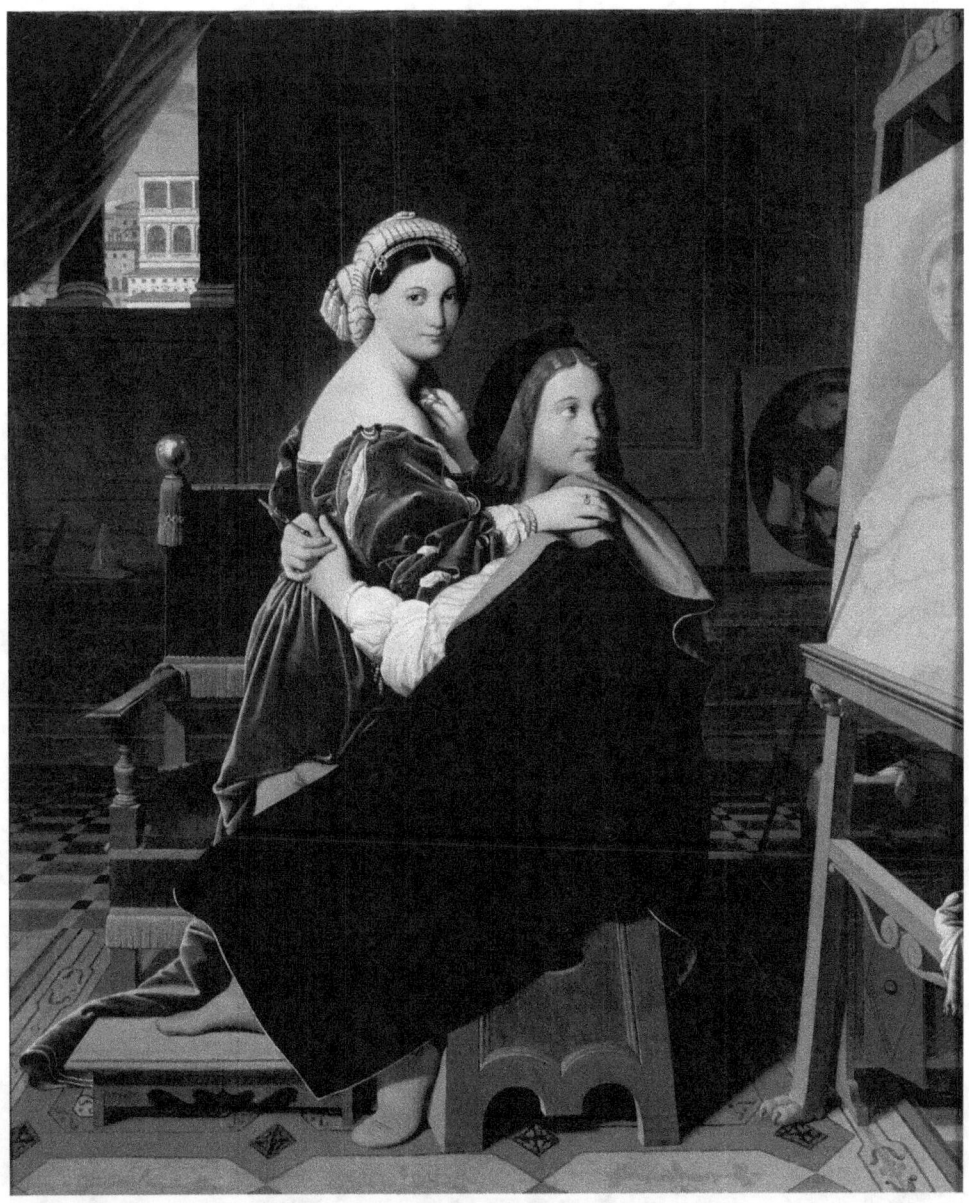

FIG. 17. Jean-Auguste-Dominique Ingres, *Raphael and la Fornarina*, 1814, oil on canvas, 66 × 54 cm, Fogg Art Museum, Harvard University Art Museums. Harvard Art Museums/Fogg Museum, Bequest of Grenville L. Winthrop, 1943.252. Photo: Imaging Department © President and Fellows of Harvard College.

cascaded onto the pavement from the open oculus, designed by Hadrian and Agrippa to frame the sky. As it has been falling since Roman times. The pavement of the Pantheon is sublime: it duplicates the plan of the building itself, echoing the great coffers of the domed ceiling, their remarkable power. It is designed of circles of marble enclosed in squares, repeated like a motif, like sacred music. The water was flowing towards the centre of the building, between the statues, the tombs, the plaque in honour of the Virtuosi. I looked. The statue of the Madonna above the sarcophagus, Bembo's verses, reflected in the mirror of marble, lay suddenly at my feet, framed in a circle traced inside a square. The composition was perfect. On that day, I saw harmony. The sphere of the Pantheon was spinning around me like the vault of the sky with its stars, its planets, its comets. It was then I first envisioned my great tondo, my Virgin of the Host, a mother venerating the circle of unleavened bread that is her son, creator of the universe and of infinity. I saw it in a pool of water. Everything I loved was there, laid out before me, a Pentecost like the one that fell on in a great ball of flames on the heads of the peasants of Orgueil: the beauty of the ancients, the beauty falling from the sky, the beauty of Rome, the beauty of the girls painted by Raphael.

★ ★ ★ ★ ★

Today in Montauban, city of forgotten palaces, across from the episcopal citadel, which houses the Ingres Museum, stands a brick building that tourists hardly ever visit. It looks like it could be a school, or maybe a convent. The Natural History Museum occupies the top floor. Its glass cabinets dating from the time of Jules Verne are filled with tropical birds, butterflies and wild animals.

On this morning in January 2013, a group of primary school children are admiring the Pinder Circus's elephant, Punch, who died in 1894. Next, the curator guiding them, a young woman in a grey suit, tells them about a graphite baluster that was offered to the famous artist of Montauban, Monsieur Ingres, in the nineteenth century. It's a piece of pure graphite, which the owner of a paint shop presented to the artist as a publicity stunt. Her colleague of the Ingres Museum has kindly lent it to her for the minerals display. But small children aren't terribly interested in mineralogy, and no one dares ask what a baluster is. A little girl asks why there is a refrigerator next to it. Amid the glass-eyed foxes and pythons, the young woman in a grey suit laughs. It's not a refrigerator, it's a safe, she says. Inside it is the most precious object in the city, more precious than all of Mr Ingres's paintings and beautiful drawings put together. A stone that the world's greatest scientists have come to observe and study, though its significance was understood only in the late twentieth century, after NASA had analysed it. This black rock that looks a bit like volcanic lava is older than the sun; it comes from another galaxy. An extraordinary witness to the birth of the stars, it fell in the village of Orgueil in 1864, as shown by this engraving of an old newspaper of the time, the *Journal du Tarn-et-Garonne*. What you see here is a reproduction; the original is in the archives of the Ingres Museum. The children listen. And stare at the newspaper. The stone in the white cabinet, like something from the space shuttle, contains diamonds, extra-terrestrial

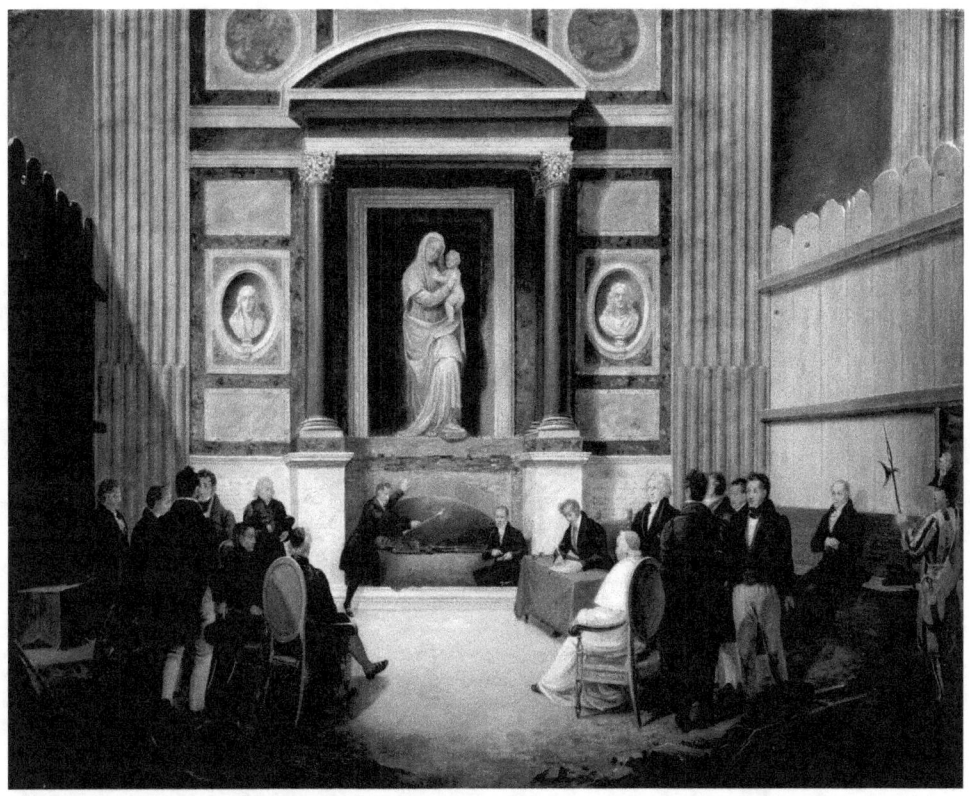

FIG. 18. Francesco Diofebi, *The Opening of Raphael's Grave in 1833*, 1836, oil on canvas, 54.9 × 70 cm, Thorvaldsens Museum, Copenhagen.

water, and a substance that no one has been able to identify. It may hold the key to the birth of the universe.

In the Ingres Museum, under the large painting *The Dream of Ossian*, a fantastical composition inspired by the Homer of the North, the curator has placed a memento of the excellent Monsieur Ingres's strange folly; surrounded by a frame of palmettos designed by the great architect Hittorff, turned humble framer for the occasion, is a glass box containing bits of stone and human bone. On the back, in Ingres's own hand, it says that these are the lovingly collected remains of the divine Raphael. After Ingres died in his apartment on Quai Voltaire, on 14 January 1867, this strange profane reliquary, along with the contents of his studio, his paintings, drawings, books, violin and musical scores, were returned to the city of his birth. Francesco Diofebi's painting of the opening of the tomb of Raphael is now in the Thorvaldsens Museum in Copenhagen.

CHAPTER 8

Niccolò to Himself

Carlo Ossola

Tibi scribo...[1] to you I write... but no, it is not to you I write, for I have not yet found a horse to carry me to you, oh my Conscience. But I consign these words to paper anyway, for *whoever is besieged, above all, ought to take care not to be attacked in times of repose*. Watch, observe, examine, decide: this is what I advise in my book on the art of war. *Counsel with many on the things you ought to do, and confer with few on what you do afterwards.*[2] And so, I now debate with myself, *solus ad solum*, since the art of this war is both against me and within me. I keep my *Prince* always on the table in front of me; completed years ago, it has not yet been published — indeed, it cannot be printed at present. In this book I wrote — and still firmly believe — *that the injury that is to be done to a man ought to be of such a kind that one does not stand in fear of revenge*. But am I really capable of such a thing? Between force and prudence I hesitate, perpetually knotting and unknotting the same idea: *for it is found in ordinary affairs that one never seeks to avoid one trouble without running into another; but prudence consists in knowing how to distinguish the character of troubles, and for choice to take the lesser evil.*[3] Not to mention that *in all our deliberations, we ought to consider where we are likely to encounter least inconvenience, and accept that as the course to be preferred, since we shall never find any line of action entirely free from disadvantage.*[4] And so I envelop myself in prudence, and there I remain, like a lotus flower in its leaf.

I have written nothing in the last few days, being preoccupied with the question of the 'dictator': *Nominating a dictator was not without difficulty for the consuls*. The stars in the sky tonight are tiny and beautiful, and as I turn to face at the hills, the words of the Poet come to mind:

---

1   This imaginary monologue takes place in the space of a single night, sometime between the completion of *The Prince* in 1513 and the publication of *The Art of War* (Florence, Heirs of Philippo di Giunta, 1521), in the period following the publication of Erasmus's *Education of the Christian Prince* (Leuven: apud Theodoricum Martinum Alustensem, 1516). Direct quotations from the works of Machiavelli appear in italics. I discussed the influence of Erasmus on Machiavelli in the following article: C. Ossola, *C'è Erasmo dietro il 'Principe'*, in *Il Sole 24 ore*, no. 54, Sunday 24 February 2013, p. 27.

2   Niccolò Machiavelli, *The Art of War*, trans. by Christopher Lynch (Radford, VA: Wilder Publications, 2007), pp. 135, 137.

3   *The Prince*, Ch. 3 and Ch. 21. All quotations from *The Prince* are from the W. K. Marriot's 1905 translation (Project Gutenberg e-book downloaded from <http://www.gutenberg.org/ebooks/1232>).

4   Niccolo Machiavelli, *Discourses on the First Decade of Titus Livius*, trans. by Ninian Hill Thomson (London: Kegan Paul, Trench & Co., 1883), p. 74. (A Project Gutenberg e-book is available at <http://www.gutenberg.org/ebooks/10827>.)

> As many as the fireflies the peasant
> (while resting on a hillside in the season
> when he who lights the world least hides his face),
>
> just when the fly gives way to the mosquito,
> sees glimmering below, down in the valley,
> there where perhaps he gathers grapes and tills —
>
> so many were the flames that glittered in
> the eighth abyss; I made this out as soon
> as I had come to where one sees the bottom.[5]

He, too, in both his heart and his verse, deplored the state of our city, which was also his own: 'Be joyous, Florence, you are great indeed | for over sea and land you beat your wings | through every part of Hell your name extends!'[6] However, his great talent — which I do not possess — led him to feel the bitterness all the more keenly, as exiled and wandering through Hell he looked up at the lovely night sky, filled with stars flickering like fireflies. I should feel appeased and come to you, oh my Conscience, as he did long ago. Or should I follow Michelangelo's example and abandon Florence to work for the popes in Rome, as many other men plan to do?[7]

I, for my part, would like to stay and serve my Republic, and I am all the more resolved to do so seeing that they have force but I possess prudence and discernment. These virtues are of limited use, however, *because this is to be asserted in general of men, that they are ungrateful, fickle, false, cowardly, covetous, and as long as you succeed they are yours entirely; they will offer you their blood, property, life and children, when the need is far distant; but when it approaches they turn against you.*[8] I gave this chapter to several of my friends to read, and they found it harsh, but for me it simply reflects everyday reality. At night I follow the example of my fellow-citizen Giovanni di Pagolo Morelli, and turn to the classics:

> You shall have the most capable men under your orders and shall be able to sit in your study reading Virgil for as long as you like; and he will never say no to you, and he will answer your questions, and he will counsel you well, and he will teach you without demanding money or gifts of any kind in exchange, and he will banish your melancholy thoughts and worries and bring you joy and consolation. You will be able to enjoy the company of Boethius, Dante and the other poets; of Tullius, who will teach you to speak perfectly, and of Aristotle, who will teach you philosophy. You will understand the cause of things and will derive great pleasure, if not from all, at the very least from each small part.[9]

I know very well that violence is the true 'cause of things'. I recall, for instance, that the famous Bonaccorso Pitti, who, after travelling widely throughout Europe as a merchant, was sent as captain to Castrocaro in November 1423, wrote thus of his methods of government:

---

5   Dante Alighieri, *Inferno*, XXVI, v. 25–33, trans. by A. Mandelbaum (New York: Bantam, 1982).
6   Ibid., XXVI, v. 1–3.
7   The Altoviti (Bindo Altoviti in particular), along with Cosimo I of Tuscany and the Neri family (to which San Filippo Neri belonged), fled to Rome shortly after.
8   *The Prince*, Ch. 17.
9   Giovanni di Pagolo Morelli, *Ricordi*, quoted in V. Branca, *Mercanti scrittori* (Milan: Rusconi, 1986), p. 200.

In the month of February [1424] at Castrocaro, I came across a band of seven men from Forlì, all of them Ghibellines; they were plotting to take the Duke of Milan's people in Castrocaro during the night of Carnival, using keys made by one of their number, who was a locksmith. I caught all seven, but two escaped. Those I caught were decapitated on my orders. Note that, in the fortress and county of Castrocaro, there are more Ghibellines than Guelphs.[10]

Hence, my Prince *ought to inspire fear in such a way that, if he does not win love, he avoids hatred; because he can endure very well being feared while he is not hated.*[11] I will grant you that force may suffice, but force alone produces only hatred; prudence suggests that it is preferable for the Prince to be feared by his subjects rather than hated. So I also write that *a prince ought to take care never to make an alliance with one more powerful than himself,*[12] and an officer is thus all the more duty-bound to warn him.

That is why I tried so hard to unite the lion and the fox, while ensuring that the fox and not the lion holds the reins of power and manages it with the intelligence proper to humans.

I return to my room now, as a stiff Tramontane is starting to blow. Inside, my mind turns from celestial objects to my memories. I remember again how poorly Fra Girolamo managed things. He understood that the disorder of the Republic, the confusion of roles, and the impotence of the magistrates favoured the arrogant rise of tyrants. There are echoes of Dante ('For all the towns of Italy are full | of tyrants, | and each townsman who becomes | a partisan is soon a new Marcellus'[13]) in his description of these pretentious upstarts:

> Many want to govern the state but cannot, because they are not capable. Many also are capable but do not want to. Neither are in their proper place. In the other state, many who wanted to govern could not, and many who both could and wanted to govern ought not to have. They too were not in their proper place.[14]

I remember his sermons of 1494 as if they were yesterday. I was twenty-five, full of hope and fury, and I would never forget the fiery homily he delivered from the pulpit on the first Sunday of Advent:

> I urge all citizens to donate to the poor the money they would normally spend on studying, because at this time charity dictates that the needs of the poor are greater. And if this does not suffice, we shall draw from the coffers of the Church to support the poor of Christ. The other good resolution is to open the workshops so that everyone, but especially the poor, might have work to support themselves. We must especially strive to lessen the hardships of those who most need our help.[15]

He could already envision the scene: everyone happily at work, the priests throw-

---

10 Bonaccorso Pitti, *Ricordi*, in *Mercanti scrittori*, p. 499.
11 *The Prince*, Ch. 17.
12 *The Prince*, Ch. 21.
13 Dante Alighieri, *Purgatorio*, VI, v. 124–26, trans. by A. Mandelbaum (New York: Bantam, 1982).
14 Girolamo Savonarola, 'Predica quinta', in *Prediche del Rev. P. F. Hieronymo Savonaruola dell'ordine de' predicatori sopra alquanti salmi e sopra Aggeo Profeta, fatte nel mese di Novembre e Dicembre l'anno MCCCCLXXXXIIII* (Venice: Bernardino Bindoni, 1544), pp. 36a–b.
15 Girolamo Savonarola, 'Predica settima fatta la prima domenica dell'Advento sopra del Salmo "Dilexi quoniam. 114"', in *Prediche [...]*, pp. 53b–54a.

ing open their treasures, the corporations renouncing their privileges. But things did not go as planned. The poor streamed in from the countryside; hunger and hardship worsened. Those who opposed him from the beginning — the priests, scholars, and merchants — banded against him, and in the end sent him to the stake.

What should I do? I looked for consolation in great books, but was reminded of poor Pulci and the other unfortunates who had nothing but bad luck. I also searched among beautiful things and recalled a story crowded with characters, an allegorical tale that seems to me a parable of our times — the *Hypnerotomachia Poliphili,* or *Dream of Poliphilus* — but found there only horror and pain and violence, even in the dream:

> Falling into a first deep, pleasant, and sweet slumber, my tired and exhausted body was overcome, and in the silent night I fell asleep. [...] With hurried and agitated steps, two horrible executioners ran towards me; their lips were thick and swollen, their clothing rough, their demeanour vulgar and hatefully coarse, their aspect savage and disagreeable, their menacing and terrible eyes rounder than those of the deadly basilisk, under thick and bushy eyebrows with hard bristles. Their faces were wide and their lips huge, swollen, drooping, screeching, and thick, of a cadaverous hue; gigantic, uneven molars as black and rotten as old iron protruded from bared gums, which their retracted lips no longer covered, and jutted out of their wide-open, fetid, filthy mouths like the foaming tusks of a hunted boar. [...] Suddenly they seized me in their evil, muscular, sacrilegious, profane arms and began groaning and pulling my hair with their dirty, foetid, greasy, bloodthirsty hands, tearing the blond locks from my head and disfiguring me mercilessly.[16]

Humaniores literae! Ferocious beasts and ragged sacks of excrement that we are! My friends would prefer my Prince to behave like the subtle and sophisticated courtiers with whom Baldassar Castiglione surrounds his princes, wretched lackeys who call *elegance* what is in fact a miserable sham.

No, I want to show the Medici the true infamy of power; I want to overwhelm them with so many Latin examples and maxims from Livy and Caesar and Cicero and Tacitus that they will imagine themselves as their successors; yet my fox will be greater than their lion. And I will not follow the example of Pier Soderini, who, as my friend Filippo Nerli wrote, made sure that they had to judge 'whether he was able to sustain the broad popular acceptance that power enjoyed'.[17] Not 'popular acceptance' but the Prince alone: feared, ready to inflict ruin, wreak revenge, and cause offence, ready to pay for bread with blood...

Now that all is quiet, these words resonate in my soul; the night is long and I must stay awake, or else I might dream that the Friends of Mercy are knocking at my door to lead me to the priest for the last rites. Never meddle in the affairs of priests: the decision to hold the second Council of Pisa here a few years ago was the cause of our downfall, as it brought Ramon de Cardona's band of bandits to the Prato, with the Medici at their backs. But what council? What did those four

---

16   Venice, Aldus Manutius, 1499. In Vulgar Latin.
17   F. Nerli, *Commentarii de' fatti civili occorsi dentro la Città di Firenze dall'anno MCCXV al MDXXXVII*, (Augusta: David Raimondio Mertz and Gio. Jacopo Majer, 1728), Book V, p. 93.

cardinals do,[18] if not precipitate not so much the schism — they knew nothing of what Fra Martino was preaching in the Magna — but rather our own demise?

I had a model: he had sudden glimmers of wisdom, like slowly dying embers; he was a Batavian who aspired like Fra Girolamo to the simplicity of the Gospel. He esteemed Lorenzo Valla and understood that we live out of folly alone. He did not disdain politics and was a friend of Thomas More, who, I am told, has recently published his perfect island of *Utopia*. When he came to Italy, he was received like a prince by Aldo in Venice and stayed there awhile to complete his collection of ancient wisdom. I keep his *Adagia* close at hand (the young Pier Vettori, though barely more than a child, already considers him his idol); they are most useful and succinct, and confirm many of my intuitions about the powerful. I find his adage 'Rulers know each other' (III, IX, 84) especially helpful. It concludes as follows: 'Tyrants, while in appearance warring with each other and clashing with a terrible uproar, in fact continue to communicate in secret and to act of a common accord to ruin each their own people, for by weakening civil society they reinforce their tyrannical rule.'

I readily admit that it was the Batavian Erasmus who showed me a way out of my predicament. In the examples of the ancients, it is either the lion or the fox that commits fraud. Cicero, in his *De officiis*, would not keep them together and, moreover, condemns both as 'wholly unworthy of man'.[19] Father Dante, himself no stranger to horrors, did not wish to see them united, even in the character of Guido da Montefeltro, whom he depicts as saying: 'The wiles and secret ways I knew them all | and so employed their arts that my renown | had reached the very boundaries of earth' (exactly like my Prince). He then distinguishes the lion's arts from the fox's wiles:

> While I still had the form of bones and flesh
> my mother gave to me, my deeds were not
> those of the lion but those of the fox.[20]

But the Batavian sage dared go where Dante feared to tread: 'if the lion's pelt is too short, add the skin of a fox'.[21] Erasmus provided many examples to explain this saying, which is based on one of Lysander's maxims, and concluded: 'If you cannot obtain something by force, employ ruse [*dolus adhibendus*]'.

Having nothing more to add to this decree, I wrote: *Everyone admits how praiseworthy it is in a prince to keep faith, and to live with integrity and not with craft. Nevertheless, our experience has been that those princes who have done great things have held good faith of little account, and have known how to circumvent the intellect of men by craft, and in the*

---

18 Bernardino López de Carvajal, Federico Sanseverino, Guillaume Briçonnet and René de Prie.

19 'While wrong may be done, then, in either of two ways, that is, by force or by fraud, both are bestial: fraud seems to belong to the cunning fox, force to the lion; both are wholly unworthy of man, but fraud is the more contemptible. But of all forms of injustice, none is more flagrant than that of the hypocrite who, at the very moment when he is most false, makes it his business to appear virtuous.' M. Tullius Cicero, *De Officiis*, I, 41, trans. by Walter Miller (Cambridge, MA: Harvard University Press, 1913).

20 Dante, *Inferno*, XXVII; 76–78 and 73–75, respectively.

21 *Adagia*, III, v, 81.

end have overcome those who have relied on their word.²² And so I concluded: *You must know there are two ways of contesting, the one by the law, the other by force; the first method is proper to men, the second to beasts; but because the first is frequently not sufficient, it is necessary to have recourse to the second. Therefore it is necessary for a prince to understand how to avail himself of the beast and the man [...] A prince, therefore, being compelled knowingly to adopt the beast, ought to choose the fox and the lion; because the lion cannot defend himself against snares and the fox cannot defend himself against wolves. Therefore, it is necessary to be a fox to discover the snares and a lion to terrify the wolves. Those who rely simply on the lion do not understand what they are about. Therefore a wise lord cannot, nor ought he to, keep faith when such observance may be turned against him, and when the reasons that caused him to pledge it exist no longer. If men were entirely good this precept would not hold, but because they are bad, and will not keep faith with you, you too are not bound to observe it with them. Nor will there ever be wanting to a prince legitimate reasons to excuse this nonobservance.*²³

Dawn is breaking, and the roosters crowing in the yard remind me of Peter in the Gospel. But I at least was faithful to this adage, unlike the proteiform Batavian — as Fra Martino della Magna called Erasmus — who twists this way and that, corrects himself, waxes Ciceronian. At the beginning of the *Adagia*, he offhandedly murmurs the ruse to end all ruses: 'The fox knows many ruses, the hedgehog only one, but it is the most important one of all'.²⁴ Soon after, he reminds us that the fable refers to 'those wily persons who become involved in conspiracies', and ironically notes that often, those same persons are caught in there own snares, whereas the hedgehog defends itself from attack much more successfully by rolling into a tight ball so that only its spines are visible. He ends with this sentence: 'The fable means that often it is more effective to have only one aim, rather than a wealth of inconsistent ruses and plans.'

I now recall that Erasmus's motto is *nulli concedo*, 'I submit to no one'; in other words, the hedgehog, not the fox, is his emblem. And princes, according to him, ought to be taught not the art of war but the art of peace, since 'war appears beautiful only to those who do not know it' and brings people only suffering. The best war, he adds elsewhere, is the war one wages against oneself and one's own vices, presuppositions and ignorance.²⁵

What a hedgehog he is! Although the *Education of the Christian Prince*, which he published quite recently, is dedicated to the most powerful prince of all, the 'most illustrious Prince Charles, grandson of the invincible Caesar Maximilian', this is how he begins his treatise: 'Plato is nowhere more meticulous than in the training of his guardians of his republic, whom he would have surpass all the rest not in riches and jewels and dress and ancestry and retainers, but in wisdom only.'²⁶

There is my servant, that peasant pulling his cart along the road, already belching oaths and wine, and here am I, in the treacherous company of the Medici and the Batavian. I aspired to master the art of war and consort with heroes and energetic

22   *The Prince*, Ch. 18, 'Concerning the way in which Princes should keep Faith'.
23   Ibid.
24   *Adagia*, I, v, 18.
25   See *Enchiridion militis christiani (Handbook of a Christian Knight)*.
26   Erasmus Roterodamus, *The Education of a Christian Prince*, ed. by Lisa Jardine (Cambridge: Cambridge University Press, 1997), p. 2.

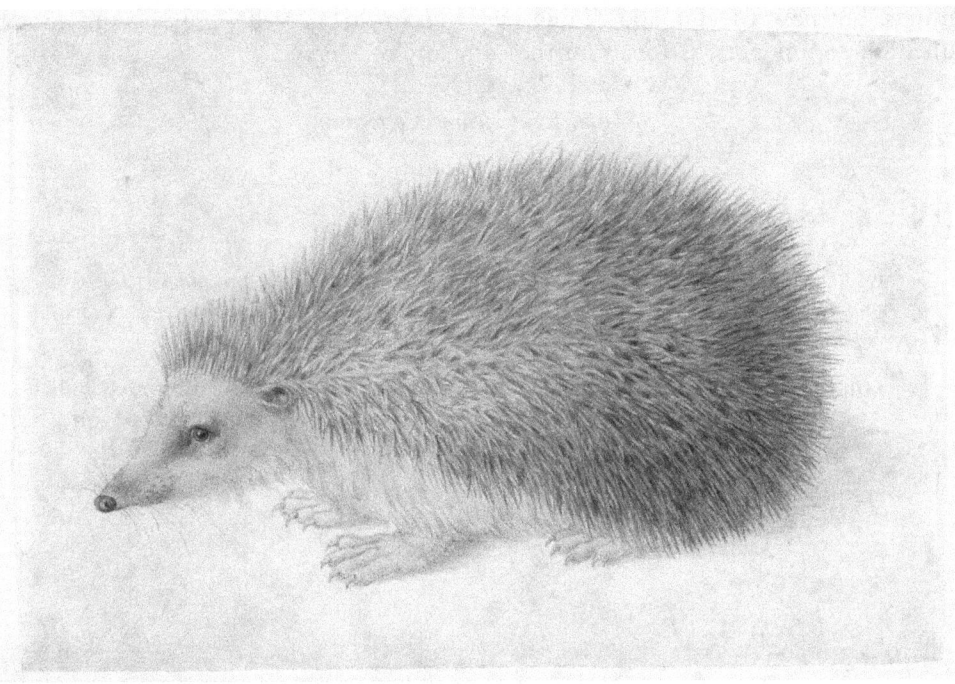

Fig. 19. Hans Hoffmann, *Hedgehog*, before 1584, watercolour and gouache on parchment, 20.7 × 30.7 cm, Metropolitan Museum of Art, New York. Met Purchase, Annette de la Renta Gift, 2005/www.metmuseum.org.

minds, but now I feel a clod sliding over me, in this gravelly, grey dawn, among uncouth commoners, as I wait for the company of Mercy...

Stilum volui meum esse regnum

[The pen is my kingdom]

Hoc monologium, in tabulis Faesulanis inclusum, a Carolo Ossola inventum et fideliter summa diligentia transcriptum, nunc ad maiorem Desideri Erasmi Roterodami et Nicolai Maclavelli gloriam producitur

[This monologue, which is included in the *Tabulis Faesulanis*, was discovered and transcribed with great care by Carlo Ossola, and is now presented to the world in homage to Erasmus of Rotterdam and Niccolò Machiavelli]

CHAPTER 9

Petrarch in Naples

Pascal Quignard

In early June 1345, in Verona, a young monk brought Petrarch a collection of Cicero's letters, which scholars throughout the Middle Ages had believed were lost forever. Petrarch rolled the old parchment out on the table. He read. He saw that it was true: until this moment, no one had known of the existence of this roll, which he now gently and piously unfurled before his eyes, flattening it delicately with both hands. He read with wonder — or rather, he *reads*, for when reading is so intense, so fervid and electrifying, it forgets time. At once, Petrarch's excitement is at fever pitch. On 16 June, he picks up his pen. He begins to write in Latin. He wishes to thank Cicero for the pages he has just discovered. *Franciscus Ciceroni suo salutem...* Francesco salutes his dear Cicero... He describes how the letters have reached him after a journey of one thousand four hundred years. He describes the course of the world since Cicero departed it. He believes in the presence of the man he is addressing beyond death. He rebukes him for his political errors, his questionable commitments, his astonishing acts of cowardice. He lists everything that troubles him, that he doesn't understand, that he admires, that he loves in Cicero. He praises his incredibly silent and heroic death by the sea in Gaeta.

The last paragraph of this letter from Francesco Petrarca to Marcus Tullius Cicero is simply extraordinary: '*Apud superos ad dexteram Athesis ripam in civitate Verona Transpadane Italie, XVI kalendas quintiles anno ab ortu Dei illius quem tu non noveras, MCCCXLV*' [Written in the land of the living, on the right bank of the Adige, in Verona, a city of Transpadane Italy, on the sixteenth day of June, in the year 1345 of a God whom you never knew]. Writing delocalises, just as speaking anachronises. Saying 'I' (when speaking to you) extends the other forever in oneself. Petrarch is actually speaking to Cicero, while at the same time emphasising that a new era has unfolded and a new God has taken humans under his protection — or subjected them to his wrath. His dialogue places both persons in the mouth that is speaking. Writing gives the reading subject access to both times. All of a sudden, the time of loss alternates with the time of arrival. The pure state of loss echoes the original loss of one's mother at birth. The child's arrival on the shore of light — *in luminis oras* — signals the disappearance of immediate, uterine satiety. This arrival is, at first, a violent influx of air into the body, then the gradual learning of the spoken word through the newly domesticated breath, the acquisition of writing that follows, reducing to silence the recently acquired language, and finally the

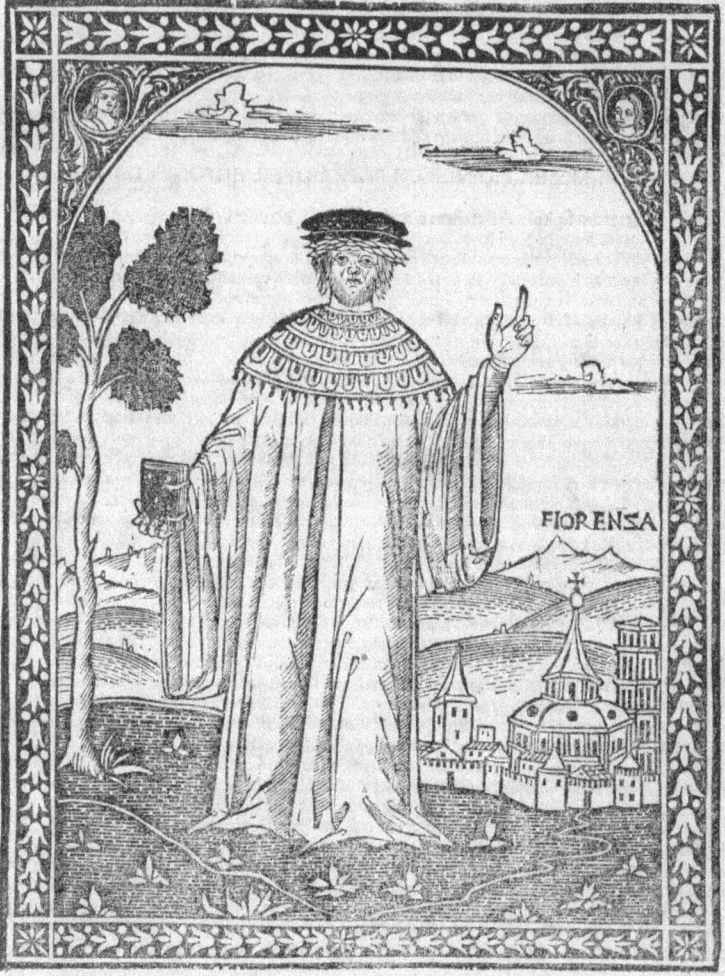

Fig. 20. Engraved portrait of Petrarch with Florence in the background, in Francesco Petrarca, *Canzoniere i Triomphi*, Venice, Albertino Vercellese, 1503, title page. Known as the "three commentaries" edition. Fondation Barbier-Mueller pour l'étude de la poésie italienne de la Renaissance, University of Geneva.

representation of the innumerable through the opposition of a finite number of consonants and vowels. Thus is knowledge always passed down, from the old to the young. The descendant proceeds from the ascendant. The stream below welcomes and contemplates that which flows from the stream above. Human time, in which this transfer takes place, is, therefore, a neoteny at first. The flow — the loss — then becomes a wellspring. Finally, time become the singular liturgy particular to every invisible grammar, immanent in every invisible vernacular, whose various rites all converge in an equally invisible sexual scene, before transmigrating from one generation to the next through death, which comes to every one of us in turn.

It comes to us through the death of those who taught us to speak, and in whose name we are fated to be reborn, or so we believe.

★ ★ ★ ★ ★

French emerged from Latin during the early Middle Ages in the same way that fear, in early childhood, emerges from the original terror. The words of Latin became the magical words of French. On the poster announcing the first performance in Vienna of *L'Enfant et les sortilèges*, composed by Colette and Ravel, the title was translated as *Das Zauberwort*, 'The Magic Word'. In Sanskrit, a *brahmodya* — literally, 'to-be-spoken-about brahman' — is a ritual riddle. The *brahman* is the formula's silent carrier. The enigma (*brahman*) carries its *littera* like the Palaeolithic hunter carries his throwing stick. Retention of the concise utterance, brainwave, invigorating word. Louis Renou wrote: 'The *brahman* is an energy that uses the word to express the inexpressible in the form of an enigma.' This is exactly what writing does. To write is to leave behind the spoken word and to become an enigma. *Brahman* should in fact be translated in the Vedic texts as 'secret of the sacrifice'. This secret is the *significe*. The original meaning of *brah* was probably to speak in tongues or to speak in animal cries. Riddle-talk, which may have originated in shamanic speech, harks back to a place halfway between riddle and enigma, in the dreamlike images that run through the souls of many animals, including humans, as they sleep. It is the Sphinx spewing riddles from her open maw. This riddle is not original so much as it is precedent. It is asemantic, always beginning, always surging, always flowing, always Venusian.

The riddle appears again in the shattering of the letters of the written language.
This regression is enigmatic.
This enigmatic regression defines the act of reading.

★ ★ ★ ★ ★

Why do I resemble Petrarch? Why do I have this irresistible and annoying tendency to sprinkle Latin quotes all over my texts, like a farmer sowing wheat in his fields? The European intertext was Latin: Roman Latin under the Empire, Christian Latin in medieval times, academic Latin in the Age of Enlightenment. This intertext, which survived for over two millennia, still spread its branches and sowed its values amongst my own people. The city where I learned to walk, and later to read, was the hideously mangled ruin of a port city that had been razed to the ground. The

Middle Ages were my childhood. My given name evokes the passion of a dead God, and I entered childhood by serving Mass in the cramped chapel of a boys' school. I departed it as a teenage organist, perched high in an organ loft near the banks of the Loire, pulling out the stops in the golden half-light of the church of Ancenis.

★ ★ ★ ★ ★

We pass through others to exist. Through others we are born. Through others we learn to speak. Through others we acquire knowledge. We are not creators with the power of self-begetting. We are creatures *ab alio* — from others. From two others at conception. From the sex of another at birth. From the mouth of others when we learn to speak our natural, vernacular language. Through the gaze of others when we read.

When absorbed in reading, withdrawn and silent, we are deep in the other.

★ ★ ★ ★ ★

In the entire continent of Europe, the scholar to whom I feel closest is Petrarch. The first Hermit, the first Renaissance man. A man who preferred Rome to Paradise, who wrote his *Secretum* in Latin, who addressed his secret to the dead, who called Cicero 'my dear Cicero' and Saint Augustine as 'my dear Augustine'. The *Secretum* is a dialogue between Petrarch and the *umbra* of Saint Augustine, which takes place in 1342. But Petrarch wrote the dialogue in 1353, in Milan, so that it contains both times at once — it is a bichronic message, like ours. It is beautiful: 'Leave me to my veil of tears, they wash away the stain of the world, and my childhood loses itself in them, so secret is the struggle of my sorrows.' Late-medieval Petrarch is as beautiful as late-Republican Ovid. As beautiful as Montaigne at the time of the Wars of Religion.

★ ★ ★ ★ ★

In 1305, a child fell from the saddle while crossing the Arno on the back of a mule and drowned. Some boatmen dived in to save him. They dragged him streaming onto the riverbank.

Consequently, for the rest of his life, the greatest, most amazing scholar of the Renaissance never ceased to see himself as a shipwrecked Ulysses.

Searching everywhere, like Ulysses, for his Ithaca.

Aeneas shipwrecked on the sands of Carthage.

An exile, a wanderer, who lifted up his life by shaping it as a voyage.

Peregrinus ubique. A traveller everywhere.

This was Petrarch's dream: a community of hermits on the slopes of Vesuvius, surrounded by vines.

Throughout his life he repeatedly declared that he would have liked to live in the Republic of Naples, on the shore of that magnificent bay, where paradise and hell exist peacefully side by side, in the shadow of the past and of the double-mouthed volcano that long ago buried Pliny the Elder as he sat reading.

Five hundred years later and only a few kilometres from there, Sade had the same idea as his ancestor Petrarch. He wrote: 'I would have liked to live next to the most beautiful, and by far the most criminal bay in the world, in the affectionate company of volcanoes.'

CHAPTER 10

Petrarch on Stage

Francisco Rico

'*Fama est propter quam poetae, sicut propter amicas suas amatores, canunt*': poets sing for fame, just as lovers sing for their beloved.[1] A celebrated author of poetry and prose, whose authority was enhanced by his regular relations with popes, kings and magnates, Francesco Petrarca, or Petrarch, admitted to being moved by an 'insatiable appetite for glory', and constant public scrutiny was merely the price to pay for the fame he so passionately desired. The curiosity he inspired in his admirers was so intense that they were known occasionally to steal or intercept letters that were not intended for them: 'Let them be [...], let them keep our letters, so long as they love and admire what they steal.'[2]

Like every other mortal, he wanted to be loved, but unlike many, the admiration he wished to inspire was motivated not merely by personal vanity (though he was, in fact, remarkably vain) but also by intellectual necessity. The main message that emerges from his prose writings is that literature should be the foundation of all human knowledge and that, contrary to general opinion, it is an excellent *vade mecum* of true Christian *pietas*. However, Petrarch also understood that knowledge was not transmitted only through doctrine, but was more effective when it took the form of an existential model, supported by a fascination with the lifestyle of the person who embodied it. This goes a long way towards explaining the rather subjective viewpoint and autobiographical tone of his mature works, from the *Familiares* to the *Seniles*, large portions of which take the form of a manifesto, which aims to describe a paradigmatic trajectory — from philology to philosophy, if you will — and, through the portrait of a specific individual, present an ethical proposition and a cultural programme.

In Petrarch, this strategic need to cultivate a seductive image — not necessarily exemplary, but invariably rich, complex, fascinating and lively, at the price of a few distortions — was combined with an inherent modesty and instinctive prudence, a useful mindset for someone destined for universal acclaim. It is in your best interest, Augustine reminds him in the *Secretum*, to 'guard your reputation', since your name is constantly on the lips 'of those who speak about you, and they are many, because maintaining a good reputation requires a great deal of effort'.

It is no wonder that Petrarch often recalled Seneca's injunction to act at all times as if Epicurus was watching: '*Sic fac omnia tamquam Epicurus spectet*'. Cicero offered

1 *Familiares*, X, iv.
2 *Familiares*, XIX, ii.

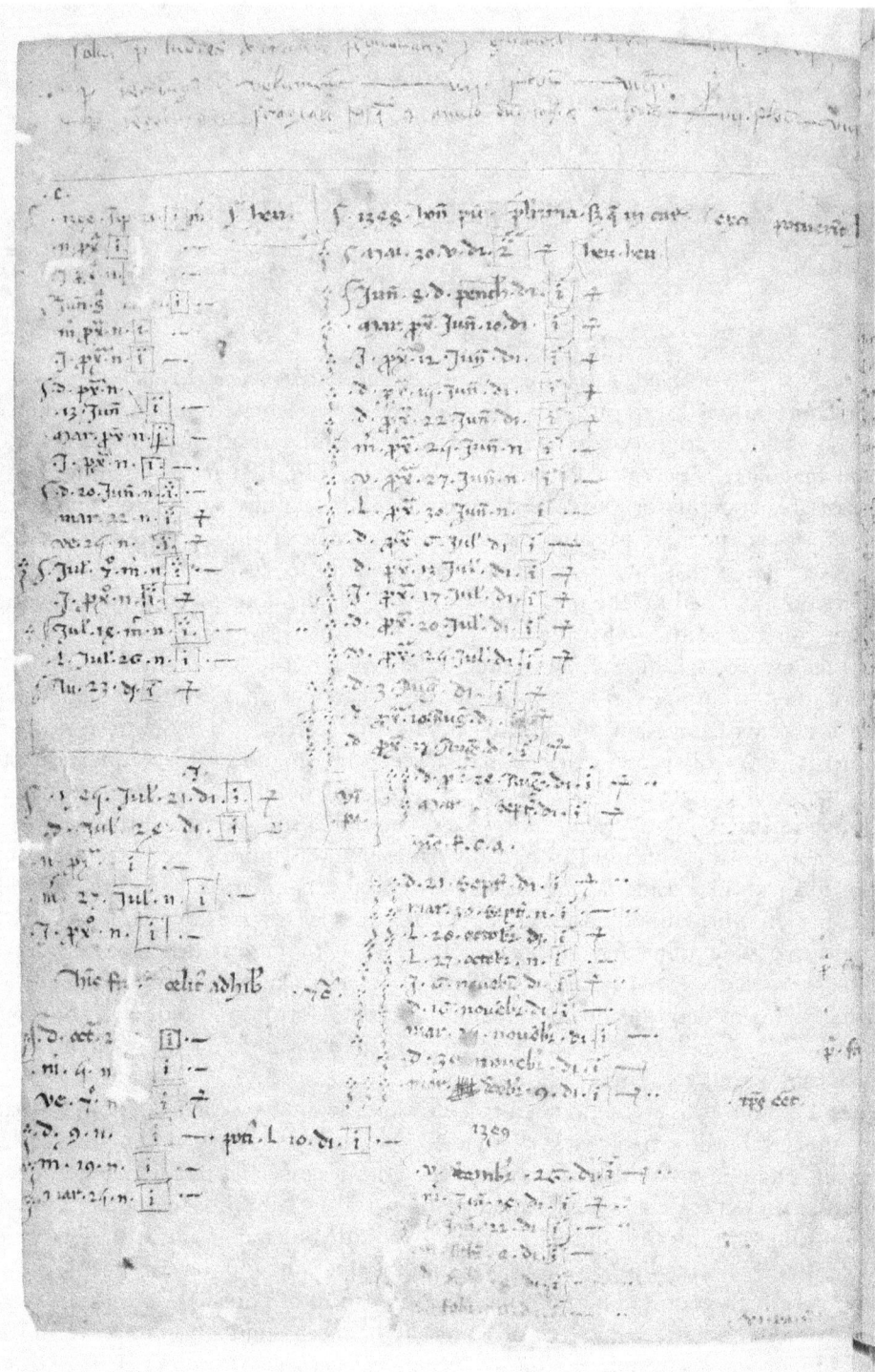

Fig. 21. Petrarch's notes in Cassiodorus, *Berengarius Pictavensis*, Latin manuscrit 2923, folio 178v, Bibliothèque nationale de France, Paris.

similar advice: live your life as if a great man were observing your every action. As Christians, however, do we really need such fictions? Our guardian angel, if not Christ himself, watches over us, hears our words and reads our thoughts as Epicurus could not (*Ad posteritatem*). Clearly, Petrarch gave greater weight to these divine witnesses; but that does not mean he neglected those of a more profane nature, and it was certainly with them in mind that he wrote nothing without considering that unknown eyes might read his words critically.

In fact, the autobiography that he began, but never finished, appears as a response to the curious gaze of posterity: 'It is possible that some word of me may have come to you [...] and you may desire to know what manner of man I was, or what resulted from my labours, especially those of which some description or, at any rate, the bare titles may have reached you'.[3] What appears as a hope for the future, however, was a disquieting reality in the present: 'It is no longer in my power to live in solitary silence. At present I am known, read, judged. I can no longer escape the diatribes of men or hide my thoughts away; whether in the public eye or in the privacy of my house, I am always on display'.[4]

Petrarch thus always viewed himself as living, and especially writing, under the scrutiny of contemporary and future witnesses as exacting as Epicurus and Cicero. In terms that are less metaphorical than they might seem at first, he always felt like an actor onstage. This sentiment manifests itself in his sizeable corpus of letters and several of his books, but it also influenced his choice of themes, and led him to adopt attitudes and behaviours that seem free and spontaneous, but in fact reflect his impression — real or imagined — of being constantly observed by sceptical spectators. I offer a few examples below.

The poet's preoccupation with his public image appears strikingly in his private notes. The glosses crowding the margins of manuscripts from his library offer unquestionable proof of the ceaseless conversation he carried on with books (which also had a physical dimension, since at the time, reading was invariably aloud). For him, reading was a way to commune 'with saints, with philosophers, with poets, with orators, with historians'.[5] Moreover, he insisted on treating these improbable conversational companions as contemporaries: '*quasi coetanei sui essent*'. He was fond of measuring himself against them and treating them as witnesses of his actions or idle pursuits.

At times, these annotations contain a distinctly subjective or biographical element. For instance, next to the section in Pomponius Mela describing a nation whose chief goal is laughter and amusement, the poet added this note: 'These are a people with whom I have nothing in common', in essence, the same sentiment he expressed in the *Canzoniere*: 'And I am one whom weeping delights' (XXXVII). Many of his observations allude to his feelings ('Read with trembling and weeping') or are couched in a tone of personal penitence. For instance, when Saint Ambrose exclaims: 'Lord Jesus, I am of no use to anyone', the humanist, deeply moved, wonders: 'If he speaks thus, then what of you?' There are countless other examples

---

3 *De vita solitaria*, I, v.
4 *De vita solitaria*, preface.
5 *Familiares*, XVI, vi.

like these among his many marginalia. And yet, I cannot recall a single annotation in which Petrarch portrays himself in a negative light or reveals a real defect; his greatest fear was that his notes might fall into the hands of a malicious reader, and be turned against him.

An especially subtle example of this fear of others appears, by omission, in the many manuscripts from his private library that are entirely devoid of annotations. It is true that Petrarch deeply disdained most medieval authors, to the point of refusing to mention them by name; including those he had not only read but practically knew by heart. He expressed a certain admiration for Dante, but nonetheless avoided quoting him by name; he implied that he had read his work only superficially and had no desire to own his books. At any rate, he refrained from annotating the copy of the *Commedia* that he received as a gift from Boccaccio, except for a single remark at the very beginning (and a few symbolic marks without any accompanying text). This single note was probably added in a moment of inattention, following his usual habit of tirelessly annotating the books he read; it seems likely that he then made a conscious decision not to add any more, since the presence of marginalia might reveal that he was not as unfamiliar with Dante as he claimed.

Folios 178^v–179 of the Paris manuscript comprising the *Historia Calamitatum* and the letters of Abelard and Heloise enclose a mysterious list of dates, abbreviations and various symbols in Petrarch's hand, which no one has ever successfully deciphered (Fig. 21). It may represent a meticulous record of his sins of the flesh, but in any event, there is no question that Petrarch intended to make it forever impenetrable to prying eyes (and succeeded). One wonders why he took such precautions in relation to a volume from his private library. Perhaps he knew that prying minds would someday scrutinise its contents.

Today, this evidence, *ex contrario*, offers us a better understanding of an important aspect of the most important annotation in Petrarch's private manuscripts: Laura's necrology, which appears in the front endpapers of a splendid Virgil, now in the Biblioteca Ambrosiana in Milan. In this list, he recorded the date, time and place of his meetings with his beloved, and those of her death (Fig. 22). This necrological note has traditionally been described as a 'private document' or 'private note', in which Petrarch had 'no reason to deceive himself by falsifying a date'. However, I think

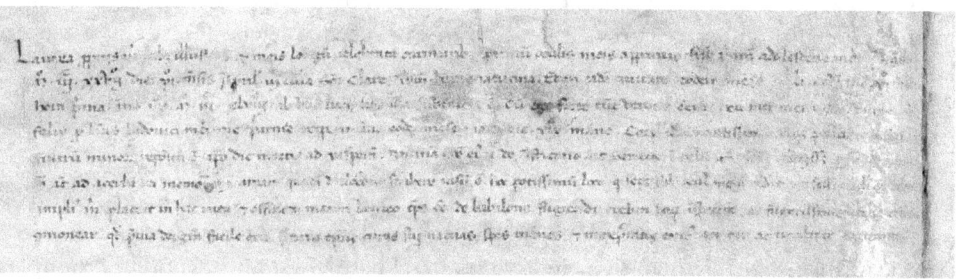

FIG. 22. Petrarch's notes (necrology of Laura), in a manuscript of the collected works of Virgil, known as *Virgilio ambrosiano* or 'Petrarch's Virgil', A 79 inf., Biblioteca Ambrosiana, Milan.

that it most resembles what Armando Petrucci has called 'exposed writing'. Having handled many manuscripts annotated by famous men, the poet was perfectly aware that a manuscript as remarkable as the Ambrosiana Virgil — which, moreover, had belonged to a famous figure such as him — would be carefully preserved and minutely scrutinised, especially if it was deposited in a public library like the one he had proposed for Venice. The gloss about Laura, which he transcribed in a good hand from a draft and theatrically placed upfront, may be a sort of discreet nod *ad posteritatem*, aiming to establish the 'official version' of his great passion as he wished to present it at the time of writing.

Petrarch had a profound sense of the fleetingness of time, which made him the greater poet: 'I know how the days, the minutes and the hours, carry off the years, and there's no trickery [...]'.[6] This attitude reveals his perpetual impulse to seize life as it slipped past him by chronologically labelling both real and imagined experiences. In this way, he transformed these moments into fragments of a unified narrative, provided with a recognisable overall form. Assigning a date to a significant moment in time was a way for him to give it shape and meaning within the broader landscape of his existential experience; similarly, refraining from dating it could indicate the intention to forget it or maintain its uncertainty. Dating an event thus amounted to recording it in the book of his life.

This anxious concern with time explains why he organised the *Canzoniere* according to anniversaries of life and death, and from greater to smaller, and also why he scrupulously dated many of his other works. The first version of *De ignorantia*, for instance, is dated 'around the end of the year 1367', and the final version 'June 1370, as the day leans towards its end', while the dedication letter he wrote in 1370 is dated 'The Ides of January, lying on my bed of pain, eleven o'clock at night'. The dating of the various drafts of the *Canzoniere* is also remarkably detailed; in his obsession with the passing of time, he added profuse notes specifying when he modified his text, even when the changes concerned a single line, and he sometimes recorded the exact time when he stopped working: 'Wednesday 9 June 1350. After dusk, I intended to start [revising poem CCLXX] but I was called to supper'. It is impossible not to wonder why he was so meticulous in recording these *nugae* and, conversely, why the years he spent revising *Africa* are shrouded in such deep silence. The answer is obvious: writing poetry in the vernacular was a deliciously enjoyable pastime, whereas *Africa*, which occupied him for several decades ('Oh Africa, which cost me so much effort!'), was increasingly a source of embarrassment and disappointment as he became progressively aware that he would fail to deliver what he had promised to his audience: namely, an epic rivalling the *Aeneid*. He preferred to leave no traces of this artistic and cultural fiasco.

In addition to the personal notes and the obsession with chronology that the drafts of the *Rerum vulgarium fragmenta* reveal — not to mention the curious list in *Historia calamitatum* — another set of writings shows how Petrarch sometimes performed for an imaginary spectator, as if on an open stage and according to a pre-written scenario, which alternated between life and writing.

At various times and in different places — between 1348, in Parma, and 1369, in

---

6 *Canzoniere*, CI, 9–10.

Arquà — the humanist scholar recorded, in a manuscript of *De agricultura*, now in the Vatican Library, the agricultural and horticultural labours he undertook in the gardens and orchards that he always planted next to the houses in which he lived. Before 1353, these notes show him busily tending his vines, apple orchard, rosemary and sage bushes, spinach patch and so on, most often with poor or meagre results. He first tried to plant laurels in 1357, in Milan, and persisted with this tree to the exclusion of all others, though most of his attempts to cultivate it failed until he retired to Arquà and finally declared himself 'a gardener through and through'.

Petrarch's love of laurels was not exclusively literary. He was extremely afraid of storms, and believed the laurel offered protection from thunder (though laurel compresses are powerless against lovesickness, he may have used them to treat an old leg wound). His orchard in Milan thus fulfilled objectives both poetic and prosaic, material and immaterial; consider, for instance, this note from 1357:

> On 4 April at sunset, when the moon was full or almost, the soil damp, and the weather unusually cold for the season, we took six laurels and an olive tree that had been brought from Bergamo and planted them in deep trenches in the garden of Saint Ambrose, in Milan. There are apparently two impediments: a delay of a few days and the type of soil, which is particularly unsuited to olive trees. However, the plants are all quite tall, and though some are frailer and others sturdier, all have formed a trunk.

A little later, Petrarch added, '*Omnes penitus aruerunt*': they all dried and perished.

It was 1357, the fourth of April and not the sixth, the date of his first vision of Laura thirty years earlier, in 1327. But he planted six laurels. And it was not Easter Monday, the day of his consecration as poet laureate in 1341, but the Tuesday of Holy Week. What was the poet alluding to: Laura in 1327, or the laurels of 1341? Either way, through these horticultural activities, he rewrote parts of his own life story and created literature *with*, or rather, *in* his actions and his conduct. As often in his poetry, Laura and laurels are fused; the woman merges with the tree. But several of his writings also contain elements of self-criticism; he remarks, for example, that the much-coveted crown has brought him neither wisdom nor eloquence (*Ad Posteritatem*). This feeling, combined with the disappointing realisation that *Africa* did not — and probably would never — meet his expectations, led him to turn instead to the traditional occupations of a *philosophus*. He penned his critical remark in April 1357, after planting the six laurels and one olive tree, an attribute of Minerva, 'who invented the first olives' (XXIV). Although he could never forget either Laura or the laurel crown he received 'in memory of the one I love so much',[7] the poet now took shelter under the tree of wisdom.

Traces of the words he wrote in his garden in Milan can be discerned throughout his life and work. In 1357, in the *Canzoniere*, he compared the laurel and the olive, to the latter's advantage ('Not the laurel or palm, but the peaceful olive [...]', CCXXX), and described his scattered verses as a 'land' or 'field', which, for lack of water, produce no reeds but only 'burdock and weeds', to be cut 'with a sickle'. 'The olive-tree is dry, and the water that springs from Parnassus, through which at one time it flowered, flows elsewhere. So fault or misfortune will deprive me of all

---

7 *Triumphus Cupidinis*, III.

the finest fruits, unless eternal Jove pours his grace on me from above' (CLXVI).

'The olive-tree is dry'. 'My laurel that was once so green has dried due to bad weather [...]'. Although all six laurels and the olive tree 'dried and perished', Petrarch persisted in trying to plant both varieties. It seems that the olive tree finally took root. All of his efforts to plant laurels, however, proved vain: the five 'holy saplings', sent by a friend in Como and planted with the help of Boccaccio, and the two fully grown trees given to him by Lombardo della Seta, which he planted 'very solemnly' on a lovely spring day, 'failed to flourish: both dried'. Many years earlier, in the third eclogue of the *Bucolicum carmen*, Daphne, transformed into a laurel by Apollo, teaches Petrarch the art of poetry before crowning him with laurels at the Capitoline Hill. In the tenth eclogue — *'Laurea occidens'* — Silvano mourns the death of a laurel he has tended with great devotion, but Socrates consoles him by explaining that the 'sacred' plant is now sending up new shoots in the Elysian Fields. In March 1359, while Boccaccio was helping the master with his laurels in Milan, both men were also busy revising the *Bucolicum carmen*. In Petrarch the gardener, life imitates art: both follow the same script, the same stage directions.

The *Rerum vulgarium fragmenta*, composed around 1357, contains no anniversary sonnet or allusion to the years of love-servitude or sorrow for Laura. Would it be implausible to suggest that the gardening endeavours of the Holy Week served this function? What Petrarch didn't write, he put into action; and he behaved as if writing. The gardening notes show him enacting a ritual, a performance. In 1357, this can be deduced from the number of laurels, the olive tree and the date; in later years, his choice of words ('very solemnly', 'sacred saplings') suggests a continuation of the ritual. In a note from 1348, the poet blames a failed attempt to transplant some shoots on his not having followed the teachings of the *Georgics*, 'against the doctrine of Virgil'. In his mind, his orchard in Milan was to be a veritable Parnassus, but it was in fact modelled on his literary *oeuvre*: as in the latter, laurel and laureate were ultimately one and the same.

In addition to the marginalia and annotations that Petrarch addressed specifically to his public, I could quote others that reveal his wariness about the possibility of someone witnessing his words or actions. He can be seen dealing with the same situation in many other places. But let us focus, instead, on one of the central aspects of his biography and his literary production: the solitary life.

In 1337, the author bought a house in Vaucluse, on the banks of a river, a few steps away from the castle of one of his admirers and patrons: the powerful Philippe de Cabassoles, Bishop of Cavaillon. He retreated whenever possible to his country home, sometimes only for a few days, sometimes for longer periods, to read and write while enjoying the beauty of nature, fishing and gardening. His love of solitude and beautiful scenery was both sincere and profound, but his desire to distinguish himself through these character traits was equally keen; in mythicising Vaucluse, he was also turning himself into a legend. Thus, the solitary life became a performance, a display, a public recitation.

In fact, Vaucluse did not always involve pure solitude: Petrarch liked to share his house with friends (several indications suggest they included female friends) and, of course, used it to promote himself and his work. According to his account, 'many Roman cardinals and great men of the world', when passing through Avignon, made an excursion to Vaucluse at his invitation, 'sometimes to see the source of the Sorgue River and sometimes simply to visit me'. More specifically, 'to visit me and observe the tenor of my life in this countryside'.[8] The *Baedeker* of the highly desirable tours he offered his guests on these occasions — who then became real, rather than fictive, witnesses — can be reconstructed through the many pages he devoted to praising the region's natural beauty and the wonderfully creative *otium* of the austere life he led there.

He discovered, and brilliantly practised, a first-rate method for disseminating his *oeuvre* and his ideas: he associated them with an attractive image of their author. A triumphant image like that of the '*poeta et historicus*' receiving the laurels on the Capitoline, or the symmetrical image of the solitary walker, dressed in peasant's clothing and immersed in his reveries, surrounded by the magnificent landscape of Vaucluse. A unique, fascinating, evocative image, which contributed significantly to the initial success of his work.

That location had all the essential qualities, including a probable classical genealogy, to serve as an attention-grabbing backdrop and add a unique, original attribute to the figure of the humanist: a figure with a landscape, rather than a landscape with a figure. Petrarch was convinced that Vaucluse was more indebted to him than he to Vaucluse, and at times was bold enough to say so: 'With all due respect to the mountains, springs and forests of this land, is not its greatest claim to glory the fact that I, Francisco, lived here?'[9]

Here, at last, is Petrarch on his great stage: '*Tel qu'en lui-même enfin l'éternité*' — or posterity — '*le change*'.[10]

---

8 *Familiares*, XII, 12.
9 *Familiares*, VIII, II–V, gamma.
10 'Such as into Himself at last eternity changes him' (Mallarmé, 'Tombeau d'Edgar Poe').

CHAPTER 11

Ludovico's Secret: A Fantasy

Cesare Segre

He was walking with his granddaughter, as he often did, through the city of Ferrara.

— Please, Grandfather, tell me about the time you argued with the Pope and he threatened to throw you in the Tiber!

For the little girl, Ludovico was a perpetual storytelling machine. And although his life had not been particularly eventful or adventurous, he had a knack for recounting its most unusual episodes, such as the years he spent in Garfagnana as governor. His granddaughter could easily imagine him riding through that wild land at the head of a small band of soldiers, charged with keeping the peace and arresting troublemakers. In fact, there was no lack of bloody skirmishes during his time there.

— But how did you occupy yourself when you got back to the fortress?

It was difficult to explain how he had felt at the time: lonely, but also weary of representing a government that was so deeply disliked, maybe even hated, by its subjects. Nor was it easy for him to talk about the precious few hours he would devote each week to reading or writing by the light of candles dripping with wax. Even in the daytime, he had to wrap himself in blankets against the cold wind rushing down from the Apennines.

From time to time, the little girl tried to move the conversation towards local issues; even in the lives of the Ferrarese and Romans, she thought — and didn't hesitate to say — there must have been exciting or painful experiences, and examples of both admirable and contemptible behaviour. This was a topic Ludovico was reluctant to discuss: he worried that it might give his granddaughter a jaded view of life. He preferred to talk about the beauty of nature, the joys of reading, the comfort of knowing that one's behaviour towards others and one's family and friends was beyond reproach. He hoped, in this way, to instil in her the idea of conscience.

— But Grandfather, aside from feeling calm and at peace with your own conscience, what can you do to ensure that others also follow their conscience and reject the base and vile actions that we alluded to previously?

Finally, the fundamental issues were emerging: one's obligations towards others

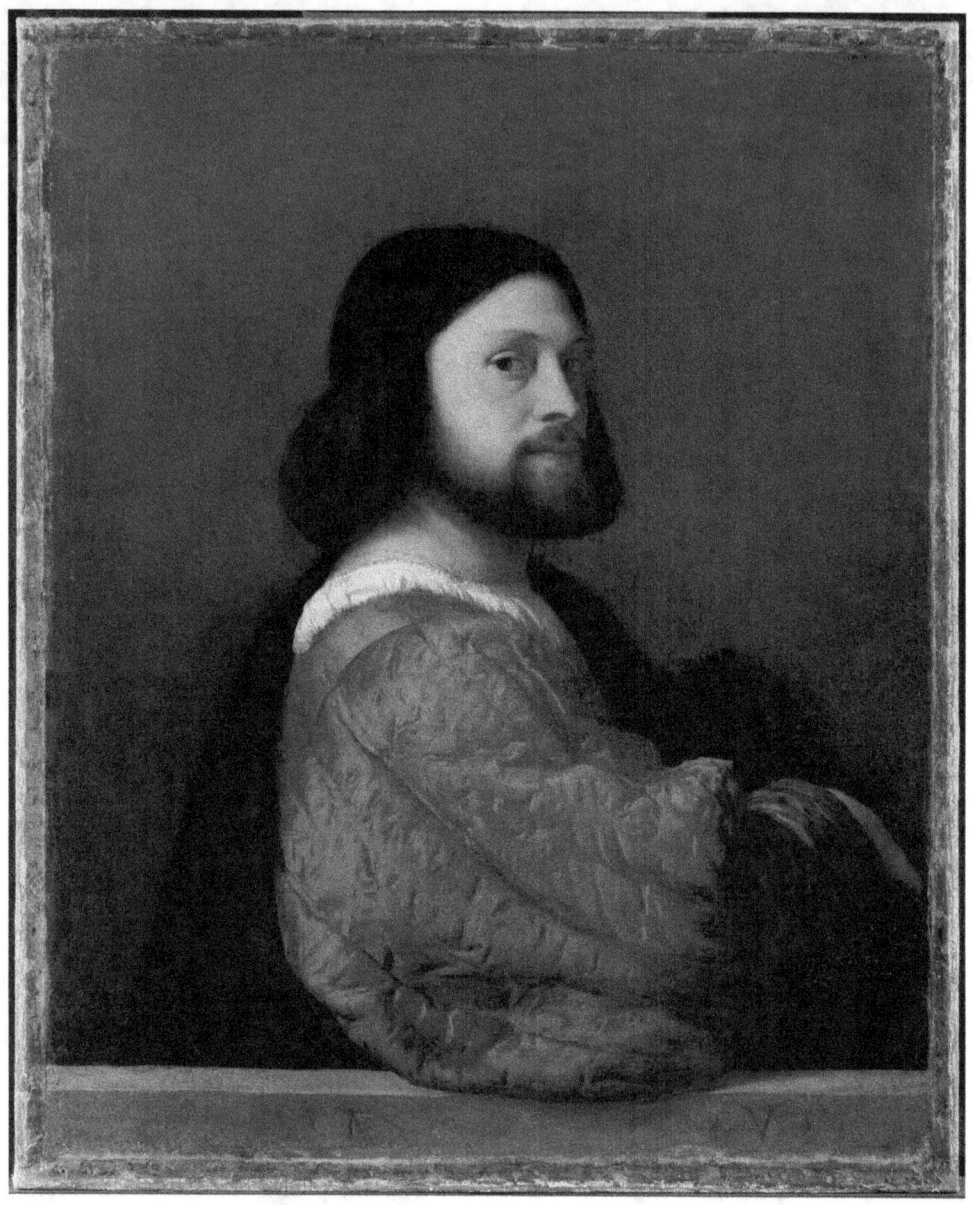

Fig. 23. Titian, *Portrait of a Man (Gerolamo (?) Barbarigo or Ariosto)*, c. 1512, oil on canvas, 81.2 × 66.3 cm, National Gallery, London. © 2015 The National Gallery, London/Scala, Florence.

and the political authorities, the 'social contract' of coexistence, and so on. In fact, even if one behaves well, the grandfather thought out loud, one must respect certain nuances and rules. Virtue ought to shun ostentatiousness so as to avoid offending the less virtuous.

'You're a famous writer, Grandfather. Couldn't you use your art to teach to other people the wisdom you try to impart to me?'

'My darling girl, you have almost unmasked me. For many years now, I have been working on a memoir in verse inspired by certain Latin models. In this work, I denounce all of the misdeeds and injustices I have observed in public life in Ferrara and in the capital of Christendom, or at least what I have seen in the course of my travels. Naturally, this account is satirical in form and based mainly on anecdotes.'

'I haven't learned to read yet, but I can already make out most of the letters. Won't you read me some of your satires, please, Grandfather?'

'I'm sorry to disappoint you, my dear, but I promised myself never to show these texts to anyone, including my own family, at least for the moment. If you insist, I could read you a few important passages. But don't you think our time together would be better spent conversing about beautiful landscapes and artworks, or about my youthful memories and the joys of study?'

'But your secret satires intrigue me. Please make an exception just this once! Next time we can return to your favourite topics. Besides, if your secret verses are so dear to you, that indicates that you have certainly devoted a great deal of time to them.'

'All right, my love, but just this once! To simplify things a bit, let me summarise the main sins that I denounce in my verse. As you will see, sinners are terribly boring, not to mention tediously repetitive. The most common, though not the most serious, sin is flattery: in other words, the act of praising the qualities of powerful people in the hope of obtaining their patronage and protection. I too sang the praises of the powerful in my *Rolando furioso*. But I slipped subtly critical allusions and ironies into these tributes, which their powerful recipients, luckily for me, failed to discern. There are many ways to obtain high offices and establish one's power. If you aspire to a lofty position, you must wage a daily battle to achieve it. You may win or you may lose, but if you are not victorious, the people who would have been your victims, had you won, will surely take their revenge!

'Whether the advantages one seeks are large or small is of no consequence. He who thirsts for power must have a high opinion of himself: if he wants to be considered important, he must above all see himself as such. The yearning for riches and power finds fertile ground at court, for instance, because it is the scene of a constant struggle for self-affirmation and the accumulation of wealth. The princes themselves are forever competing to extend their dominions and their influence abroad. And they will go to any length, including murder, to satisfy their ambitions. Even here in Ferrara, as you may know, the duke's relatives conspired against each other to seize power.'

'I can tell that you are speaking in very general terms, because you want to avoid telling me about any specific events. I won't insist, given how reticent you are to speak about such matters.'

'Thank you, my dear, and be sure never to tell another living soul about these writings.'

'What is it you fear? Do you think someone will try to steal your ideas?'

'Ha! That is the least of my worries. On the contrary, I wish more people shared my ideas! The truth is, I hold some very powerful people accountable for many of the errors and crimes I denounce, and I don't think my patrons would be very happy to hear that. Moreover, I reveal many secret little altars kept by many famous people, and though I refer to them by aliases, they might recognise themselves and sue me for defamation, plot their revenge, or blackmail me. In other words, it could become dangerous for us in Ferrara. I am sensible enough to distinguish what can be divulged from what cannot.'

'Does that mean that no one will ever read your *Satires*?'

'I plan to stipulate in my will that my *Satires* be published only after I have been twenty years in the grave. By then, the people I criticise will certainly be dead, and, more important, I will not fear the reactions of their friends and family, since I will have long departed this world.'

'Do you keep these inflammatory texts in a secret hiding place?'

'As you know, my darling girl, I have a workshop where I make copies of my writings. Once in a while, a poetry enthusiast requests my permission to transcribe one of my lyrical compositions — sometimes even an entire series of poems. I abandoned the idea of collecting all my works in a single volume long ago; anyone who wants to publish them is therefore free to choose any number of poems to print. But in the case of the *Satires*, this task is impossible. Moreover, only very few people are aware of their existence.'

'Do you keep the book in a safe in the cellar?'

'If we go to my workshop, you can see it with your own eyes...

'This small table is reserved for people who come to the workshop to read or copy my poems. All of my manuscripts are there, to the side, arranged in a somewhat disorderly way at this little bookshelf. Here you can work undisturbed, and there is plenty of light.'

'Grandfather, when I learn to write, will you let me help you with your work? I could copy your poems or do anything you want!'

'That would be wonderful, my love; I thank you in advance for your precious assistance. Now, back to my *Satires*. Do you see that little cabinet to the left, the one with the lock? Here's the key. Have a look inside.'

'But there is just one book in here!'

'Take it out. As you can see, it is written entirely by hand, with many corrections. I destroyed all my drafts to ensure that they would not circulate without my consent. My secretary Bruno made this fair copy, and from time to time I go over a few pages and revise them. I have made dozens of corrections. This is the only existing copy. To transcribe even a small part of it requires my express permission. I have allowed only a small number of people to make copies of a few of the satires, and I made them promise not to disseminate them. To know that this book exists, and lay hands on it, you would have to be a spy.'

'And what if a spy did find out about it?'

'He would have been sent by my princes, but I don't think they are particularly preoccupied with this sort of thing. What they fear most is a scandal; they are not particularly concerned with what each of us thinks. I am also known as a faithful subject — at least, as long as no one finds out about these *Satires*! And no one knows how explosive this small book could be.'

'So now, when I play with my friends upstairs, I shall have a great secret: we are running and jumping on top of a powder keg!'

The Satires *were published in 1534, a year after Ariosto's death, in a clandestine edition with no indication of the publisher's name or place of publication. Some have attributed it to Francesco Rosso da Valenza, a typographer and friend of Ariosto responsible for the 1532 edition of* Orlando Furioso, *but no proof exists. The first authorised edition of the* Satires *was established by Anton Francesco Doni, on the basis of Ariosto's manuscript, and printed by Gabriel Giolito Ferrari. The Ferraresi apparently did not take offence to Ariosto's criticisms: on the contrary, they continued to honour the poet's memory. The Church, however, did not forgive him, and in 1583 added the* Satires *to its index of prohibited books.*

CHAPTER 12

A Feast on Île Barbe:
The Italians at the Court of France

Lionello Sozzi

> I went to his Majesty with the cup and basin;
> then, upon entering his presence, I kissed his knee,
> and he received me very graciously.
>
> BENVENUTO CELLINI, *Autobiography*

It was a lovely spring morning, the fifteenth of May 1539 to be exact. On Fourvière Hill and along the banks of the Rhône the trees were flowering and the meadows greening. Birdsong filled the air. All of Lyons rejoiced, for on this day, King François I of France, who rarely ventured beyond the Louvre, Fontainebleau, Tours, Amboise and such places, was travelling by river, sailing down the River Saône from Lyons to Île Barbe on an elegant schooner with his entire court. He intended to stop at the island to join the annual celebration of the feast of Saint Martin, patron saint of the abbey. He planned to attend Mass in the church of Our Lady and follow the procession, then spend the rest of the day on the island with his guests, entertained by dancing, music, singing and various other performances. The famous Italian lutenist Alberto da Ripa was to play delicious melodies composed by fashionable musicians of the time: gigues and courantes, passacaglias and gavottes.

In truth, the King was not expected to take part in the outing; therefore, his *lieutenant* was attending. However, the monarch managed to free himself from his obligations, and appeared at the party, majestic and imposing, draped in the beautiful ermine robe reserved for the grandest occasions. By his side was his sister Marguerite, Duchess of Alençon and Queen of Navarre, her eleven-year-old daughter Jeannette (future Jeanne d'Albret, wife of Antoine de Bourbon and mother of King Henri IV) and another Marguerite, the king's *mignonne*, a lass of fifteen, born of his first wife, Claude de France. His second wife Éléonore, sister of Charles V, may have been present as well, though no sources mention her; whereas the presence of the aforementioned *lieutenant général* of Lyons, Jean Du Peyrat, who had held the position for more than fifteen years, and that of Cardinal Jean de Lorraine, Archbishop of Lyon and titular Abbot of Saint-Martin, who would celebrate the Mass, is documented.

There were many others present, of course. The guests included publishers, such as François Juste, representing the prosperous Lyons book trade (he was accompanied

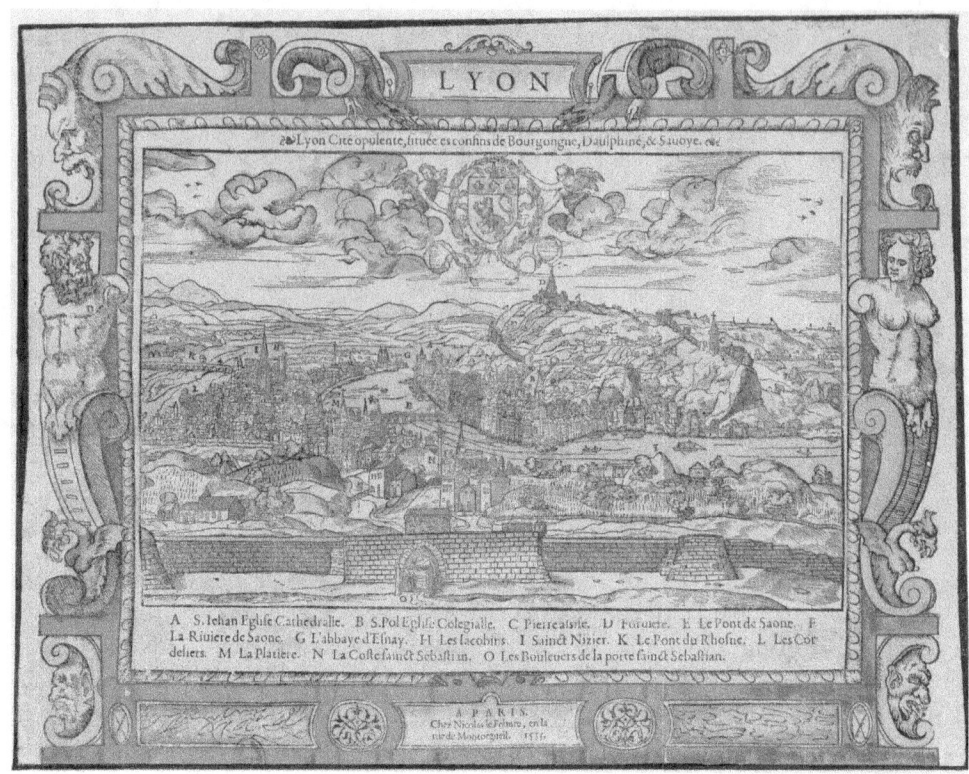

Fig. 24. Nicolas Le Febvre (attributed to), *Lyon Cité opulente, située es confins de Bourgongne, Daulphné et Savoye*, 1555, paper glued to wood panel, 340 × 260 cm, Bibliothèque nationale de France, Paris.

by Vincent de Portonariis, a Piedmontese typographer who settled in Lyons in the footsteps of Baldassare de Gabiano), writers and poets, musicians and painters, actors and jugglers and, among the French authors, Bonaventure des Périers, Marguerite's *valet de chambre*, who would later describe this day and the *voyage* in a charming poem. The company included many foreigners, too, many of whom were Italians, such as Ripa and Portonariis, and others whom we shall hear more about later. During the first quarter of the sixteenth century, the French travelled to Italy to admire the ruins of ancient Rome or to attend the lectures of Pietro Pomponazzi in Padua, while the Italians ventured to France for more prosaic reasons: to seek favour from the King and his sister, or to live at court and obtain advantages and benefits from the 'Father of Literature'. Many Italians attended the party on Île Barbe, although most came not from Lyons but from elsewhere: Fontainebleau, for instance, where famous artists such as Rosso and Primaticcio had founded a school and were busy painting the rooms of the castle with splendid frescoes.

After Mass, a sumptuous banquet was laid out in the abbey's vast refectory. The meal proceeded in an atmosphere of relaxed, almost familiar simplicity — at least at first — which was disrupted, as we shall see, only towards the end of the *liesse* by the troublesome clouds that des Périers alludes to in his poem. After the opening prayer, *hors-d'œuvres* of cured meats, eggs and vegetables were served. As the servants passed around the dishes, they invited the guests to enjoy the meal by saying, '*C'est pour vous mettre en appétit*'. Jeanne sat next to her cousin, giggling and joking and eating with gusto. No doubt the two young women were exchanging amused comments about the guests, many of whom they found highly entertaining. 'Look at that fellow's hat! And that man's huge moustache! Did you notice the gentleman flirting with the Comtesse de Saint-Rambert? Oh, look, I think that Italian is Girolamo Fondulo, a scholar from Cremona whom the King hired to tutor young Henri; everyone says he is terribly clever and talented and knows all the Latin authors by heart and is a veritable fountain of wisdom, but what a funny-looking man — he seems so strange and *exténué*, and did you ever see anyone as tall and skinny as him?'

Sitting to the right of the King, his sister the Queen of Navarre was deep in conversation with the cardinal to her right. In lowered voices, they discussed pious and serious matters. Marguerite recalled the good Briçonnet, who had died several years earlier. He had been a much-revered spiritual guide for her, and she wished to have the cardinal's opinion of him. In one of his letters, Briçonnet had advised her to avoid the specious theories of the Neoplatonists, which he condemned as '*semence platonicque et aristotelicque, superstitieuse et pestifere*'. Did he not judge them too severely? Marguerite wanted to know. She had read Marsilio Ficino's *Theologia Platonica* and thought it a wonderful book, finding in it nothing particularly objectionable or dangerous... The cardinal answered, with perfect aplomb, that the risk of heresy was always present, and one must guard against it at all times, of course, but it was equally true that the voice of God sometimes made itself heard in works which appear far removed from the true faith and the doctrine of our Holy Mother the Church. The cardinal, clearly unwilling to take sides, thus deftly evaded the question.

The Queen and the churchman were speaking in low voices, almost whispering, their words covered by the tumult of the other banqueters. Many of the guests loudly proclaimed their devotion, admiration and reverence for a monarch known for his humanity and appreciation of culture and art (or so they claimed, hoping to be overheard). According to one, the King was watching Leonardo at work one day when the artist dropped a paintbrush; the King stooped to pick it up and handed back to the artist with devout admiration. Another recalled that the monarch had sat by the great artist's bedside as he lay dying at Amboise. The Italians told each other these stories partly out of sincere reverence, partly in the hope of being rewarded in a similar way, though preferably more tangibly, with shiny gold coins rather than words or gestures of sympathy and human courtesy. Lowering their voices, they made fun of the way the French called Leonardo 'Vinci', unaware that this was not his family name but merely the place he came from. Moving on to politics, they praised the King's victory over the Swiss at Melegnano. ('And why the French call the place Marignan is still a mystery!' they added.) They expressed little alarm that Italy had become a battleground for foreign armies; the area of Milan now belonged to France, though after the Peace of Cambrai it would in fact be controlled by Charles V. Some laughingly quoted the popular saying, '*Francia o Spagna, basta che se magna*' ('France or Spain, so long as we have enough to eat'). Others reviled the Connétable de Bourbon for his treachery, and deplored the defeat at Pavia and the King's capture and deportation to Spain, where he was forced to sign the Treaty of Madrid. Yet they had nothing but praise for his sister Marguerite, who, during her brother's captivity, had managed state affairs with a combination of pious devotion and remarkable political acumen.

As was to be expected, many celebratory speeches were given. Luigi Alamanni, who had fled to France after being banished from Florence for backing a plot to overthrow the Medici, recited from memory verses extolling the monarch's 'majestic spirit, which prizes glory above riches and kingdoms.' Evil tongues whispered, 'See how he flatters him and butters him up! Mind you, he is bound to praise the King, since the monarch has granted him money, missions and a garden in Aix, which we can all enjoy.' 'A garden in Aix? Are you serious?' others muttered. 'He has received more than that: a castle in Dauphiné, a thousand écus *en récompense* paid to him by order of the King, not to mention that in January last year he published his *Opere toscane* in Lyons, and dispatched copies left and right to serve as his ambassadors.' 'Do you know what Benvenuto Cellini told me?' another added. 'That Luigi Alamanni has mastered only one art, according to him: the art of flattery. He also told me he intends to tell all in the memoir he began recently, which will undoubtedly be both beautifully written and full of the most amusing anecdotes!' Still on the topic of Alamanni, others discussed the various encomiums he had penned. 'Have you read the dedication of *Coltivazione*?' one asked. 'Pure, unabashed sycophancy!' 'Are you familiar with his eclogue *Admeto secondo*?' his neighbour replied. 'He mourns the death of Louise of Savoy, which is well and good, and extols Marguerite of Navarre, which is also fine, but he then describes the King of France as the monarch who "with greatest honour reigns and governs" and claims that, if fortune had favoured him, the golden fleur-de-lis would have spread over the entire world, from the Ganges to the Pillars of Hercules. He is the biggest bootlicker at court!'

Others, meanwhile, discussed money-lust and the thirst for riches. The Tuscan Gabriello Simeoni was eager to make himself heard; he described some satirical verses he had written in the style of Francesco Berni, on the topic of avarice as Queen of the World. In his view, even the most bitter truths about human misery should be stated concisely, through short, pithy maxims rather than long, tedious speeches. He himself was amassing a collection of such *entreprises sentencieuses*. Other writers were doing the same: he happened to know that at this very moment (he was keen to appear well informed) Paul Jove was working on a *Ragionamento delle imprese* and Claude Paradin was completing a collection of mottos, *Devises héroïques et emblèmes*, a clear sign of the direction in which literature was now headed.

From avarice in general, the conversation shifted abruptly to the character of Italians in particular, namely their cupidity and greed. However, the discussion was constrained by the presence of several bankers from the peninsula; everyone knew of the important role that the Gondi, Guadagni, Del Bene and Strozzi played in France at the time. Consequently, someone changed the topic to the Italian character more broadly, by remarking on the Peninsulars' natural inclination to falsehood (turning to his neighbours, he whispered anti-Italian verses, of the type '*Italiens villains*') and contempt for the law: Benvenuto Cellini, imprisoned in Castel Sant'Angelo in Rome for brawling and fighting, perfectly embodied this trait. At this point, however, François I intervened. 'Benvenuto is a great artist, and I know for a fact — for all my sources are trustworthy — that with my help he will soon escape from the Castel and join us in France. I shall welcome him with every possible honour and grant him a pension. For his part, he promised to give me a beautiful salt cellar he made for Ippolito d'Este.' All those present emphatically expressed their approval, especially the Italians, for whom the idea of a pension was irresistibly attractive.

After Cellini, they discussed Aretino, another famous Italian who was admired and reviled in equal measure. 'Do you know his *Ragionamenti*?' one asked. 'They are very beautiful, droll and racy.' Many disagreed, however, and the discussion grew heated, with some deploring the freedom of tone and the obscenity of Aretino's writings, and others remarking that he had recently adopted a milder tone and turned out pious works like the *Humanità di Cristo* or lives of the saints. 'And you believe he is sincere?' scoffed one of his detractors. 'He is just an opportunist who hopes to win a cardinal's hat'. Again, the King spoke: 'I have held Pietro Aretino in high esteem since 1525, after Pavia, when he sent me a touching letter expressing his solidarity. There is only one of his works that displeases me, namely his overly polemical response to my plans for an alliance with Suleiman. He clearly did not understand that it was only a temporary alliance against the pact between the emperor and the pope; I never intended to set Christ and Mohammed on an equal footing, but merely to impede Charles's progress. Such is politics: sometimes the Devil and holy water get along famously.' 'I, for one, immediately comprehended His Majesty's purpose', Alamanni boastfully interjected. 'In fact, I defended him in some *stanze*, in which I argue that although some may find it unconscionable for a most Christian king to extend a friendly hand to the heathens, their criticism is wholly unfounded. I also added a couple of lines, which, in my humble opinion, are rather good: "What glory is there in banning | those who humbly and peacefully approach you?" Suleiman had sent our King a handsome letter filled with feelings of respect, affection and devotion. Was His Majesty to respond with hostility and ill will?'

At this point, the discussion grew more impassioned, moving from the literary to the political. 'Damned Turks!' someone exclaimed. 'They sail their boats up the coast to France and Italy, to Sicily and Liguria, robbing, pillaging, raping and killing! Let them stay home, or get what's coming to them!' 'Are we really so different?' others shouted. 'What of the New World? They say the Dominican missionary Bartolomé de Las Casas is writing a report on the extermination of the Indians by the Spanish — a massacre, a truly terrible thing. We Europeans have killed many innocent souls, and imposed our laws and customs on the survivors. And to make matters worse, we boast of spreading our civilisation and faith.' Yet others placatingly wished that a climate of civilised concord, not unlike the one that prevailed between the Romans and the peoples they conquered, would eventually spread among nations.

Next, the discussion moved to the topic of cultural achievements. Some guests continued to mock the faults of the Italians, while others praised their merits. The Piedmontese typographer Portonariis lauded the Italian art of printing, epitomised by Aldo Manuzio, and boasted of his own modest contribution: if Dante, Petrarch, Boccaccio and many other Italian authors were so widely read in Lyons today, he noted, it was thanks mainly to Baldassare de Gabiano and himself. The conversation then turned to Italian writers and scholars who had recently returned from France to Italy, such as the famous legal scholar André Alciat, who previously taught in Bourges; the fame of his book of *Emblemata*, published a few years earlier and universally admired, had spread rapidly across Europe. The prince of poets of Lyons, Maurice Scève, who until then had remained silent, suddenly spoke up. 'I found this work extremely useful when writing my *Délie*', he said, 'which is a collection of *dizains* divided into sections introduced by a highly symbolic emblem. Everything in poetry is symbolic, and, if it is authentically poetic, every verse alludes to a hidden meaning beyond objective facts. Alciat helped me understand this. One of his emblems, for instance, expresses clearly that, in love, joy and pain are indissolubly linked. I imitated him in a *dizain* in which I tell the woman I love, "*quand il touche, il point plus doux, aussi plus grièvement*".' A beautiful woman seated opposite the poet shot him an amorous, languid look, and he smiled back at her tenderly. Her name was Pernette du Guillet; she had not been invited to the party, but the poet had brought her anyway, to the indignation of many. Meanwhile, another beautiful woman sitting nearby signalled her disagreement. Her eyes and lips were those of a woman of passion, a devoted disciple of Eros. 'When love is true passion', she said, 'it knows no pain, only joy — joy of the heart and pleasure of the senses. To die in one's lover's embrace: one cannot hope for a sweeter death.' She was Louise Labé, known in Lyons as 'La belle Cordière', a poetess whose unpublished sonnets — the poem that begins '*Baise m'encor, rebaise moy et baise*', for instance — circulated from hand to hand. Some of the ladies glanced at each other in horror and disgust: who was this strumpet? How dare she describe carnal love in such coarse and lubricious terms? Louise turned to them with a smile and recited the first lines of another sonnet: '*Ne reprenez, dames, si j'ay aymé, | si j'ay senti mille torches ardentes*'. Marguerite, following the conversation from afar, felt obliged to intervene: 'You should really read Ficino. He will help you understand that "love desires only that which is moderate, modest and honourable; violent, frenzied pleasures confound the spirit and their immoderation is contrary to true Love, which is the celebration of beauty." I am currently writing a collection of short stories narrated by *devisants*', she continued. 'One of these narrators, commenting on a particular event, explains that we are mistaken if we look to love as a source of pleasure or advantage: love fades as soon as it has obtained what it desires. The true lover would rather renounce and abstain than risk extinguishing the powerful feeling that burns in his breast.'

La Belle Cordière did not dare reply, but her face clearly expressed her disagreement. To the more fearful among the assembly, the air seemed heavy with menace, and an embarrassed silence fell. Luckily, at this point, the servants reappeared with platters of appetising *entrées*: chickens and pheasants, fried fish from the Saône and exquisite *quenelles*, a delectable speciality of Lyons. As everyone reached eagerly for the food, the atmosphere grew more relaxed and the discussion less contentious. Some of the Italians turned to the question of emblematic and poetic language. Antonio Brucioli, for instance, argued heatedly that philosophy should nourish poetry, and quoted in support a remarkable letter from Pico della Mirandola to Ermolao Barbaro, which opposed the density of philosophical and theological thought to the predominance of rhetoric. Another invoked the example of Rabelais. 'What a shame that Master François is not with us here! He usually lives in Lyons but is in Montpellier at present, visiting patients. The marvellous adventures of Gargantua and Pantagruel that he so wittily recounts in his novel — which he will no doubt continue to write — may seem comical, but in fact contain a "substantial marrow". Literature, beneath the veil of form and the intention of pleasure, gives rise to a lesson, an idea.' 'But can this idea truly be expressed freely', another diner asked, 'in the face of prohibitions and censorship?' The conversation was again moving onto dangerous ground.

One of the writers, possibly Dolet, decried the severity with which the authorities condemned free philosophical and creative activity. 'How many authors,' he lamented, 'how many thinkers are thrown into prison or exiled simply for expressing their opinions or doubts, or inviting us to explore new paths? Remember poor Marot! First they lock him up, then they force him to flee to Italy. And why? For allegedly eating bacon during Lent! Culture and literature can bear witness to *dignitas hominis* only if they enjoy complete liberty.' Though seated at some distance, François I overheard this tirade. As an embarrassed silence fell over the table, he said: 'Liberty does not mean *libertinage*. As a most Christian king, it is my duty to correct errors and snuff out heresy.' The *lieutenant general's* severe mien no doubt served to signal his agreement, but it was the King's sister Marguerite who spoke next; she had been close to Marot and deeply admired him. 'Indeed, my brother is right,' she said, 'but he knows that our God is sometimes a *deus absconditus*. Whoever searches for the truth walks the path of the Lord, and the paths of the Lord are infinite.'

The conversation grew progressively less perilous, as the guests began discussing the vast new expanses that had been laid open to human enquiry thanks to the new culture: ancient authors rediscovered, new knowledge to explore, new books to read, new concepts to remember! How many things have we read, studied and forgotten! But how could we possibly remember everything? And keep in mind all the expressive devices that give substance to eloquence and the art of speech? Suddenly, a figure that had remained somewhat apart from the company until then, as if unconcerned by the lively debate, spoke. His name was Giulio Camillo Delminio. Portly and with a slight stutter, he hailed from Friuli but boasted of noble Croatian roots. He had wandered from city to city across Italy: from Venice to Padua, Bologna to Rome, Genova to Milan. It was rumoured that he had invented a sort of 'drinkable gold', which he administered to one of his admirers with the promise that it would restore his youth, though in fact it caused his death. It was also said that he made a public show of devotion but was known to spend most of his time in taverns and brothels. Nonetheless, many praised him, including Erasmus, who admired his eloquence. After leaving Italy and passing briefly through Geneva, he arrived in France and managed to win the King's favour. He presented himself as an orator, poet, alchemist and Kabbalist, but especially as the inventor, by the grace of God, of 'a miraculous potion — according to the words of a very learned lady present here today — which has the power to grant universal understanding of words and objects, and give writers access to the most hidden beauties of the Latin tradition and literature in the common tongue.' Charlatan, actor or brilliant inventor? Opinions were divided.

During the banquet on Île Barbe, raising his voice to ensure the King could hear him, Delminio spoke on the subject of culture and memory. 'I have devised a system that allows one to remember everything one has learned, making the flow of human speech easy and unimpeded.' The revellers stared in bewilderment as Delminio explained his *Idea of the Theatre* or *Idea of Memory*, a machine that looked something like a wooden theatre, possibly modelled on that of Vitruvius (but no one present quite understood it), which could be used to memorise any number of concepts by associating them with images or specific expressions. 'His Majesty', this strange character continued, 'has already ensured me of his support and promised me a cash prize.' François I nodded in confirmation, but many of the guests, clearly displeased, showed signs of perplexity and even veiled irritation. 'Is that all you need to do these days to get a handsome reward: propose some preposterous idea?' one muttered. 'As for those among us who labour in obscurity without giving ourselves airs — who helps us, who thinks of us?' The most irate of Delminio's detractors was Étienne Dolet, a famous Latin scholar and humanist, who would be burned at the stake in the Place de Grève a few years later for holding views sympathetic to the Reformation. He was overheard confiding his angry feelings to his old friend des Périers, seated beside him.

The atmosphere grew more impassioned, and conflict soon erupted between the

Italians and the French, with accusations of low moral character and jealousy flying back and forth. The Italians rejected the criticisms and denied that their native land was a den of charlatans, emphasising instead its many accomplishments. The new poetry, they argued, was born under the auspices of Petrarch, while prose style was deeply indebted to Boccaccio. Their opponents responded by quoting the views of Lemaire de Belges and Symphorien Champier, who denounced the political cynicism of Machiavelli and the greed, cruelty, disloyalty, *fourberie*, inclination to *tromperie* and usurious ways of the Italians, more specifically the Lombards. 'What honest folk are the Lombards!', one of the Frenchmen exclaimed, quoting a popular satirical play; he added that he would take the Neapolitans and Romans over the Lombards any day, for he appreciated the joie de vivre of the former and the good humour and tolerance of the latter in the face of the endemic corruption and rampant simony of the Roman clergy. One of his compatriots noted that, according to Erasmus, the Italians cultivated false eloquence and cared not a fig for the truth. Even the style popularised by Petrarch, he added, was dull and tedious, and expressed nothing truly personal or authentic. In matters of religion, another rejoined, the Italians viewed worship as an essentially formal, superficial and even theatrical act, devoid of true spirituality. But everyone agreed that the Italians' most detestable characteristic — here the discussion turned again to the discord generated by Delminio's speech — was the *outrecuidance*, the *vantardise*, the arrogance with which many of them claimed to possess and transmit a certain knowledge, when in reality they had nothing at all to teach.

Angry jibes and sarcastic remarks flew back and forth for a while longer, until a less choleric man, Bonaventure des Périers, intervened. This peace-loving writer was himself quite willing to follow the invitation to silence which he had set forth the year before in his *Cymbalum Mundi*, inspired by Thomas a Kempis (the book was condemned, but its author avoided arrest, likely thanks to Marguerite). He bade the antagonists, Dolet in particular, to calm down and take things in good humour. Yet in his heart he regretted that a strange character like Delminio had succeeded in taking advantage of the King's trusting nature. Bonaventure no doubt considered Delminio a charlatan, even a swindler, but wisely realised that this was neither the time nor the place to question the King's decision. 'In truth, many Italians are cunning scoundrels, rascals and swindlers', he continued, in a humorous and pleasant tone. 'But it is also true that many are clever, original, resourceful, sometimes even brilliant. Would you like me to tell you a story I wrote recently, which I plan to include in a book of short stories? I called it *"D'un singe qu'avoit un abbé, qu'un Italien entreprinst de faire parler"* [Of a monkey owned by a priest, which an Italian undertook to teach to speak]'.

To cries of 'Yes, tell us a story!', Bonaventure began his tale. 'Once upon a time, there was a priest...' His fable was inspired by the plots of two farces by Poggio and Astemio, in which the main protagonist was not an Italian but a humble *subditus*. In des Périers's version, however, the character of the *princeps* or *tyrannus* — the King in the actual event — became a simple *abbé*, and Delminio an anonymous Italian, to avoid any suspicion of irreverence. The *abbé* of the story owns a pet monkey, an unusually clever and cunning creature, which seems to lack only the power of speech. 'If parrots can be taught to speak', the priest wonders, 'why not a monkey? I would gladly give a whole year's earnings to one who could achieve this.' 'Hearing these words', des Périers continued, 'the Italian in question approached the *abbé* with his nation's natural assurance and, bowing low and with many *excellences* and *magnificences*, said: 'Nature created this animal that so resembles man precisely so that man might improve and perfect this similarity. In the past, have not elephants and donkeys been known to speak?' For the priest, the fact that these philosophical arguments were *italicques* made them all the more persuasive', the author added, 'for we French have a particular tendency to put more faith in the words of foreigners than in those of our countrymen. The wide-eyed priest then asked the Italian if he would be kind enough to undertake this *entreprise*, and how long it might last. The Italian was difficult to persuade: he demanded excellent terms, as he would need to stay with the monkey night and day and feed him only the rarest, most exquisite and most expensive food. "Money is no object," the priest replied. The cunning Italian estimated that it would take at least six years, and demanded a large handful of *écus* as an advance.' The Italians in the audience laughed to themselves, even as they loudly criticised their compatriot's attitude — they feared being implicated against their will in an affair that might damage their reputation. They therefore warned the *magister* that this *folle entreprise* could bring dishonour on their entire nation, that the King would certainly be angry when he found out, and so on. But des Périers replied, 'Why are you so worried? Don't you understand that a lot can happen in six years? The priest might die, the monkey might die, I myself might be dead and buried. In any case, all accounts will be settled.' The outcome was that the Italian not only profited from the large sum he had extorted from the priest, but also took away the monkey on the pretence of teaching him *certains secrets*, thus depriving the priest of both his money and the amusement provided by the antics of his extraordinary pet.

When Bonaventure had finished, everyone laughed. 'A very amusing story', someone remarked, 'but how does it relate to Delminio?' 'Why, in no way at all', des Périers replied. 'My goal was simply to entertain you.' The analogy was obvious, others objected: in both cases, a fabulous result was promised, one of the characters was duped and one of the characters was the duper. But the author had prudently named no one and avoided any direct allusion to the credulity of the King or the cunning of the Friulian adventurer, so that even Delminio laughed at the story, along with Dolet and all the others. The tension and conflict that had threatened the gathering a moment before dispelled, and the atmosphere again grew friendly and cheerful.

The banquet continued until late afternoon, when a final course of delicious *chèvre* cheeses (the island had many goats) and *profiteroles* was served. The guests then took leave of each other one by one, the musicians laid down their instruments, and the King and his court boarded his handsome schooner and returned to the place from which they had started. The first shadows of evening fell over Fourvière. In a few hours, the peaceful radiance of the full moon would bathe Lyons and the island.

CHAPTER 13

Montaigne in Rome: A Fantasy in Four Voices

Edna Stern

During the year 1580–81, Montaigne travelled from his hometown near Bordeaux, through Germany and Switzerland to Italy and, in particular, Rome. He was accompanied by a secretary, who began writing a journal of this trip. In December 1580, just as they reached Rome, the secretary was dismissed and Montaigne took it upon himself to continue writing the journal.

I was walking through the city of Montpellier, where I was later to give a concert, when I was drawn to a small library. It is there that I found a copy of this *Journal de Voyage*.

Returning to my hotel, I leafed through the book. The written characters began to form a picture of a rolling carriage, and all of a sudden I was sitting inside it with Montaigne, Gesualdo and Palestrina in the midst of a conversation.

PALESTRINA: 'I do not meddle in religious affairs, why would the cardinals meddle in mine? As you know, they had the most extraordinary discussion at the Council of Trent on the possibility of banning polyphony in favour of plainsong. It was already twenty years ago, but the subject still intrigues me. Was the matter of such importance, given all the problems affecting the Christian world, that it deserves a special discussion? At the time I felt it almost as an insult to be dictated the proper way of composing.'

MONTAIGNE: 'The Church was perhaps trying, during that period, to suppress divergences in all fields. If you look at the matter metaphorically, one voice is the voice of one opinion. It is the voice of a unique Church. And what are multiple voices but an obstacle to hearing the principal, most important voice?'

EDNA: 'In polyphony, the whole makes the one. No single voice is more important than the others; they each contribute together and, by their clever juxtaposition, form a greater and richer masterpiece. This, rather, is the philosophical idea behind polyphony.'

GESUALDO: 'Your definition is not very precise, Edna. I would not say that all voices are of equal importance; this would not be in the nature of things. One voice leads more than the others in that it is the harmonic base. Another voice may be essentially the rhythmic base, while yet another may appear to be the most important because it attracts the listener's attention with its melody. I would not say

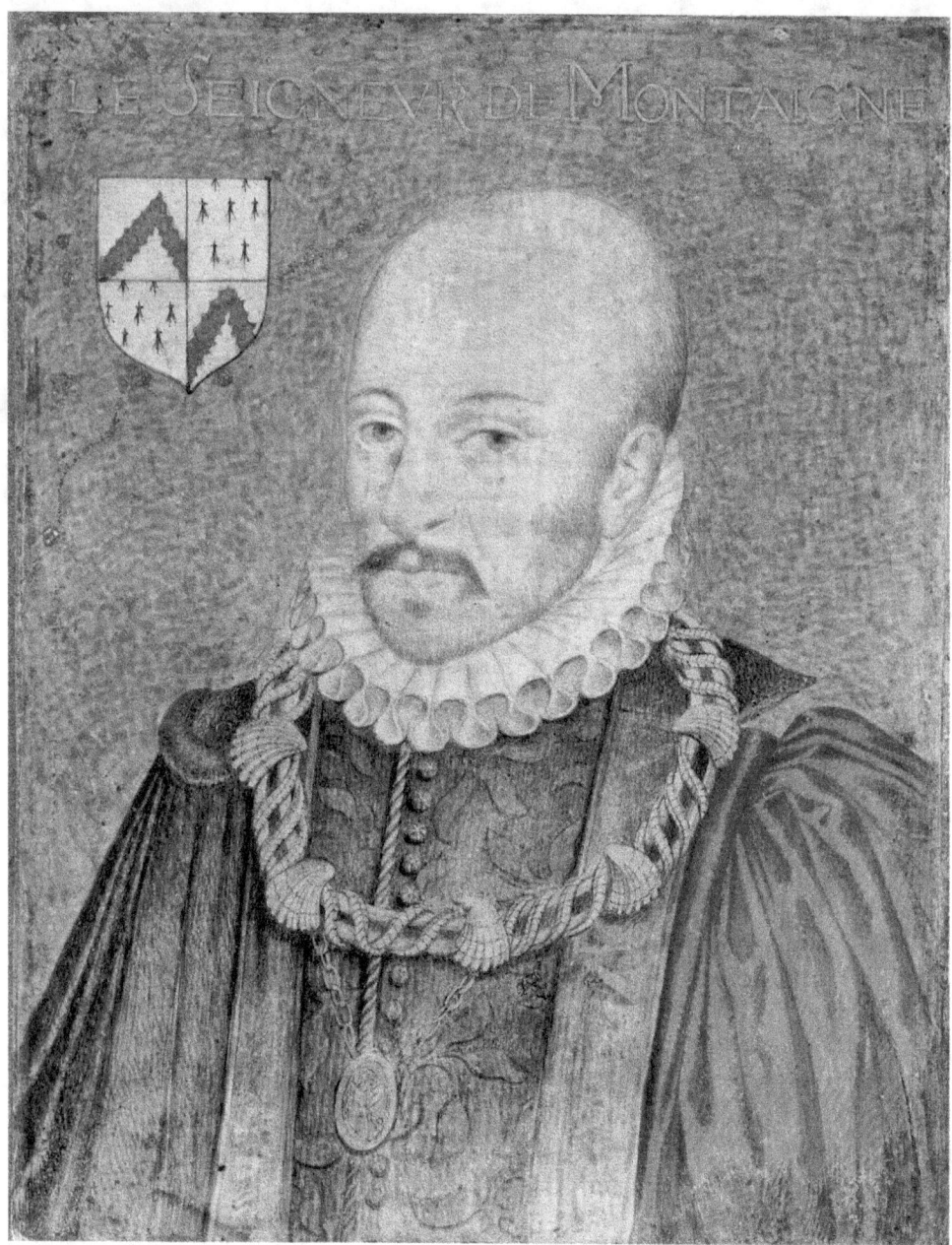

FIG. 25. Anonymous, *Presumed Portrait of Michel de Montaigne*, late sixteenth century, oil on canvas, 13.2 × 14.5 cm, Musée Condé, Chantilly. Photo © RMN-Grand Palais (domaine de Chantilly) / René-Gabriel Ojéda.

that all voices are of equal importance, but rather that they all have equally essential functions within the broader scheme of the musical piece.'

PALESTRINA: 'Quite so, quite so. It is very much like a king governing the people and entrusting different functions to members of his government. In that sense, I can understand the wish of the Church to control all that is going on underneath it. Indeed, even seemingly unimportant matters, such as musical compositions for the celebration of religious ceremonies, can have important consequences.

'Yet one cannot go against one's own time. The contemporary fashion in musical composition was bound sooner or later to influence the style of Church music as well. The members of the council knew very well that they could not fight this development, so they finally adopted a rather broad policy, consisting in limiting the influence of secular elements and insisting on the intelligibility of the words of the sacred texts. In this way, the real decisions were taken locally. I would not have liked to be the Kapellmeister of Modena, for example, where Bishop Giovanni Morone completely abolished polyphony in his cathedral in 1538.'

MONTAIGNE: 'I see what you mean. Naturally they could not go against fashion; it is a sacred establishment in its own right! Allow me, however, my dear Palestrina, to return to my previous metaphor of the Church favouring music in one voice as being the voice of one Church and one God. So, you would not compare polyphony to polytheistic religion and see plainsong as representing monotheism?'

PALESTRINA: 'Heavens no, Montaigne! I am a pious Catholic. I almost took holy orders just a few months ago, after the death of my beloved wife. Yet all my compositions are written in the style of today, that is, in several voices. Our Lord created an intricate world, and the music we compose today is in its image.'

MONTAIGNE: 'If I understand you correctly, you consider polyphony to be the natural way of producing — or rather, shall I say, creating — music similar to the natural way the earth functions?'

PALESTRINA: 'Yes. It is but one mechanism constructed from separate, independent elements that are all subjected to the same, unique rhythm. Like the rising and setting of the sun, the flow of the rivers into the seas and the flight of birds in the sky.'

MONTAIGNE: 'This makes me wonder. To try to recreate the world's mechanism through music — that is an interesting idea. But is it at all advisable, and won't the simple mind of man be confused by the sound of so many voices?'

GESUALDO: 'On one of my recent travels, I heard the most awe-inspiring piece of music. Written by an Englishman named Thomas Tallis, the piece is a Motet for forty independent voices, called *Spem in Alium*. Its magnificence was beyond anything I have heard so far. It is only natural that in all fields man strives to develop and improve. If he can build the most elaborate constructions and fool the eyes with the most lifelike paintings, why shouldn't he do the same in music?'

MONTAIGNE: 'Well said, Gesualdo. And what do you think would be considered polyphony in writing then?'

EDNA: 'I would tend to think that what we are doing now — having a conversation — is the most faithful expression of polyphony, and conversations are nearly always an integral part of every literary composition.'

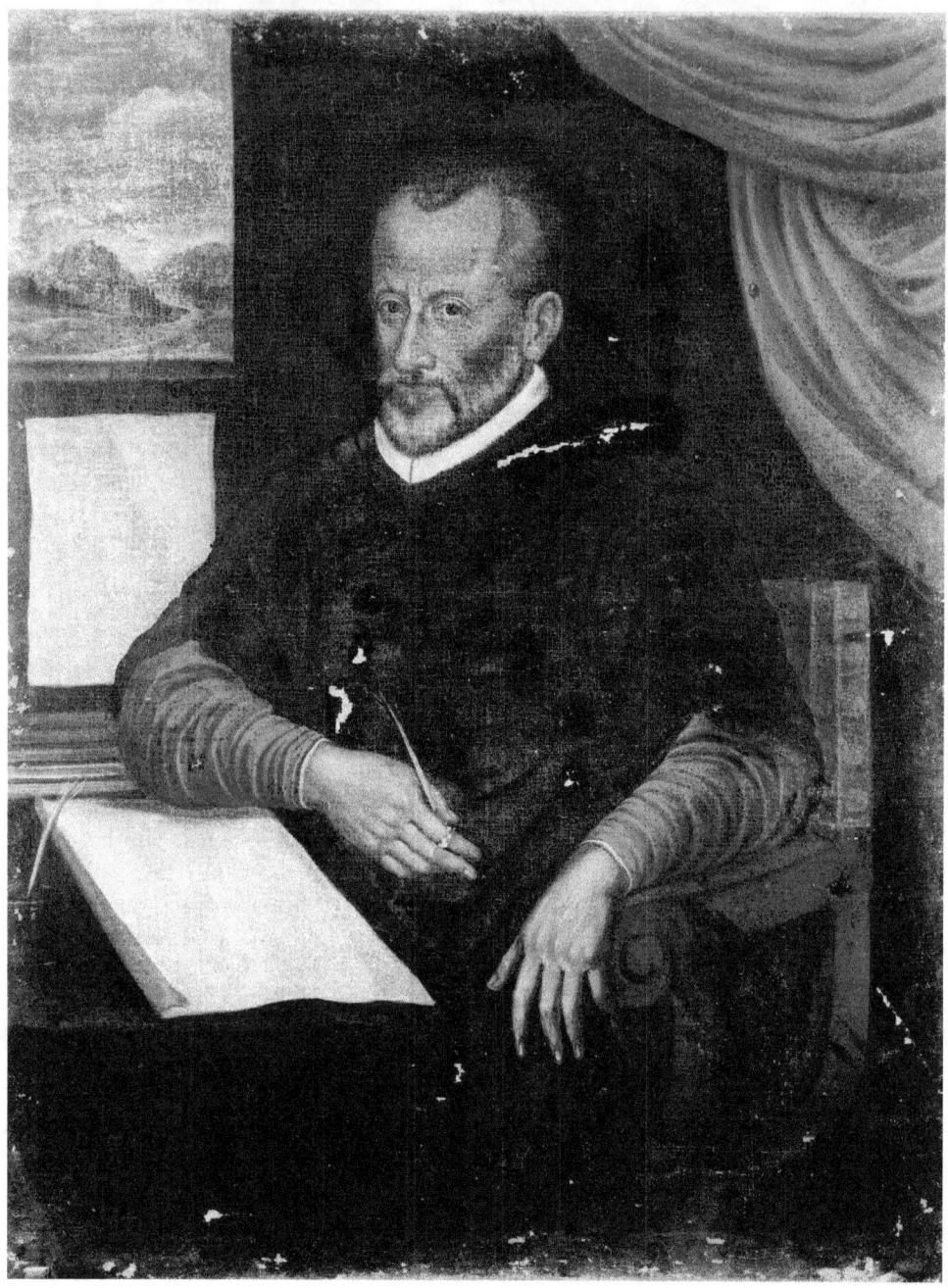

FIG. 26. Anonymous, *Portrait of Pierluigi da Palestrina*, late sixteenth century, oil on canvas, 86.50 × 112 cm, Oratorio di San Filippo Neri, Rome. © 2015 Photo Scala, Florence.

MONTAIGNE: 'If this were the case, how could we converse with forty people? How are we to understand this multiplicity without being overwhelmed by its density?'

EDNA: 'Your *Essays*, Montaigne, only *seem* to be a monologue with yourself. In fact, they contain a great variety of voices, since your abundant quotations are really conversations with authors from the past. I dare say that future writers will converse with you too, as this is the way philosophy works, through great exchanges across centuries.

'On the other hand, it has just occurred to me that I might have to reconsider my statement that conversation is the most faithful expression of polyphony. It is a good example of polyphony, but not the only one. I refer to another kind of polyphony that appears in your writings and is expressed through a feigned split in your opinion. After you clarify one point of view, you go on to show us its opposite — demonstrating equal understanding of this second perspective, thereby making us doubt your true position.'

MONTAIGNE: 'My dear, I may contradict myself but I never contradict the truth.'

At that very moment, a bee flew in through the open window of the carriage and landed on Montaigne's arm. Gesualdo raised his hand to kill it, but Montaigne stopped him in time, jokingly remarking that the bee might seem unimportant to us, yet fulfil an essential function in our world, which is hidden from us.

MONTAIGNE then continued, unperturbed: 'Yes, I am a man of conversation, and indeed I like to make use of the wisdom of the ancient writers. I also miss their greatness and feel even more deeply the shallowness and decadence of our times.'

THE BEE: 'Nonsense. I can say with complete confidence that I was fortunate to live in one of the most brilliant courts that ever existed. Even then, they praised bygone times and denounced the present, saying that all things are continually going from bad to worse.'

PALESTRINA (laughing): 'And what court would that be, little bee?'

The bee turned suddenly into a man: BALDASSARE CASTIGLIONE was looking at us humorously.

CASTIGLIONE: 'The court of Guidobaldo da Montefeltro, Duke of Urbino, of course! We took great pleasure in our discussions, which were full of sharp exchanges of quick retorts. There many men of talent there, including Ottaviano Fregoso, his brother Messer Federico, Giuliano de' Medici, known to all as the Magnifico, Messer Pietro Bembo, Count Ludovico and many other noble gentlemen.'

EDNA: 'I remember that you explained your view on our understanding of decadence, and how it is related to the body's decay. You wrote that the glamorous past is lived by the young, with the advantage of a body that has full enjoyment of all the capacities imparted by good health, the energy of youth, and beauty, whereas the past is remembered at a time of bodily decay, thus leading us to glorify the past and making us unable to enjoy the present. Perhaps another reason for this idea of yours on the glory of the past comes from the exploration of old paths versus new ones. Old paths have an established structure, whereas new paths are still being explored and therefore seem less promising at the moment. However, let us continue our discussion on polyphony and composing music in the image of our intricate world. I am sure you have interesting thoughts on the subject, or you wouldn't have come in.'

CASTIGLIONE: 'Indeed, I do have some thoughts on the subject. Is the world simple or is it intricate? That is the first question. Are all things planned, or are they improvised and happen, so to say, naturally? To return to your question about polyphony, I believe that whether it is written in one, two, three or forty voices is of little importance, so long as the musical discourse is fluid and pronunciation effortless. As my dear friend Count Ludovico used to say, one should "Practice in everything a certain nonchalance that shall conceal design and show that what is done and said is done without effort and almost without thought".'[1]

EDNA: 'You seem pensive, Montaigne. Has the word *sprezzatura* prompted a thought?'

MONTAIGNE: 'I am still reflecting on polyphony, nature and grace. All the time we conversed, it reminded me of an experience I had, but I couldn't recall it exactly. As you know, my memory is rather poor...

'During my voyage here, I had the chance to see and hear the famous organ of the gardens of Ferrara...'

At that precise moment, I heard my alarm clock ring. I woke up, still clutching the book in my hands, and my eyes fell on the following passage from Montaigne's *Travel Diary*:

> The music of the organ, which is real music and a natural organ, though always playing the same thing, is effected by means of water, which falls with great violence into a round arched cave and agitates the air that is in there and forces it, in order to get out, to go through the pipes of the organ and supply it with wind. Another stream of water, driving a wheel with certain teeth on it, causes the organ keyboard to be struck in a certain order; so you hear an imitation of the sounds of trumpets. In another place you hear the song of birds, which are little bronze flutes that you see at regals; they give a sound like those little earthenware pots full of water that little children blow into by the spouts, this by an artifice like that of the organ; and then by other springs they set in motion an owl, which, appearing at the top of the rock, makes this harmony cease instantly, for the birds are frightened by his presence; and then he leaves the place to them again. This goes on alternately as long as you want.

---

1 Baldassare Castiglione, *The Book of the Courtier*, Book I.

CHAPTER 14

Dark Shadows from the Youth of Giordano Bruno

Carlo Vecce

Several years ago, I was conducting research in the State Archives of Venice when a thick, dusty folder with a reference number that was not the one I had requested somehow landed on my table. It was too late to tell the archivists that they had made a mistake. The room was almost deserted, the light had grown dim, and sudden, bright flashes of lightning and the hammering rain outside indicated that a storm was rising. Intrigued, I untied the laces of the folder and opened it to see what lay inside. Among the mountain of documents, my eyes were drawn to a cloth bag containing a sheaf of folded paper. The seal was broken, but it bore the unmistakeable mark of the Venetian Inquisition of the late sixteenth century. On the first page, in the neat hand of a chancellery clerk, I read the following words:

> Venetiae, die XXVI de mense Maii 1592.
>
>   Coram supradictis conductus quidam vir communis staturae cum barba castanea, aetatis et aspectu annorum quadraginta circiter, cui delato iuramento de veritate dicenda, qui tactis scripturis iuravit etc. Et cum moneretur ad dicendum veritatem antequam ulterius interrogaretur, dixit ex se:
>
>   I will tell the truth. I was summoned before this Santo Offitio on several occasions and always considered it a joke, since I was always prepared to defend myself.
>
>   *Subdens ad interrogationem:* Last year in Frankfurt I received two letters from Signor Gioanni Mocenigo *(omissis)*
>
>   *Interrogatus* regarding his family and given name, whose son he is, his place of his birth and nation, *respondit porrigens aliquam scripturam:*
>
>   Knowing that you would certainly wish to question me about my person and works, I resolved to bare my soul to Your Excellency in this document, which describes in detail my nation, homeland and youth, and with your permission, I shall continue this account of my life until the present day.
>
>   *Quibus habitis, cum hora esset tarda, fuit remissus ad locum suum, animo etc. cum monitione etc.*
>
>   *Ex ordine Inquisitoris Generalis fratris Iohannis Gabrielis de Salutiis, transcribitur in actis solum quod oportet, et omittitur omnia quae pertinent ad privatam personam*, and seems irrelevant to this dispute, *quoniam prolixe et verbose enarrat de pueritia sua et adulescentia, etiam in minimis.*[1]

---

1   The Latin text in this passage is translated below for ease of comprehension:
Venice, the 26th of May 1592.
   A man of average height, with a chestnut beard, around forty years old, appeared before the

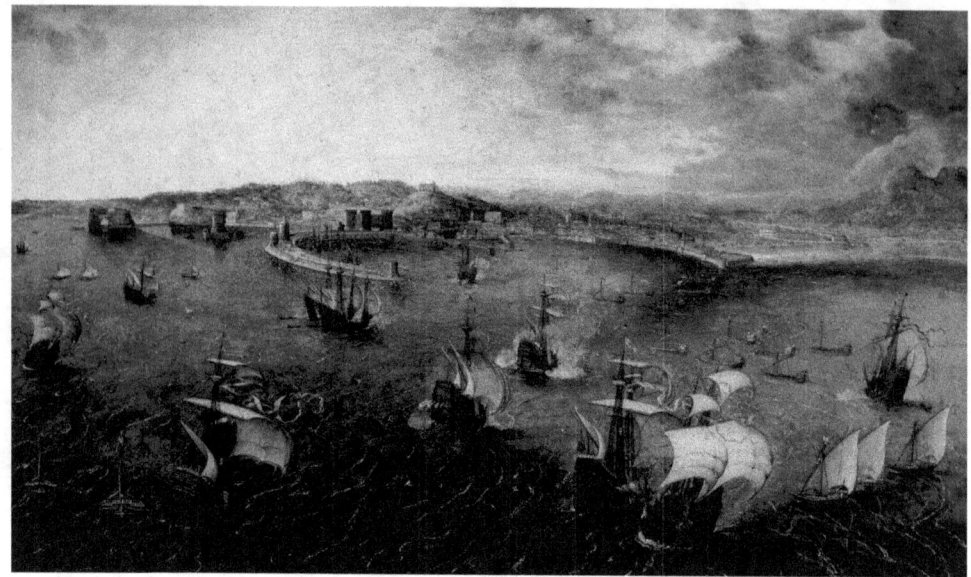

FIG. 27. Brueghel the Elder, *Port of Naples*, 1560, oil on wood, 70 × 41 cm, Doria Pamphilj Gallery, Rome. Amministrazione Doria Pamphilj srl con socio unico.

In contrast, the pages in the folder, which numbered no more than ten, were covered in a hurried, nervous scrawl, as if the author had been in a great rush to finish writing, and were much harder to decipher. I transcribed them as fast as I could, filling in the abbreviations and modernising the spelling and punctuation somewhat as I went along. I had almost finished when the archivist came to tell me that they were closing. I handed him the folder, fully expecting to be able to continue studying it the following day.

I never saw this document again. Overnight, the water rose until it surrounded the building, causing considerable damage and forcing the Archive to close for an extended period. When I finally had an opportunity to return, a few months later, I was unable to consult the folder, as I had not noted the reference number. Many years have passed since, and my memory of this event is gradually fading, its contours blurring, as if it had all been a dream. These notes are the only trace I have of the interrogation conducted by the Venetian Inquisition in 1592. The

aforementioned authorities and swore on the Bible to tell the truth. And since he was urged to tell the truth before any question had yet been put to him, he said:

I will tell the truth. I was summoned before this Holy Office on several occasions and always considered it a joke, since I was always prepared to defend myself. Being questioned: Last year in Frankfurt I received two letters from Signor Gioanni Mocenigo (not in the file). Questioned regarding his family and given name, whose son he is, his place of his birth and nation, he answered while presenting a written note: Knowing that you would certainly wish to question me about my person and works, I resolved to bare my soul to Your Excellency in this document, which describes in detail my nation, homeland and youth, and with your permission, I shall continue this account of my life until the present day.

These having been received, and as it was growing late, he was led back to his cell and to his soul, etc. with due warnings, etc. By order of the inquisitor general, Fra Giovanni Gabriele de Salutiis, the record transcribes only the pertinent details and omits everything related to his private life as irrelevant to this dispute, for he writes at length and verbosely about the smallest details of his childhood and youth.

prisoner had answered in writing with his autobiography, the story of his self, the fragments of a secret youth.

My name is Giordano, from the family of Bruni. I was born and raised in the city of Nola, twelve miles outside of Naples. My profession is, and has always been, that of a man of letters and science; my father's name was Gioanni and my mother's Fraulissa Savolina; my father was a soldier by trade and is now dead, as is my mother.

I am about forty-four years of age: my parents told me I was born in '48.

Before I took holy orders I was known by the name I received at baptism: Filippo.

My family home was a pretty little estate with a house of four or five simple rooms, on a narrow lane outside the city of Nola, at the foot of Monte Cicala, not far from a ruined chapel dedicated to Saint John which stands next to the path leading up to the cliff of Cesco.

My mother had a strange name, Fraulissa, like all the members of her family, who were named after stars, knights and fairies: Luna and Mercurio and Febo, Scipione and Franzino, Morgana and Cassandra.

My father was a soldier and rarely at home.

He would return after several months of absence, tired and quiet, and once I saw his sword still stained with dark blood.

'Bandits and cutthroats who rob and kill people crossing from Airola through the forest of Cancello', he said. Lowering his eyes, he continued: 'If we catch them, we hang them from posts by the roadside. Foreigners coming to our lovely Campania would do well to take the road that leads from Rome to Naples if they relish such things, for along the way they can admire a great many robbers hanging from the gibbets, and at every step find enough fresh meat to feed the grandest banquet the world has ever seen.' Since he often spoke in this fashion, he was known as the philosopher-soldier.

One night, after supper, a neighbour said: 'I have never been so happy as in this moment.'

My father replied: 'You have never been so foolish as in this moment.'

He was fond of telling the story of Don Paulino, the parish priest of Santa Prima, a village near Nola, and his good friend Scipione Savolino. On Good Friday, Scipione went to confession and was absolved without much difficulty, even though his sins were considerable in both number and gravity.

This happened a first time.

The following year, Scipione didn't bother with an explanation, saying to the priest: 'My father, you already know last year's sins.'

Don Paulino answered: 'My son, you already know last year's absolution. Go in peace and sin no more.'

I learned to read from another priest, Gian Dominico de Iannello, and I studied grammar with Bartolo di Aloia.

My father was friendly with Cola di Gianbernardino Tansillo, a cousin of the poet Luigi Tansillo, and I remember a magnificent Messer Luigi who used to visit when my father was away.

Messer Luigi and I wandered the countryside like two pilgrims, discussing poetry and stopping in the vineyard of our estate at harvest time to watch the games and songs of the peasants.

Smiling, he recited this poem of his own composition:

> Let my floors be made of flowers and grass,
> branches be my roof, black oaks my marbles,
> and a wine cask the safe where I keep my treasure.

I remember the lovely summer days, and the jujubes falling from the tree in the courtyard and hitting the ground and turning to pulp and being eaten by worms. Vasta, Albenzio's wife, tried to curl her fringe, but instead burned her hair because the iron was too hot; cockroaches crawled out of the manure pile and Albenzio crushed them underfoot.

Laurenza's hair fell out in handfuls when she brushed it; Antonio Savolino's bitch had five pups; a cuckoo sang in La Starza and then we ran to the ruins of Cicala Castle and on to Scarvaita. Messer Danese cut a skirt on his worktable and folded it; the boards of Costantino's bed were always crawling with bedbugs.

The third mill was in the old part of Fiurulo; Ambrigio made love to his wife; their son Martinello entered puberty and hair grew on his chest and his voice changed; Paulino strained to lift a heavy bar off the ground and broke his red belt with the effort and swore prodigiously. I also remember soups with too much salt which tasted of smoke.

The earth gave us fruits and flowers year-round, olives and grapes, and in autumn the cellars were full of the delicious smell of new wine, heady Asprinio and fragrant Greco.

I truly believed I was born under a lucky star.

Sometimes my earliest memory emerges like a dream, a dark shadow, an enigmatic prophecy.

I thought I saw a huge snake emerging from a crack in the wall and slithering towards me, and I cried out for my father and he and others in the house ran around looking for a stick to kill it.

Another marvel I saw one night was a blazing beam flying through the air above the roofs of the houses, or perhaps it was a creature of heaven, and it flew straight ahead and rose above Monte Cicala before disappearing from sight.

Another time, invisible evil spirits chased me from the foot of Monte Cicala, near the plague cemetery, all the way to Santa Maria del Porto, throwing rocks at me the whole time, though I was not hit.

But for me the greatest marvel of all was the wondrous spectacle of nature.

I roamed alone through the fields and woods all the way to Summonte, white-capped with snow in winter, and the hills above the towns of Domicella and Carbonara.

I returned home with a face so dirty that my mother laughed and told me I looked like a man who had spent thirty years making charcoal on Monte Scarvaita, a place beyond Monte Cicala, above Carbonara.

Oh, sweet Monte Cicala, covered in ivy, olive trees, dogwoods, laurels, myrtle and rosemary, chestnuts, poplars and elms in a happy union with vines.

From its highest point, I could see its brother Vesuvius, scarred and hunchbacked, black with smoke, and since I could see no farther I imagined there was nothing beyond.

As a child, this marked the outer boundary of my world.

I would later go beyond it, on the day I went to Naples.

The road passed next to Vesuvius, whose lower slopes were blanketed with vines and trees and the fruits of all shapes and colours that Mother Nature produces in such abundance. Turning to look behind me, I saw Monte Cicala: it looked grey and miserable.

I realised in an instant that I was the victim of a false image, and that reality does not end where our senses allow us to go.

I was fourteen when I arrived in Naples in 1562.

Through the damp fog of the marshes, on the other side of the bridge, I saw the royal city of Naples, a veritable theatre of the world, and the walls, doors, towers, steeples and churches, the Monte Sant'Eramo and the black and menacing fortress. We entered through a gate adorned with the image of an ancient king on horseback, holding a sword in his hand. We passed in front of houses with fires lit by the door out of fear of the plague.

Advancing through the maze of lanes and marketplaces, I gazed up at the façades of the palaces and churches, at the spires and fountains, amid the tumult of sounds and cries, songs and church bells and the dull hammering of blacksmiths, surrounded by a multitude of men, women, ragged and barefoot children, laughing girls with bright dresses and uncombed hair. At the top of a small hill, we finally arrived at a house in the noble quarter of Nido.

I had come to Naples to study literature and humanities, logic and dialectics. I attended the public lectures of Gioan Vincenzo de Colle, commonly known as Il Sarnese, a philosopher who read Aristotle with Averroes' comments and held that ideas were more precious than words.

I also took private lessons in logic from an Augustinian monk, Fra Teofilo da Vairano, who later taught metaphysics in Rome. He read Plato to me, and we practised reasoning as we strolled in the cloister of San Gioanne in Carbonara where he took me every day to read the books left there by Cardinal Seripando.

At sixteen or seventeen I joined the order of Dominicans in the monastery of San Dominico in Naples.

I decided to become a monk after I witnessed a dispute at San Dominico; its protagonists seemed like gods of this earth, and the convent's library was their Olympus.

The most eminent Neapolitan doctors had lectured in these halls, including the greatest of all, Thomas Aquinas, of which Jesus Christ on the cross reportedly said: 'You wrote about me well, Thomas.'

In the vast church, I contemplated the beauty of the sinner Mary Magdalene, and in the chapel of Carafa, in Sanseverino, the figures of the night sky, which I thought resembled triumphant beasts, and I began reading Sacrobosco's *Sphæra* and Copernicus's *De revolutionibus*.

I dreamt that my soul, in the throes of a heroic ecstasy, flew above the horizon of natural affections and, overcome with other thoughts, as if dead to my body, aspired to something higher.

I was given the name Iordano Bruno on becoming a friar, and this is the name I have used everywhere since, except when I fled from Rome and used my old name Filippo when crossing the mountains.

I was received in the order by a friar who was prior of the convent at the time: Master Ambrosio Pasqua. At the end of my probationary year he introduced me to my profession, which I solemnly practised in the same convent, since at that time, as far as I know, convents were the only place one could do so. When the time came, I was admitted to the sacred orders and the priesthood. I sang my first Mass in Campania, some distance from Naples, in the Dominican monastery of San Bartolomeo.

Soon after, however, I returned to the convent in Naples. I refused to go to the College of Adria, and finally I officially became a student in Naples in 1572.

In July 1575, I defended two theses on Saint Thomas's *Summa contra Gentiles* and Pietro Lombardo, and was awarded the degree of Lector in Theology.

As I sat reading in the library, my mind wandered across unknown worlds, through the works of Aristotle and Plato and *omnes commentatores*, both ancient and modern: Averroes, Thomas, Pietro Lombardo, Ficino, Cusano and the Church Fathers — Augustine, Jerome, John Chrysostom.

Raimondo Lullo taught me an art more powerful than writing: the wondrous art of memory, which, according to Plato, is the writing of the soul.

I read the works of Erasmus of Rotterdam in secret; they were reputed to be heretical and dangerous and therefore kept in a secret library. Fra Ambrosio, the stupid beast, spent a lot of money trying to remove all the annotations by Erasmus and other heretics from the books in our library.

One of these, Erasmus's *Manual of the Christian Knight*, was a powerful weapon against the idolatry of sacred images. The only true image of Christ, he says, is the one found in the Gospel.

Erasmus taught me how to separate gold from iron and uncover truths that time or men have occulted or perverted; in other words, he schooled me in the art of philology, which served me as a sharply honed sword to slice through the mask of hypocrisy behind which power hides its true, violent and bestial face.

By May 1568, I had become well-versed in Hebrew, and was therefore sent to Rome to recite the psalms of Zion, Mother of Nations, on the conversion of heathens and heretics, before the Holy Father Pius V and Reverend Cardinal Inquisitor Rebiba.

I remember that I travelled to Rome by coach, like a rich man, and wore a broad-brimmed hat that the convent had bought for me.

Along the Via Appia I saw countless corpses by the side of the road, either murdered by cutthroats or decimated by malaria.

I appeared before the Pope and recited the psalm both forwards and backwards, astonishing many in the audience with my powers of recollection. On the same occasion, I met the converted Jew Andrea de Monte, who taught me about the secret teachings of the Kabbalah.

In truth, Naples was the theatre of the world for me.

It was in this theatre, on Piazza del Mercato, on 4 March 1564, that I witnessed the execution by fire, with the most terrible contortions and suffering, of two noblemen condemned for heresy and impenitence: Gioan Francesco Alois and Gioan Bernardino Gargano.

I also witnessed the revolt of the Neapolitan populace against the Inquisition and the Spaniards, whom they held responsible for the terrible famine and extreme poverty. Those who have neither bread nor money lack not only stone, grass and words, but also air, earth, water, fire and life itself.

Novices and young friars like me often slipped out of the convent at night to visit the nuns of the convent of Sant'Arcangelo in Baiano or the prostitutes who plied their trade in the Piazzetta, Fundaco del Cetrangolo, Borgo di Santo Antonio and another place near Santa Maria del Carmino.

The women pilgrims to the Madonna di Piedigrotta, glistening with sweat and with their blouses unlaced in the heat, were also a fine sight to behold. They cried and sang: 'Jesus Christ, Holy Mary, Blessed Mother of Piedigrotta, Holy Virgin of the Rosary, Our Lady of the Mountain, Holy Mary Appareta, Advocate of Scafata! Alleluia, alleluia, evil be gone! Saint Cosmas and Saint Julian, keep evil at bay! Begone, begone, away, away, a thousand miles away!'

But my greatest pleasure was to visit the Lady Morgana.

Her admirable, black-veiled face reminded me of the face of the sinner Mary Magdalene in the chapel of San Dominico.

In her house in Nido was a large mirror in which I discovered my face, which looked always as if it was contemplating the fires of hell.

I was the sort of man who laughs only when others are laughing. Most of the time I appeared uneasy, with a serious and strange countenance, never happy, as solitary and withdrawn as an old codger, as erratic as a dog fed a diet of blows and raw onions.

One day, after eating in a tavern and feeling somewhat disinclined to pay the bill, I told the innkeeper: 'Innkeeper, let's play a game.'

'What do you wish to play?' he said. 'I have tarot cards.'

I replied: 'I never have any luck with that accursed game, because I have a very bad memory.'

He said: 'I have ordinary cards, too.'

I replied: 'They could be marked and you would certainly know the markings. Have you a new pack that has never been used?' He answered in the negative.

'All right then, another game.'

'I have tablets.'

'I don't know that game.'

'I also have chess.'

'I would rather deny Christ three times than play chess.'

The innkeeper suddenly lost his temper: 'By all the devils, what do you want to play? Choose something!'

I said: 'Let's play ball and mallet.'

He said: 'What the hell is that? Do you see a ball and mallet here? Does this look like the place for such a game?'

I said: 'All right then, let's play *mirella*.'

'That's a game for porters, peasants and swineherds!'

'How about five dice?'

'What in God's name is five dice? I've never heard of such a game. But we could play three dice if you want.'

I told him that I never had any luck at three dice.

'The devil take your soul!' he said. 'If you really want to play a game, you need to think of one we can both play.'

I said: 'All right then, let's play *spaccastrommola*.'

'Now you have gone too far', he said. 'You should be ashamed of yourself, suggesting such a vile, whoreson's game!'

'All right, all right,' I said. 'I'll race you.'

'I refuse,' he said.

I retorted: 'By the blood of the blessed Virgin, you shall race me!'

'If you want to do the right thing,' he said, 'pay me. After that, you may go to God or to the Devil for all I care!'

I said: 'By the blood of all the whores in Christendom, you shall race me!'

'And if I won't?' he said.

'You shall!' I said.

'But I've already told you that I don't want to race you today, or tomorrow or ever...'

'How about right now?'

'And if I say no?'

'And if you say yes?'

In the end I paid him with my feet, so to speak, by jumping up and running away. And would you believe it, that fat pig who not a minute earlier insisted he would not play — not today, not tomorrow, not ever — suddenly decided to race me after all, with two of his kitchen boys in tow. They chased me for a good while, but caught me only with their cries. And then I swear by Saint Roch's horrible wound that I never heard from them again, and they never laid eyes on me.

Another time, at a tavern in Cerriglio, after we had eaten well and no longer needed anything from the innkeeper, we amused ourselves by sending him out to search for all sorts of rare delicacies and sweetmeats.

We eventually ran out of ideas, but when the innkeeper ran up with a jug of vinegar in response to some ridiculous request from one of my companions, I said: 'You stupid moron, have you no shame? Fetch us some orange flower water and Malvasia wine from Candia, and make it quick.'

Rage suddenly darkened the innkeeper's face. 'In the name of the Devil,' he shouted, 'are you dukes or marquises? Can you pay for what you have just ordered?

I wonder how you'll manage when the bill comes. You have not stopped asking for things that can't be found in a simple tavern!'

'Scoundrel, thief, impudent wretch!' I berated him. 'Do you imagine you are addressing your equals? A fine rogue you are, you insolent ruffian!'

'A curse upon your lying mouth!' he cried.

Then we rose from the table all together to defend our honour, and each grabbed a spit from the fire, some of which were still adorned with fine pieces of roasted meat. The innkeeper ran to fetch a halberd, and two of his servants grabbed rusty sabres. There were six of us, armed with long rods and makeshift shields and helmets fashioned from pots and pans. Thus equipped, we defended ourselves valiantly while backing slowly down the stairs towards the door to the street, occasionally pretending to counter-attack. Before long, the innkeeper, persuaded for some reason of our superiority and fearing for his life and the safety of his servants, capitulated; he threw his halberd to the ground, and no doubt fearing our revenge, ordered the servants to retreat.

Turning to us, he said: 'Gentlemen, forgive me for losing my temper. I had no intention of offending you! Pay me what you owe me, and may God bless you!'

'Traitor, you tried to kill us!' I said. By then we all had a foot in the street.

Then the innkeeper, realising with despair that we would accept neither his courtesies nor his submission nor his prayers, picked up his halberd and called to his servants, and his wife and son. What a racket they made! 'Pay me, pay me!' one shouted. 'Scoundrels, thieves, cheats!' the others shrieked.

But they were not stupid enough to chase us, for the obscurity of the night streets was more in our favour than theirs. Fleeing the innkeeper's rage, we met at another place near Carmini and had enough money to last us three days.

There were many people there: some enjoyed themselves, others lamented the state of the world; some cried, others laughed; some offered advice, other described their hopes; some smiled, others frowned; some argued in one direction, others argued in another. It was like watching a comedy and a tragedy at the same time, a choir singing the Gloria and another singing the Requiem. No man who hopes to understand the ways of the world would want to miss such a sight.

I was still wearing the habit of a Dominican friar and celebrating masses and other divine services under the orders of my superiors and the priors of the various monasteries and convents of my order where I officiated. This was when all the fuss began.

When I was a novice, my master Fra Eugenio Gagliardo reported me, perhaps only with the aim of frightening me, for throwing away images of the saints — Saint Catherine of Sienna and Saint Anthony, if my memory serves me — while keeping the crucifix, and also for asking a novice why he was reading the *Seven Joys of the Virgin* and advising him to throw it out and read something else instead, such as the *Lives of the Holy Fathers*.

In May 1572, Fra Augustino da Montalcino, a lector in theology at the Minerva in Rome and a haughty and scornful man, visited our convent. One day in the cloister, in front of the other novices, I debated him on the Incarnation and the Trinity.

I said that, according to Arius, the Word was neither creator nor creature but rather the medium between the two, because the Word lies midway between the speaker and the spoken, although it is considered the first link in the chain. And it is not that by which but that for which everything was created, not that by which but that unto which everything refers and returns to in the end, which is the Father. I especially insisted on this last point.

For this and probably a few other reasons, I was accused and, unknown to me, tried in secret by the provincial superior, Fra Dominico Vita. I was not aware of it at the time, and I soon forgot about the dispute.

Four years later, in 1576, I heard a knock on the door of my cell.

It was a fellow friar warning me that the Inquisition had opened a secret inquiry against me.

After glancing at the books on my table, he warily backed out of my room.

The books he saw were old copies of Saint Jerome and Saint John Chrisostom with the annotations by Erasmus which Fra Ambrosio, dumb beast that he was, had half-erased.

I wrapped them in rags and threw them into the latrine.

The paradox of wisdom hiding in excrement made me laugh, and reminded me of a story by Giovanni Boccaccio that tells of a certain Andreuccio, a young man not unlike me, who also falls into shit while roaming the mean streets of Naples, the Malo Pertuso and Rua Catalana.

I packed my few belonging into a bag, my most precious possession being safely hidden away in my memory; it contained all the things I had read in books, and no one could ever take it from me.

After nightfall, like Andreuccio, I climbed out of a small window into the lane, and wrapped myself in a cape.

At dawn, they opened the city gates.

I walked out through the Porta de Santo Ianuario and across the narrow valley of the Vergini and Santa Maria Antesecula.

From the other side, I looked back as the city awoke to the daily illusion of life and pleasure, and saw for the last time its walls and watchtowers, its chiming church-bells, its domes of green and gold majolica glistening in the sunlight.

Then I turned my back on it, and have wandered since like a pilgrim through every part of this great and terrible world, and visited many of its kingdoms.

Here is one who has vaulted across the air, penetrated the skies, studied the stars, pushed the boundaries of this world, razed the imagined walls of spheres and intervals — the seconds, octaves, ninths and tenths — devised by worthless mathematicians under the blind gaze of vulgar philosophers!

Guided by good sense and reason, and through careful investigation, he opened all the hidden gardens of truth that were in his power to open, laid bare the secrets of nature, gave eyes to moles, light to blind men who could not steady their gaze long enough to see their image reflected in the mirrors arrayed all around them, tongues to mutes who dared not express complex beliefs, and strength to the legs of the lame who feared to step in spirit across that chasm which vile and ignoble minds cannot cross.

He made these truths as real as if they were actual denizens of the sun, the moon or the other stars, and showed in what way the celestial bodies we see from afar are similar to or different from each other, larger or smaller than the one that is closest to us and to which we are bound, and opened our eyes that we might at last see this deity: our sacred mother, who conceives us in her womb, who feeds us from her back and in whose loving arms I firmly believe we will all be welcomed in the end.

By the Hudson River between Croton and Poughkeepsie (New York),
4 March 2013 at sunset.

CHAPTER 15

Filigrana Italiana

Marina Warner

While Montague Rhodes James was in his last year as a Scholar at Eton, the notorious 'public' school where England's élite is still trained for wealth and high office, a new organ screen was being installed between the choir and the ante-chapel. One day during Matins, young Monty glimpsed something on the walls in the corners at the end, images previously concealed under the chapel stalls: two female figures, shadowy and faint, standing on trompe l'oeil pedestals of curly acanthus; their heads were bare, their hair loose, and they were dressed in long white robes — virgins in paradise!

The revelation was fleeting. Soon, the new organ and its wooden screen were erected and the stalls were put back; the painted figures disappeared again. But the eighteen-year-old James, already a keen antiquarian with marked imaginative gifts, had seen a fragment of the pre-Reformation decoration in the Gothic chapel, and he did not forget.

The passions of the future scholar were crystallised by that apparition — the hidden saints announced to him that beneath the fabric of England's most English redoubts of power and privilege, there lay another picture, another story, another face.

The idea of a *filigrana* — a watermark — was invoked by Jorge Luis Borges as the underlying structure of his cunning tales, and the analogy later provided Italo Calvino with an inspired metaphor for the epiphanies that art and literature may grant to those who love them and attend to their encrypted meanings. M. R. James was one of these, and that chance removal of the chapel stalls in 1881 had revealed to him another history, woven into the fabric of the chapel. Like one of the protagonists of the ghost stories which he went on to invent, he had accidentally discovered, under the surface of the austere whitewashed walls, connections to the past and to a history to which he, as an Englishman, belonged, but which had become foreign; the effaced images had brought the grace and fantasy of medieval Europe to Britain, and transfused the storytelling curiosity of humanist courts of the Renaissance into the illustrious educational establishment on the banks of the Thames. 'I will only repeat...,' he wrote in his memoirs, *Eton and King's* (1926), 'that in these paintings Eton possesses a treasure which is, honestly, unrivalled in this country and in France. You must go as far as Italy (or almost as far: we must not forget Avignon) before you can find wall-paintings of equal importance and beauty.'[1]

༄

Gasparo Spirello was seventeen when his master, Messer Gerolamo, stopped alongside his workbench, where he was tooling a binding of the new selection of Madonna Veronica's *Canzoniere*, and beckoned him into the inner room where the workshop's books were stored before delivery to their patrons or their purchasers. Messer Gerolamo sat down at the oak table to face the young engraver, who stood before him. A *Legenda Aurea*, on which Gasparo had worked a year or so ago, lay open at the feast day of the Invention of the Holy Cross, with the woodcut of St Helena proving the true wood on which the saviour hung by holding each of the three crosses in turn over the body of a young girl, freshly laid in her grave. Stroking and patting the great volume as if it were a favourite hound, restive and yet biddable, Messer Gerolamo, master printer to the young and clever Duchess of O—, Madonna Veronica del Licorno, looked up at his assistant and smiled.

— I have a proposal for you, *Gasparotto mio*, which I hope you will find an inspiration.

Messer Gerolamo prided himself on the talent he discovered and fostered, and he had known Gasparo since he was a baby, for the boy's mother worked in the Castle for his workshop's most attentive and gracious patroness. For his part, the young man was relieved: when summoned, he had expected a reprimand (his execution of twining sea serpents on a colophon had been deemed skittish, and he'd been asked to quell his fancies in future).

— I am going to send you into England. *Che ne pensi, Gasparo mio?*

But the master printer did not give the lad time to reply, for he was already writing out a letter of credit, closing the huge book and thrusting it into Gasparo's arms.

— Wrap this well, *giovinotto*, and go home and tell your good mother to start packing. We shall be sending you there with much of our old stock. I'm putting it together — last year's prints and those from years before — in the north this is all still new to them, and they are hungry for our woodcuts. They want to feast their eyes at home on the lives of the blessed saints and the deaths of the glorious martyrs. Whereas we — and he tapped a knowing index finger below his right eye — now have a finer appreciation, under the aegis of our great lady.

Off with you, now. London awaits!

༄

Montague Rhodes James, known as Monty to his friends, was a friend of my grandfather's and was Provost at Eton when my father was a pupil there. The school inspired in him a lifelong and obsessive loyalty, at a pitch that cannot be grasped by someone who has not known an English public schoolboy, and which upset me as his daughter, with my contrary hopes and ideals. Monty presided — loomed is perhaps the better word — over the whole establishment. His scholarly and genial presence dominated that sacred enclave, when enthroned in the chapel, or when, his dark gown swirling, his canonicals lifting to his stride, he swept across the school yard and stopped to exchange a few words with a boy he knew — my father, perhaps, causing him mortification at his gaucherie in response. In the College

Hall giving out the formal grace, or at home in the Provost's elegant and princely quarters, Monty James breathed out essence of Eton. He was a Biblical scholar; a palaeographer and archaeologist and folklorist; an indefatigable cataloguer of manuscripts held by colleges and other foundations; a loving gazetteer of churches, abbeys, cathedrals and monasteries (their ruins). His scholarship was antiquarian, his talents hermeneutics and entertainment. In all the manuscripts he listed and annotated, he read the stories they told, and he correlated characters and plots, proverbs and maxims with church ornaments and furnishings that had survived the reformers' hammers and gouges: in misericords, pew-ends, and the odd decorative elements on a grille, or placed too high up for the iconoclasts to reach.

Yet, when my father recalled him in later life, this learned and celibate figure of authority always provoked a chuckle of amused affection, because M. R. James's most beloved works, the writings that earned him a vast audience and are still read — and filmed — today, were his ghost stories. The most famous feature grisly, active, charmed things: in 'The Mezzotint', which scared me terribly, the figure depicted in the foreground has moved each time the narrator looks at the picture. First he is seen creeping towards the house on all fours, then stealing away with a bundle in his arms. Later this turns out to be a baby. In 'Oh Whistle and I'll come to you my lad!' the protagonist excavates an ancient pipe, disregards the warning inscribed on it, and blows on it; in the night the awakened phantom comes and torments him — with fatal consequences.

Gory, hair-raising, yet semi-comic, these are winter's tales in the tradition of the source books for religious frescoes, which later nourished Shakespeare's imagination, a tradition which has continued to shape current paranoid fantasy cycles about Vatican conspirators and vampire lovers. James liked to perform them on Christmas Eve by the fireside with only a candle or two to dispel total darkness.

Some of his readers have identified his hauntedness with his repressed sexuality, or a Peter Pan complex, or other Victorian particularities of his personality. But in my view his ghosts were not his alone; they are ancestral ghosts, rising from the national imaginary, filled with beliefs in relics, icons, charms, cantrips; he raised them because he met them again where they lay dusty and forgotten in old books and on old walls.

After first reading the ghost stories in a small battered volume of my father's, I then came across James the scholar through his edition of *New Testament Apocrypha*. He includes there a résumé, translation, and commentary on the apocryphal gospel in which the child prodigy Jesus slides down rainbows, quickens clay birds into life, and adjusts timbers that Joseph has mistakenly cut too short. Subsequently, I kept encountering James in ever more heterodox texts. *The Testament of Solomon* and its directory of devils with their occult names (Epiphass, Nonoskelis) is a wilder piece of esoterica, which he also translated with amused as well as learned notes. He had a lifelong taste for the bizarre and the extreme, and once remarked that when he was a boy, 'Nothing could be more inspiring that to discover that St Livinus had his tongue cut out and was beheaded, or that David's mother was called Nitzeneth.' *The Golden Legend* was made for him.

A few years after M. R. James returned to Eton in 1918 in his supreme role of

Provost, he began the work of uncovering the paintings that he knew had adorned the chapel before the Reformation. The figures he had glimpsed were Saint Sidwell and Saint Winifred, and they belonged to a parade of saints, some familiar, some almost entirely forgotten in his time.

∾

> Messer Gerolamo went on,
> — Our esteemed English counterpart and correspondent shows sharp interest in our work. He tells me the time has come for the English language — and that he's confident that our loquacious late Bishop of Genova, our revered Jacopo da Varazze of blessed memory, could become even more popular and influential than he is already with the makers of sermons and designers of church decorations — for those poor dull spirits in the north who are ignorant of Latin!
> Messer Gerolamo nodded at Gasparo, for he had flinched.
> — Yes, you are right. My views are no longer current, as Madonna Veronica likes to remind me. What is more, they have been out of style for a long time. It is the vulgar tongue that makes the sweetest music now!
> — And our London friend does not wish to be left far behind, he writes. In his last letter to me, he declares that translation will boom in his country.
> — I could send others who are older, wiser, more experienced at our trade than you. But I have chosen you from all them (he waved towards the door and the bustling workshops beyond), and Madonna Veronica agrees that you shall go. When you are there, you may keep those bright eyes of yours wide open and your clever ears pricked — and bring back news of what those ruffians are up to...

∾

The artists who worked on the Eton frescoes remain unknown, but they show multiple influences of foreign contacts within the polity that united the storytelling imagination of Europe before the English Reformation; their slender, elongated and fashionably dressed figures display affinities to delicate Flemish and Burgundian journeymen's imagery, compositional closeness to the products of Parisian workshops, and similarities with artisans in England making stained glass, church plate, and vestments; but ultimately, they reverberate with Italian narrative verve, as in such magnificent, complex, and vast cycles as Agnolo Gaddi's chapel in Santa Croce, Florence, and Piero della Francesca's chancel in Arezzo. There, in the 1450s, Piero painted his huge complex account of the legend of the true cross, drawing the episodes from several feast days in the Golden Legend, and structuring the scheme to form a total vision of Christian triumph.

The Eton series gives evidence of artists' migrations and their curiosity; they carried stories all over Europe. The painters' identities are not known in this case, but they were working on the frescoes around 1477–87, and they dressed the figures in their frescoes in the latest stylish dress from the continent — they were scandalously fashionable as well as idolaters.

The frescoes can now be seen again,* and have been reproduced in fine photographs in a new book. They are in grisaille, so the saints' statues look as if they are standing in niches, and between them delicately painted and intricate bas reliefs

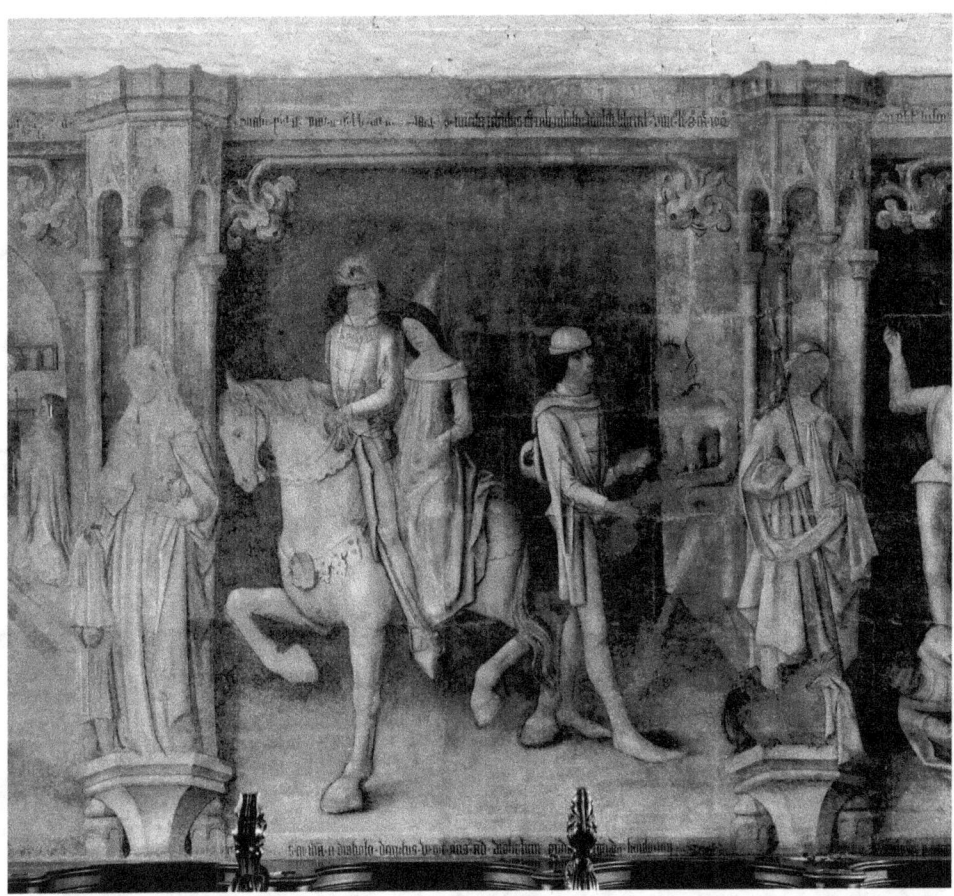

Fig. 28. Walls of Eton Chapel, 1479–87, fresco. From left to right: Amoras sells his wife to the devil; St Elizabeth of Hungary. Reproduced by permission of the Provost and Fellows of Eton College.

unfold, as in a cinematic sequence, populous narrative scenes about the miracles of the Virgin Mary, the unpleasant crushing of unbelievers, and the exploits — and sufferings — of saints. The stories come from the most popular works of devotion of the times — the *Speculum Historiale* by Vincent de Beauvais and the *Miracles of the Virgin* by Gautier de Coinci; but above all, the *Legenda Sanctorum* (*Legenda Aurea*) by the Dominican fabulist Jacobus de Voragine, Bishop of Genoa, flows into the plots. They are pictures that present the faith in a manner that was abhorrent to the Reformers who were to come within a matter of decades; the stories they tell promote typical reprehensible Catholic laxity.

They do not seem especially suited to an institution packed with adolescent boys, but they must have entertained them.

Here, the Virgin Mary is stepping in to rescue an unmarried woman from death in childbirth (in such miracles, she intervenes to protect fallen women — and men — even taking the place of a nun who is having a baby so that she can return to the convent after giving the child away for adoption, as if nothing has happened).

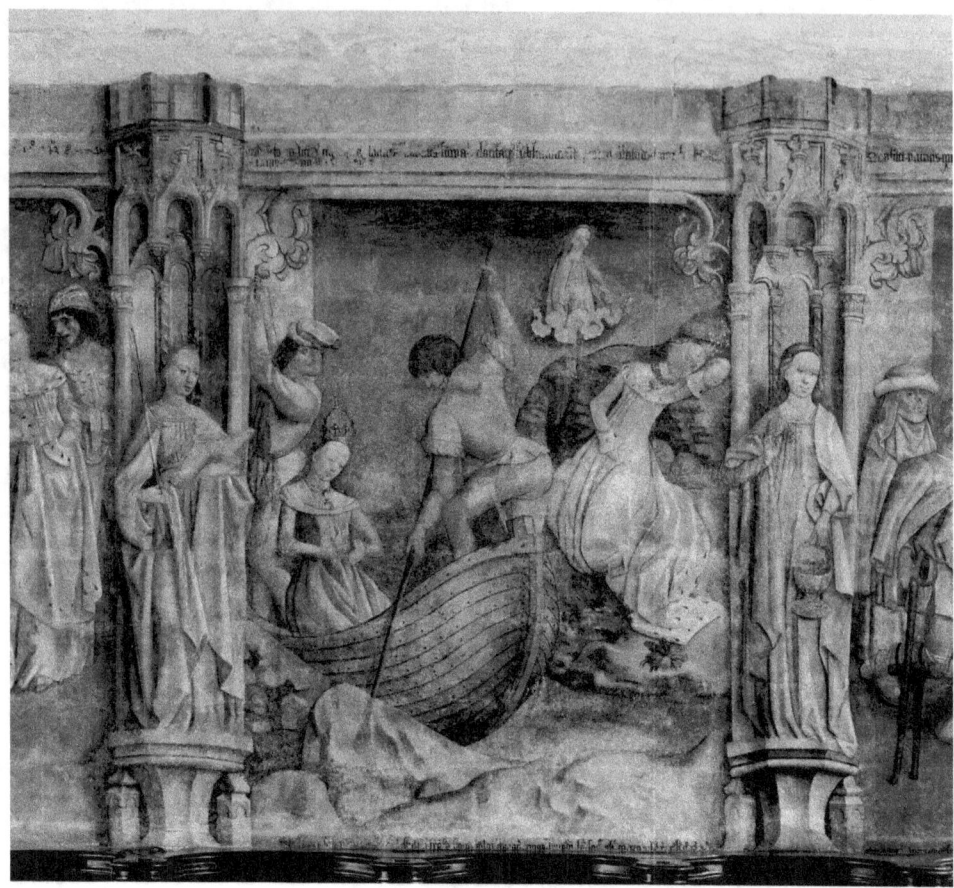

FIG. 29. Walls of Eton Chapel, 1479–87, fresco. From left to right: St Ursula; the Empress sees the Virgin in a vision; St Dorothea. Reproduced by permission of the Provost and Fellows of Eton College.

Here, a blaspheming soldier, mocking a woman praying before a statue of the Virgin, throws a stone at the image, who bleeds from the blow and strikes him dead.

Here, an innocent Empress, first assaulted by her brother-in-law, is then accused of child murder and exiled; Mary works to vindicate her in the eyes of all, gives her powers of healing, punishes her slanderers and brings her safely home — to a convent.

Here, Amoras, a wicked, dissembling youth, has made a satanic pact and is carrying off his wife, who knows nothing of his wickedness, to hand her over to the devil.

These pictures resemble many other targets of the whitewashers' buckets all over the country during the short reign of Henry's son Edward VI, and then, again, during the longer rule of his second daughter Elizabeth I, who, by a royal edict of 1559, ordered that all superstitious and idolatrous images should be destroyed. The doctrine of intercession, which gives Mary her indulgent role as the '*mater*

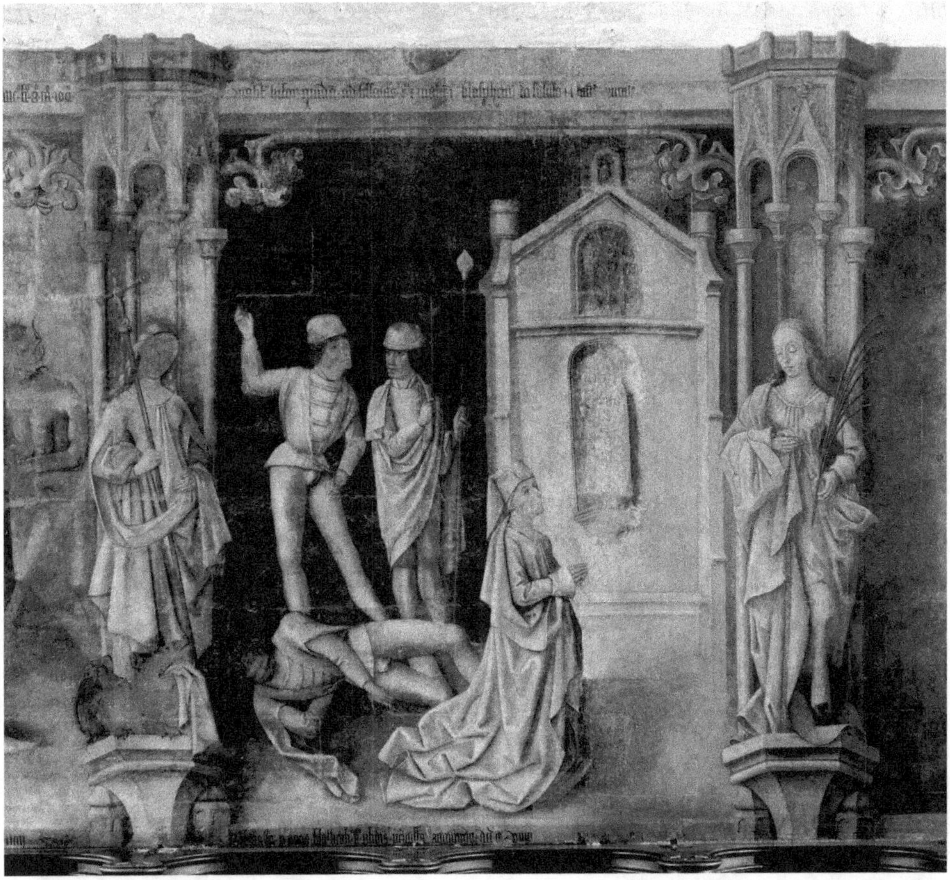

FILIGRANA ITALIANA 133

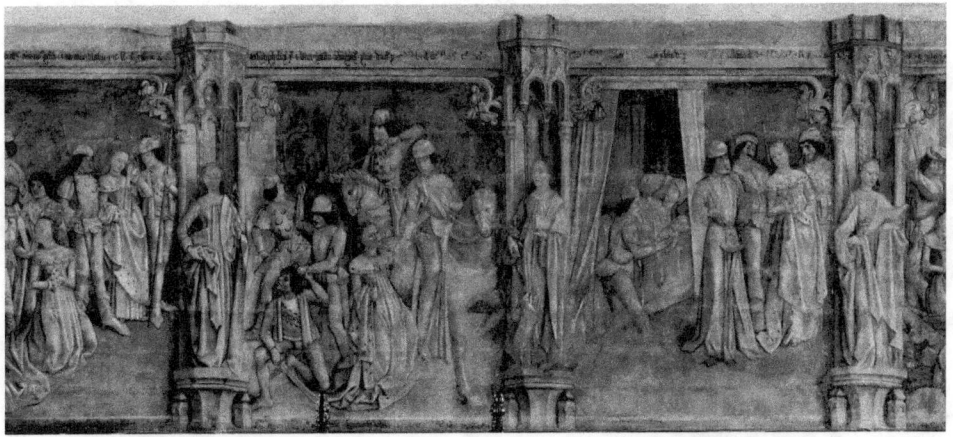

FIG. 30. Walls of Eton Chapel, 1479–87, fresco. From left to right: unidentified female saint; the miracle of the wounded image; St Margaret. Reproduced by permission of the Provost and Fellows of Eton College.

FIG. 31. Walls of Eton Chapel, 1479–87, fresco. The legend of the falsely accused Empress. Reproduced by permission of the Provost and Fellows of Eton College.

misericordiae, advocata nostra' (in the words of the *Salve Regina*), ever understanding, ever forgiving, consequently stood in the first line of attack from the Reformers, alongside the paraphernalia of efficacious prayer — holy water, rosaries, relics. Small wonder zealous Protestants scratched out the eyes and obliterated the features of this wretched uncanonical crew of dramatis personae on the wall of Eton College chapel.

∽

> A struggle instantly exploded at the very core of Gasparo Spirello's being, between thrill at the thought of adventure, and horror that he was being taken from everything he knew, from O., where he had lived all his life, from his mother who would, he knew, be stricken at his departure, from his sister, Lucia, who was almost his twin in age and who also worked for Messer Gerolamo, and from his love, his darling, his angel, his robin, his thrushling, his swallow — his Fiammetta — Gasparo Spirello never could decide which of the songbirds he loved she most resembled with her quivering throat and her dancing bright black eyes.
>
> At the door, hugging the splendid *Legenda Aurea* to his chest and feeling the leather of its rich binding warm to his blood temperature (as if urging him to remember that even if it were now so very old-fashioned it still had blood in its veins), Gasparo turned to his master and thanked him.
>
> As he did so, it flashed upon him that before he left he would ask Fiammetta to marry him.

∽

Some of the faces of the dramatis personae in the Eton chapel frescoes had been destroyed before later whitewashing covered them. These pious acts of disfigurement were not consistent: a few female saints, a few male saints, and several characters (men and women) in the stories had become blank masks, as if hidden from view like the face of the Prophet in Persian or Indian manuscripts of a similar date, when he and other Islamic saints are screened from our gaze by short veils. These figures are irrecoverable. The stories which tell of sacred images working miracles were special targets of the Reformers' outrage: the painting of the Virgin's statue, in the section that relates the miracle story of a Jew blasted for his blasphemous attack on an image, has become an empty socket, a blur, so that, in an instance of eerie duplication, the act described in the story has been repeated by the iconoclast, in a ferocious denial of the ascribed power of such holy images.

The blank damage that remains here and there in the paintings from the iconoclasm of the mid-sixteenth century is however profoundly eloquent, for it stands witness to the fervour that destroyed so much of the architecture, sculpture, stained glass, painting, ware, and so forth of England in the medieval and early Renaissance.

The original fifteenth-century scheme was even more comprehensive than the restorers would be able to rescue, for it included, in an upper storey reaching to the windows, another full cycle of stories about male saints. This band of pictures has vanished altogether.

In some way, the iconoclasts of the second intense wave of the Reformation, which began when Elizabeth issued her decree, were cultural patriots; like Caxton, who had successfully presented Chaucer as a new Ovid or a new Virgil in order to stake a claim that English literature could hold its own, the defacers of Catholic stories and images were asking for history to start again; they were radicals reshaping the landscape of imagination. In former hallowed ground they were hollowing a new space in which to plant another form of life (to adapt the neat wordplay of the historical geographer Marcus A. Doel).[3]

⁓

> ... and Fiammetta said yes. But then, with a sidelong look, the one she gave him when he knew she was going to try to get her way, she added,
> — I'm coming with you. How can I let my young and beautiful husband travel alone to a country full of sad pale girls who dream of someone like you from the warm South?
> Lucia was only ten months or so older than Gasparo, but she had since their father's death asserted the elder sister's authority, and she had worked long hours by day and by night, with a candle beside her (she loved the way the flame's softness brought out the gleam of the illuminations in Madonna Veronica's gorgeous coloured manuscripts) as she worked, pricking out the design of the illuminations to turn them into simple line drawings for Gasparino and others on Messer Gerolamo's benches to copy on wooden blocks, and when she heard that her brother was leaving for London to take a copy of the new book, she ran to find Fiammetta to share her anger and her horror, and found her future sister-in-law already trying out an assortment of her brother's clothes.
> — How do I look? she asked, smoothing the hose over her thighs and laughing as she tightened the laces to flatten her chest.
> Lucia flared up at the thought.
> — Do you think I can let you two travel alone? She cried. What would our dear dead father think of me abandoning my responsibilities like that?
> That was how three Italian youths, slender, beribboned in silk, with vari-coloured hose and velvet caps on their heads (the fashions in O. were bright and witty compared to English apparel) arrived in London during the last quarter of the fifteenth century; they delivered prints from Messer Gerolamo's workshop, showed his London correspondent the several printed volumes with woodcuts they had been despatched to sell (including the magnificent folio edition of the *Legenda Aurea* with more than a hundred woodcuts, hand-coloured), and began thriving, as they reported in letters they punctually sent back home.

⁓

Another English heartland where pictures were painted on the walls and then swabbed with whitewash to cover them was the prosperous town of Stratford-upon-Avon in Warwickshire. There, in the substantial glass-walled Gothic Guild Chapel of the Holy Cross, Caxton's illustrated edition of the *Golden Legend* provided a journeyman painter or painters with the models for the images frescoed on to the chancel walls a few years after the book first appeared in 1483. They depicted Empress Helena unearthing the cross where it had been buried in Jerusalem on the Mount of Calvary. Here, in full colour, the intrepid mission of her old age unfolded: the long journey to the Holy Land, the interrogation of the possible witnesses, the proving of the true cross by miraculously curing a leper (or, in an alternative source, a young woman, recently dead), and the scattering of splinters throughout the Roman empire in order to found churches.

What is most intriguing, however, about the destruction of these frescoes, is that the signature authorising the payment of two shillings for the work of the lime pails and brushes is that of John Shakespeare, father of William, who was alderman of the town in that period.[4]

The Shakespeares' relationship to the old religion has excited much scholarly discussion. William was born around the time his father began the work of painting over the chapel's papist pictures, and the destruction continued during William's childhood, with his father presiding over the dismantling of the rood loft and the removal of the stained glass.

Catholic memories haunt the plays — sometimes literally, when Hamlet's father's ghost rises in agony out of purgatory. The family entanglement with the old religion leaves its mark on William's dramatic imagination: it surfaces in his many spectres and sinners, goddesses and virgins, and the several subjects of hallucinations and prophetic dreams. He makes a statue of a virtuous queen (Hermione in *The Winter's Tale*), and she comes to life, silently but warm to the touch at the happy end, as in a miracle story depicted at Eton, on the south side of the Chapel, where the upper frieze includes a scene showing a young bridegroom who, smitten by the beauty of a statue, had promised eternal love to the Virgin; on his wedding night, she comes for him and reproaches him bitterly for forgetting his vow; she then takes him for her own, leaving his bride neglected in the nuptial bed (Prosper Mérimée was inspired by this for the story *La Vénus d'Ille*).

On the lower register on the same south side of the Chapel, the story of the travails of an innocent Empress unfolds in eight exquisitely painted and very busy scenes; they follow the wronged heroine from persecution to triumph. The story is much more familiar from romance and fairy tale than from hagiography, and it's a surprise to find it dramatised in this liturgical setting. In plays and poetry it takes many forms (Patient Griselda, that nastiest of instruction manuals on wifely virtue, being the most famous); but in *The Winter's Tale*, which by its very title draws attention to itself as a traditional story, Shakespeare combines it with other Marian echoes: when Hermione appears to Antigonus in a dream, the vision foreshadows her later materialisation as a living statue who inspires awed worship. In *Pericles*, Shakespeare stages a virgin martyr's triumph in the brothel against would-be violators; they are magically incapable of assaulting Marina, just like numerous villains of *The Golden Legend* when confronted with heroic virgins. Marina's eloquent defence of her person wields a form of enchantment, as does St Catherine's oratory. Her unassailable holiness shatters the wheel on which her torturers want to bind her, and deflects all other missiles they use to attack her. In the case of Santa Cristina, her pagan father cuts out her tongue, but it continues quivering on the ground and rails against him, then flies up and pierces him through the eye. Shakespeare took from Ovid's tale of Philomel the image of the severed tongue, but his Lavinia also echoes the poor afflicted young women martyrs in the *Golden Legend*.

The *Italianità* of English Renaissance culture, and its rich texture of Catholic storytelling, surfaces more obviously still in Shakespeare's dramatic scenes and their sources in fables, riddles, fabliaux, and lyric love poetry: when Portia sets the three caskets before her suitors in Belmont on the Venetian lagoon, when Juliet lies cataleptic in Verona, when Isabella repudiates Angelo's bargain, the playwright is drawing on the granary of literature from the south.

That Shakespeare knew Italian has been suggested in some quarters, and even more vertiginously, that he actually was Italian! But Shakespeare does not need to have had Italian blood or known the language; his imagination is inscribed with the filigrana that M. R. James glimpsed much later in the Chapel at Eton when he saw the shadowy saints emerge, like an apparition from the wall.

∾

> Later that year, after much successful business in London, Gasparo and Fiammetta and Lucia Spirello (the two young women still successfully passing *en travesti*), travelled west out of London and began making their way cross country, stopping to set up shop temporarily as jobbing artists; they had held on to the remaining prints in their baggage in order to draw from them for commissions they might receive.
>
> In Stratford-upon-Avon, where the prosperous burghers were eager to adorn their town, Fiammetta found she was having a baby; in the event, she gave birth to twins that second summer the family spent in England. This eventuality required they shed their disguise, and raised difficulties for Fiammetta and Lucia working in public. Besides, even in England, there were signs that the demand for painted lives of the saints was dwindling.
>
> Phidias and Anastasia struck their English friends as rather unwieldy names for such tiny scraps of life, but the parents and the children's aunt took them from *The Boke of the Citie of Ladies*, where they had executed images of the artists at their work bench and their easel, to accompany Christine de Pisan's praises of Lady Reason.
>
> The Spirello travellers had news from home: their great lady patroness was now celebrated for her poetry as well as her patronage. Love poetry, they were told, frank and fierce, but always decorous. All books, Messer Gerolamo reported, were now full of different kinds of feelings and different kinds of stories from the *Legenda Aurea*.
>
> They began longing to return. They made plans to return. They began packing.
>
> But did they?
>
> Did the twins grow up at home, at ease with the spoken Italian of their generation? Did they meet Madonna Veronica?
>
> Or could they have stayed on in Stratford-upon-Avon year after year, with their things half packed, expecting to leave but never quite managing it?
>
> Or did Lucia remain behind on her own? Could she have married there?
>
> The trail peters out.
>
> Except for traces in the plays of their contemporary, if they can be counted evidence.

∾

While M. R. James did not forget his sighting of the lost saints in the chapel of Our Lady of Eton, he also never fully acknowledged what the vision meant; or perhaps, to put it differently, he could not but disavow sympathy with its points of reference. As a conservative establishment figure, an English gentleman, and above all a devout Anglican, he had to deny certain implications of the art and stories that he loved, and close his mind to the idea that certain aspects of continental beliefs might have seeped indelibly into English consciousness. The Catholic, particularly Italian, past was not only covered up, it had been rejected and ordered into oblivion. But like the filigrana, it would appear when held up in a certain light.

Notes

1. M. R. James, *Eton and King's: Recollections, Mostly Trivial* (London: Williams & Norgate, 1926), pp. 90-91.
2. Emily Howe, Henrietta McBurney, David Park, Stephen Rickerby, Lisa Shekede, *Wall Paintings of Eton* (Milan: Scala, 2014).
3. Marcus A. Doel, 'Proverbs for Paranoids: Writing Geography on Hollowed Ground', *Transactions of the Institute of British Geographers*, 18.3 (1993), 377–94.
4. The Guild chapel designs are known only from copies made by Thomas Fisher in 1804–07, during a short period when they were uncovered before being painted over again. He left the work incomplete. It includes reproductions of 'the various grants and indulgences of the gild; with representation of one hundred and fifty public and private seals...' etc., was printed in a lavish facsimile volume by Nichols & Sons, London, in 1836, in an edition of 120 copies.

INDEX

Abelard 88
Adam, x, 26–27, 30, 32
Adiutorio, Desiderio d' 66
Aeneas 82
Agrippa, Marcus Vipsanius 68
Alamanni, Luigi 102, 103
Alberto da Ripa 99, 101
Alciat, André 104
Alcibiades 56
Aldo, Manuzio (Aldus Manutius) 2, 74 n. 16, 75, 104
Alois, Gioan Francesco 121
Altoviti, Bindo 72 n. 7
Ambrose, Saint 87, 90
Amoras xi, 131
Andrea de Monte 121
Andreuccio 124
Angelo 137
Anna (or Diamantina) 45–54
Anthony, Saint 37, 123
Antigonus 136
Antoine de Bourbon 99
Antonello da Messina x, 35–43
Apollo 56, 61, 91
Aretino, Pietro 103
Ariosto, Ludovico 93–97
Aristotle 72, 119, 120
Arius 124
Astemio, Lorenzo 107
Augustine, Saint 82, 85, 120
Augustino da Montalcino, Fra 123
Averroes 119, 120

Baldassare de Gabiano 101, 104
Balsamo, Jean 4, 15
Barbara, Duchess of Mantua 49–54
Barbara the Younger, daughter of the Duke of Mantua 52–54
Barbarigo, Gerolamo xi, 94
Barbaro, Ermolao 105
Barbier-Mueller, Jean Paul 4, 15
Bartolo di Aloia 117
Beatrice 13
Beleth, John 37
Bembo, Bernardo x, 18, 19, 21–23
Bembo, Carlo 17
Bembo, Pietro 9, 15–23, 63–65, 66, 68, 113
Benci, Ginevra de' x, 15, 19–23
Berni, Francesco 103

Boccaccio, Giovanni 3, 88, 91, 104, 107, 124
Boethius 72
Borges Jorge Luis 127
Borgia, Angela 17, 18
Borgia, Lucrezia 15, 16, 17, 18, 64
Botticelli, Sandro 32, 56
Bourbon, Connétable de 102
Bracci, Cecchino 61
Brandenburg, Margrave of 49, 54
Bréauté-Consalvi, Hannibal de 66
Briçonnet, Guillaume 75 n. 18, 101
Brucioli, Antonio 105
Brueghel the Elder xi, 116
Brunelleschi, Filippo 26, 32
Bruno, Ariosto's secretary 96
Bruno, Fraulissa 117
Bruno, Gioanni 117
Bruno, Giordano 115–25
Buti, Lucrezia 11–14

Caesar, Julius 74
Calvino, Italo 127
Camillo Delminio, Giulio 106, 107, 108
Camuccini, Vincenzo 66
Caprotti, Gian Giacomo 61
Carvajal, Bernardino Lopez de 75 n. 18
Castiglione, Baldassare 9, 64, 74, 113, 114 n. 1
Catherine of Alexandria, Saint 136
Catherine of Sienna, Saint 123
Caxton, William 134, 135
Cecilia, daughter of the Duke of Mantua 52
Cellini, Benvenuto x, 56–57, 99, 102, 103
Champier, Symphorien 107
Charles the Bold, Duke of Burgundy 21
Charles V, Emperor 76, 99, 102, 103
Charles VIII, King of France 1
Chassignet, Jean-Baptiste 65
Chaucer, Geoffrey 135
Chirico, Giorgio di 29
Christ 31, 38, 58, 61, 73, 87, 103, 119, 120, 121, 122, 129
Christine de Pisan 137
Cicero, Marcus Tullius 38, 74, 75, 79, 82, 85, 87
Claude de France 99
Colette, Sidonie-Gabrielle 81
Colle, Gioan Vincenzo de (Il Sarnese) 119
Colonna, Vittoria 55
Consalvi, Cardinal 66
Copernicus, Nicolaus 119

Cornaro, Catherine, Queen of Cyprus 16–18
Cosmas, Saint 121
Cosimo de' Medici 12, 72 n. 7
Cristina, Saint 136
Cusano, Nicola 120

Dante Alighieri 2, 65, 72, 73, 75, 88, 104
Danzi, Massimo 4
Daphne 91
David, King 56, 129
Delminio, see Camillo
Des Périers, Bonaventure 101, 106, 107–08
Diofebi, Francesco xi, 66, 69, 70
Disdéri, André 65
Doel, Marcus A. 135
Dolet, Etienne 105, 106, 107, 108
Donatello 29, 32
Doni, Anton Francesco 97
Dorothea, Saint xi, 132
Du Bellay, Joachim 2
Du Guillet, Pernette 104
Du Peyrat, Jean 99
Ducimetière, Nicolas 4

Edward VI, King of England 132
Eléonore, wife of François Ier 99
Elizabeth I, Queen of England 132, 134
Elizabeth of Hungary, Saint xi, 131
Epicurus 85, 87
Epiphass 129
Equicola, Mario 9
Erasmus 2, 71 n. 1, 75, 76, 78, 106, 107, 120, 124
Eros 104
Este, Ippolito d' 103
Eustachia 38
Eve x, 26–27, 30

Fabris, sculptor 66
Febo di Poggio 61
Fernando de Montepulciano 56
Fiammetta 134, 135, 137
Ficino, Marsilio 2, 7, 9, 11, 13, 14, 58, 101, 105, 120
Fiorato, Adelin Charles 55
Fisher, Thomas 138 n. 4
Flandrin, Paul 64, 65
Fondulo, Girolamo 101
Fornarina, La xi, 63, 67
Francesco, Duke of Mantua 49–50, 51
François Ier, King of France 3, 99, 102–04, 105, 106, 108
Fregoso, Federico, 113
Fregoso, Ottaviano 113
Freud, Sigmund 61
Frey, Karl 55

Gaddi, Agnolo 130
Gagliardo, Eugenio, Fra 123

Galileo 2
Ganymede x, 56, 58, 60
Garcilaso de la Vega l'Inca 10
Gargano, Gioan Bernardino 121
Gargantua 105
Gautier de Coinci 131
Gerolamo, Messer 128, 130, 134, 135, 137
Gesualdo, Carlo 109, 111, 113
Gigante 51
Giolito Ferrari, Gabriel 97
Giorgione 56
Giotto 26
Giovanni di Pagolo Morelli 72
Giuliano de' Medici 26, 113
Gregory XVI, Pope 65, 66
Guido da Montefeltro 75
Guidobaldo da Montefeltro 113

Hadrian 68
Hamlet 136
Helena, Saint 128, 135
Heloise 88
Henri II, King of France 1, 101
Henri IV, King of France 99
Henry VIII, King of England 132
Hermione 136
Herod x, 12
Hittorff, Jacques Ignace 70
Hoffmann, Hans xi, 77
Hyacinth 56

Iannello, Gian Domenico de 117
Ingres, Delphine 65
Ingres, Jean-Auguste-Dominique x, 63–70
Isabella 137

Jacobus de Voragine (Jacopo da Vorazze) 38, 130, 131
Jacopo della Quercia 32
James, Montague Rhodes 127, 128–30, 137
Jean de Lorraine 99
Jeanne d'Albret 99, 101
Jerome, Saint x, 35–43, 120, 124
Jesus, see Christ
John Chrysostom 120, 124
John of the Cross 10–11, 13
John, Saint 58
Joseph 129
Jove (Jupiter) 56, 58
Jove, Paul 103
Julian, Saint 121
Juliet 136
Julius II, Pope 58
Juste, François 99

Labé, Louise 104–05
Las Casas, Bartolomé de 104
Laura xi, 12, 13, 88–89, 90, 91

Lavinia 136
Le Febvre, Nicolas xi, 100
Le Verrier, Urbain 65
Lemaire de Belges, Jean 107
Leo the Hebrew 9–10, 11, 13
Leonardo da Vinci x, 3, 4, 13, 19–21, 23, 56, 61–62, 102
Lippi, Filippino 12
Lippi, Filippo x, 8, 11–14
Livinus, Saint 129
Livy 74
Lomazzo, Giovanni Paolo 56, 62
Lombardo della Seta 91
Lombardo, Pietro 120
Lorenzetto (Lorenzo Lotti) 65
Lorenzo de' Medici (Lorenzo il Magnifico) 3, 21, 61
Louis XVI, King of France 63
Louise de Savoie 102
Ludovico di Canossa 113, 114
Ludovico, Duke of Mantua 50, 51, 52, 54
Lullo, Raimondo 120
Lysander 75

Machiavelli, Niccolò 16, 71–78, 107
Mantegna, Andrea x, 45–54
Marcellus, Marcus Claudius 73
Maretsch, Lord of 49
Margaret, Saint xi, 133
Marguerite, daughter of François Ier 99
Marguerite, Queen of Navarre 99, 101–02, 105–06, 107
Marina 136
Mark, Saint 41
Marot, Clément 105
Martino della Magna, Fra 75, 76
Martin, Saint 99
Mary Magdalene 119, 121
Masaccio x, 25–34
Masolino da Panicale x, 25–34
Maximilian I, Emperor 76
Memling, Hans x, 18, 22
Mérimée, Prosper 136
Michelangelo Buonarroti x, 7, 10, 25, 26, 32, 34, 55–56, 58–62, 72
Minerva 90
Mocenigo, Gioanni 115
Mohammed 103
Montaigne, Michel de xi, 2, 82, 109–14
More, Thomas 75
Morgana, Lady 121
Morone, Giovanni 111
Mozart, Wolfgang Amadeus 63

Nanni di Banco 32
Narcissus 56
Neri, family 72 n. 7
Nerli, Filippo 74

Nifo, Agostino 7, 11
Nitzeneth 129
Nonoskelis 129

Ossian 70
Overbeck, Johann Friedrich 66
Ovid 82, 135, 136

Palestrina, Giovanni Pierluigi xi, 109–13
Pammachius 38
Pantagruel 105
Paola, daughter of the Duke of Mantua 52
Paradin, Claude 103
Pasqua, Ambrosio 120, 124
Paulino, Don 117
Pausanias 56
Perini, Gherardo 61
Perseus x, 56–57
Peter, Saint x, 28, 76
Petrarch (Francesco Petrarca) xi, 2, 4, 12, 79–83. 85–92, 104, 107
Petrucci, Armando 89
Phidias 56
Philippe de Cabassoles 91
Philo 9
Philomel 136
Pico della Mirandola, Giovanni 105
Piero della Francesca 130
Pirandello, Luigi 15
Pistoia, Giovanni 61
Pitti, Bonaccorso 72, 73 n. 10
Pius II Piccolomini, Pope 12
Pius V, Pope 120
Plato 7, 11, 21, 32, 38, 56, 58, 76, 119, 120
Pliny the Elder 82
Poggio Bracciolini, Gian Francesco 107
Poliphilus 74
Pomponazzi, Pietro 11, 101
Pomponius Mela 87
Pontormo, Jacopo da 32
Portia 136
Prie, René de 75 n. 18
Primaticcio, Francesco 101
Portonariis, Vincent de 101, 104
Proust, Marcel 15, 61
Pulci, Luigi 61, 74

Rabelais, François 2, 105
Ramon de Cardona 74
Raphael (Raffaelo Sanzio) xi, 25, 63–70
Ravel, Maurice 81
Rebiba, Cardinal 120
Renou, Louis 81
Ripa, Cesare 101
Roch, Saint 122
Ronsard, Pierre de 4
Rosso da Valenza, Francesco 97

Rosso Fiorentino 32, 101

Sacrobosco, Joannes de 119
Sade, Domitien-Alphonse de 83
Saint-Rambert, Comtesse de 101
Salome 11
Saltarelli, Jacopo 61
Salutiis, Giovanni Gabrieli de 115
Sanseverino, Federico 75 n. 18
Satan 61
Savolino, Scipione 117
Savonarola, Girolamo 58, 73, 75
Scève, Maurice 104
Sciascia, Leonardo 15
Sebastiano del Piombo 58
Seneca 85
Seripando, Girolamo, Cardinal 119
Severus Sulpicius 38
Shakespeare, John 136
Shakespeare, William 129, 136, 137
Sidwell, Saint 130
Sigismund, Emperor 49
Silvano 91
Simeoni, Gabriello 103
Socrates 91
Soderini, Pier 74
Solomon 129
Sophia 9
Spirello, Anastasia 137
Spirello, Gasparo 128, 130, 134, 135, 137
Spirello, Lucia 134, 135. 137
Spirello, Phidias 137
Strozzi, Ercole 17–18
Suleiman I, Sultan 103–04

Tacitus 74
Tallis, Thomas 111
Tansillo, Cola di Gianbernardino 117
Tansillo, Luigi 117–18
Tebaldeo, Antonio 17–18

Teofilo da Vairano, Fra 119
Terence 3
Thomas a Kempis 107
Thomas Aquinas, Saint 119, 120
Thorvaldsen, Bertel 66
Tintoretto, Jacopo 56
Titian xi, 4, 56, 94
Tommaso dei Cavalieri 55, 58, 61
Tullia d'Aragone 9
Tyard, Pontus de 9
Tyrol, Count of 49

Ulysses 82
Ursula, Saint xi, 132

Valla, Lorenzo 75
Van Eyck, Jan 41
Venus 56, 61
Verne, Jules 68
Vernet, Horace 66
Veronese, Paolo 56
Veronica del Licorno 128, 130, 135, 137
Verrochio, Andrea del 61
Vettori, Piero 16, 75
Vincent de Beauvais 131
Vinci, Leonardo da, see Leonardo
Virgil 72, 88, 89, 91, 135
Virgin, the xi, 13, 64, 68, 121, 122, 123, 131, 132, 134, 136
Vita, Dominico, Fra 124
Vitruvius, 106

Winifred, Saint 130
Wittkower, Rudolf 62
Württemberg, Duke of 52

Yates, Frances 15

Zurla, Giacinto Placido, Cardinal 66

www.ingramcontent.com/pod-product-compliance
Lightning Source LLC
Chambersburg PA
CBHW082248220526
45469CB00009B/2921